CW01360034

Critical Approaches to Children's Literature
Series Editors: **Kerry Mallan** and **Clare Bradford**

Critical Approaches to Children's Literature is an innovative series concerned with the best contemporary scholarship and criticism on children's and young adult literature, film, and media texts. The series addresses new and developing areas of children's literature research as well as bringing contemporary perspectives to historical texts. The series has a distinctive take on scholarship, delivering quality works of criticism written in an accessible style for a range of readers, both academic and professional. The series is invaluable for undergraduate students in children's literature as well as advanced students and established scholars.

Titles include:

Cherie Allan
PLAYING WITH PICTURE BOOKS
Postmodern and the Postmodernesque

Clare Bradford
THE MIDDLE AGES IN CHILDREN'S LITERATURE

Clare Bradford, Kerry Mallan, John Stephens & Robyn McCallum
NEW WORLD ORDERS IN CONTEMPORARY CHILDREN'S LITERATURE

Alice Curry
ENVIRONMENTAL CRISIS IN YOUNG ADULT FICTION
A Poetics of Earth

Helen A. Fairlie
REVALUING BRITISH BOYS' STORY PAPERS, 1918–1939

Victoria Flanagan
TECHNOLOGY AND IDENTITY IN YOUNG ADULT FICTION
The Posthuman Subject

Margaret Mackey
NARRATIVE PLEASURES IN YOUNG ADULT NOVELS, FILMS AND
VIDEO GAMES

Kerry Mallan
SECRETS, LIES AND CHILDREN'S FICTION

Andrew O'Malley
CHILDREN'S LITERATURE, POPULAR CULTURE AND *ROBINSON CRUSOE*

Christopher Parkes
CHILDREN'S LITEARTURE AND CAPITALISM
Fictions of Social Mobility in Britain, 1850–1914

Hazel Sheeky Bird
CLASS, LEISURE AND NATIONAL IDENTITY IN BRITISH CHILDREN'S
LITERATURE, 1918–1950

Amy Ratelle
ANIMALITY AND CHILDREN'S LITERATURE AND FILM

Karen Sands-O'Connor & Marietta Frank
INTERNATIONALISM IN CHILDREN'S SERIES

Michelle Smith
EMPIRE IN BRITISH GIRLS' LITERATURE AND CULTURE

Critical Approaches to Children's Literature
Series Standing Order ISBN 978–0–230–22786–6 (hardback)
978–0–230–22787–3 (paperback)
(outside North America only)

You can receive future titles in this series as they are published by placing a standing order. Please contact your bookseller or, in case of difficulty, write to us at the address below with your name and address, the title of the series and the ISBN quoted above.

Customer Services Department, Macmillan Distribution Ltd, Houndmills, Basingstoke, Hampshire RG21 6XS, England

The Middle Ages in Children's Literature

Clare Bradford
Deakin University, Australia

palgrave
macmillan

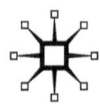

© Clare Bradford 2015

All rights reserved. No reproduction, copy or transmission of this publication may be made without written permission.

No portion of this publication may be reproduced, copied or transmitted save with written permission or in accordance with the provisions of the Copyright, Designs and Patents Act 1988, or under the terms of any licence permitting limited copying issued by the Copyright Licensing Agency, Saffron House, 6–10 Kirby Street, London EC1N 8TS.

Any person who does any unauthorized act in relation to this publication may be liable to criminal prosecution and civil claims for damages.

The author has asserted her right to be identified as the author of this work in accordance with the Copyright, Designs and Patents Act 1988.

First published 2015 by
PALGRAVE MACMILLAN

Palgrave Macmillan in the UK is an imprint of Macmillan Publishers Limited, registered in England, company number 785998, of Houndmills, Basingstoke, Hampshire, RG21 6XS.

Palgrave Macmillan in the US is a division of St Martin's Press LLC, 175 Fifth Avenue, New York, NY 10010.

Palgrave is the global academic imprint of the above companies and has companies and representatives throughout the world.

Palgrave® and Macmillan® are registered trademarks in the United States, the United Kingdom, Europe and other countries.

ISBN 978–1–137–03538–7

This book is printed on paper suitable for recycling and made from fully managed and sustained forest sources. Logging, pulping and manufacturing processes are expected to conform to the environmental regulations of the country of origin.

A catalogue record for this book is available from the British Library.

Library of Congress Cataloging-in-Publication Data

Bradford, Clare.
The Middle Ages in Children's Literature / Clare Bradford.
pages cm. — (Critical Approaches to Children's Literature)
Includes bibliographical references and index.
ISBN 978–1–137–03538–7 (hardback)
1. Children's literature—History and criticism. 2. Middle Ages in literature.
I. Title.
PN1009.5.M54B73 2015
809'.89282—dc23   2014038109

Typeset by MPS Limited, Chennai, India.

For Alan Gruner

Contents

List of Illustrations — viii
Series Preface — ix
Acknowledgements — x

Introduction — 1
1 Thinking about the Middle Ages — 11
2 Temporality and the Medieval — 40
3 Spatiality and the Medieval — 62
4 Disabilities in Medievalist Fiction — 85
5 Monstrous Bodies, Medievalist Inflexions — 107
6 Medievalist Animals and Their Humans — 132
7 The Laughable Middle Ages — 155
Conclusion — 180

Notes — 183
Bibliography — 194
Index — 204

List of Illustrations

1.1	*Hunting for Dragons* (2010) by Bruce Whatley	16
1.2	*Hunting for Dragons* (2010) by Bruce Whatley	17
1.3	*The Paper Bag Princess* (1980) by Robert Munsch and Michael Martchenko	22
1.4	*The Paper Bag Princess* (1980) by Robert Munsch and Michael Martchenko	23
1.5	*The Three Pigs* (2001) by David Wiesner	37
1.6	*The Three Pigs* (2001) by David Wiesner	38
6.1	*The Minstrel and the Dragon Pup* (1993) by Rosemary Sutcliff and Emma Chichester Clark	149
7.1	*Princess Smartypants* (1986) by Babette Cole	157
7.2	*The Knight Who Was Afraid of the Dark* (1989) by Barbara Shook Hazen and Tony Ross	159

Series Preface

The *Critical Approaches to Children's Literature* series was initiated in 2008 by Kerry Mallan and Clare Bradford. The aim of the series is to identify and publish the best contemporary scholarship and criticism on children's and young adult literature, film and media texts. The series is open to theoretically informed scholarship covering a wide range of critical perspectives on historical and contemporary texts from diverse national and cultural settings. Critical Approaches aims to make a significant contribution to the expanding field of children's literature research by publishing quality books that promote informed discussion and debate about the production and reception of children's literature and its criticism.

Kerry Mallan and Clare Bradford

Acknowledgements

I have been greatly assisted in the development of this book by many people who have provided me with suggestions and support over the years of research and writing. Several sections of this book had their first airings at conferences and scholarly events, where I gained much from the feedback of my audiences. The International Research Society for Children's Literature and the Australasian Children's Literature Association for Research have always afforded supportive scholarly networks. In particular I thank Pamela Knights, Mavis Reimer, Ingrid Johnston, Kimberley Reynolds and Helen Young, for their helpful insights. My colleague and friend Kerry Mallan has been a constant source of support and encouragement.

Many thanks to Louise D'Arcens, Andrew Lynch and Stephanie Trigg for inviting me to the 'Medievalism, Colonialism, Nationalism' symposium at the University of Wollongong in 2010, and the 'International Medievalism and Popular Culture' symposium in Perth in 2011. These events assisted me greatly in mapping out the connections between children's literature and medievalism studies.

The insights of my students have challenged and enlivened my research. Among them were students at the University of Winnipeg, where I taught in the Master of Arts in Cultural Studies during a memorable year in Canada as Trudeau Fellow, and the Honours students taking the 'Medievalism' option at Deakin University. The Children's Literature PhD support group, comprising Dylan Holdsworth, Emma Hayes, Emma Whatman, Tom Sandercock, Juliet O'Conor, Lara Hedberg, Kate Norman and Rebecca Hutton, gave me valuable advice on draft chapters.

My colleagues at Deakin have provided a collegial environment; particular thanks are due to Ann McCulloch, Lyn McCredden, Deb Verhoeven, Emily Potter and Ann Vickery. It is a privilege to work with the talented children's literature team of Elizabeth Bullen, Leonie Rutherford, Paul Venzo, Sue Chen, Michelle Smith and Kristine Moruzi.

Cecilia Rogers, Trish Lunt and Elizabeth Braithwaite have provided me with excellent research assistance, and the Deakin University library staff, especially Marina Minns, have gone out of their way to help me. In Canada I greatly appreciated the knowledgeable support of Leslie McGrath at the Osborne Collection of Early Children's Literature in

Toronto. Many thanks to Paula Kennedy and Peter Cary at Palgrave Macmillan for seeing this book through to publication.

Finally, my family have always shown a keen interest in my research and have been constant in their support. Thank you to Alice, Maggie, Luke, Phil, Shauna and the incomparable Mr Cohen.

Thank you to the following for permission to reproduce illustrations:

From the book *Hunting for Dragons* by Bruce Whatley. Copyright © Bruce Whatley, 2010. First published by Scholastic Australia Pty Limited 2010. Reproduced by permission of Scholastic Australia Pty Limited.

From *The Paper Bag Princess* © 1980 Bob Munsch Enterprises (text); © 1980 Michael Martchenko (art); published by Annick Press Ltd. Reproduced by permission.

Illustration from the book *The Three Pigs* by David Wiesner. Copyright © 2001 by David Wiesner. Reproduced by permission of Andersen Press.

Illustration © 1993 Emma Chichester Clark. Extract from *The Minstrel and the Dragon Pup* by Rosemary Sutcliff and illustrated by Emma Chichester Clark. Reproduced by permission of Walker Books Australia.

From *Princess Smartypants* (1986, London) by Babette Cole. Copyright © 1986 by Babette Cole. Reproduced by permission of Penguin Books Ltd.

From *The Knight Who Was Afraid of the Dark* by Barbara Shook Hazen, illustrated by Tony Ross. Text copyright © 1989 by Barbara Shook Hazen. Illustrations copyright © 1989 by Tony Ross. Pictures used by permission of Dial Books for Young Readers, a division of Penguin Group (USA) LLC.

Introduction: Framing the Medieval

An experience common among scholars is that once we embark upon a project of any substance, we encounter what can seem like a flurry of references to the topic in which we are engrossed. Discussions relating to this topic appear everywhere, in popular and scholarly publications; it seems that our own enthusiasm is widely shared and that our investigations tap into the zeitgeist, confirming our acumen in taking up the topic in the first place. What happens, clearly, is that our attention is sharpened because of the pleasurable state of obsessiveness into which we enter as we focus on our research, so that stories and references which might previously have escaped our notice now jostle for attention. The topic I address in this book, medievalism in children's literature, is somewhat different. It is not so much that my partiality causes me to see medievalism everywhere and across multiple genres and platforms, as that the medieval is indeed everywhere.

The terms 'Middle Ages', 'medieval', 'medievalist' and 'medievalism' are notoriously slippery, referring variously to times, cultures, practices, texts and modes of thought. Kathleen Davis and Nadia Altschul remark that the Middle Ages constitutes 'an idea rather than an internally unified entity' (2009: 1), an idea, moreover, which is always subject to change as the Middle Ages is re-envisioned in the light of changing ideas and values. As a time frame, the Middle Ages encompasses the fifth to the fifteenth century, occupying a middle position between antiquity and modernity. This middleness is not a natural or inevitable state, but was attributed to the medieval by Renaissance and Enlightenment thinkers in order to distinguish the Middle Ages from classical antiquity and from their own times; as Bruce Holsinger says, the Middle Ages constitutes 'the historical period that modernity most consistently abjected as its temporal other' (2005: 5).

In this book I consider the uses and abuses of the medieval in medievalist texts for the young – that is, post-medieval texts which respond to and deploy medieval culture. Children are introduced to versions of the medieval from infancy, through cartoons, picture books, artefacts and practices ranging from fairy-themed parties to *Shrek*; and this process is amplified in contemporary times by the expansion of global markets in which the medieval is a sought-after commodity, consumed in popular texts such as the Harry Potter series, Terry Deary's *Horrible Histories*, and multiple manifestations of gothic and paranormal romance. Many of these texts invoke the medieval in ways which might seem frivolous, far-fetched or 'inauthentic', another slippery term to which I return in Chapter 1, 'Thinking about the Middle Ages'. They may, indeed, have little to do with what we know of the historical Middle Ages; rather, medievalist texts have more to do with the valency of the medieval past in the present; the meanings and pleasures it affords; and what these allusions to the medieval tell us about relations between medieval and modern.

I proceed from the assumption, then, that medievalist texts, whether fantasy, non-fiction or fiction, are not 'about' the Middle Ages so much as 'about' the cultures and times in which they are produced. Like children's literature more generally, they cover a gamut of forms and approaches, from popular to literary, from picture books for very young children to Young Adult (YA) novels. Medievalisms are fundamentally recursive in that they draw not merely on medieval culture but on a variety of post-medieval tropes and texts. The gothic affords a vivid example. Contemporary vampire romance, including the Twilight series, calls on the traditions established in the eighteenth century, when, as Fred Botting notes, 'gothic tales were set in the Middle, or "Dark", Ages' (2014: 2), incorporating imaginings of a dark, superstitious and mysterious Middle Ages associated with 'supernatural possibility, mystery, magic, wonder and monstrosity' (2). Whether or not contemporary authors are familiar with these eighteenth-century texts, they cannot but be aware of their twentieth-century reinventions, from Anne Rice's *Interview with the Vampire* to the television series *Buffy the Vampire Slayer*, which themselves draw upon earlier texts and on gothic subcultures and practices. Gothic medievalisms are, then, inflected by the 'multiple and entangled readings and interpretations' (Botting 2014: 198) which have circulated since the eighteenth century, always responding to the preoccupations and anxieties of their own times. Similarly, medievalisms for the young call on a multi-temporal assortment of texts and cultural influences. They do not tell us about the historical Middle Ages – in any case, an impossible proposition, given that the period referred to as medieval incorporates a thousand years of social, cultural and political conditions. Rather, the texts I consider in this book disclose how the *idea* of the Middle Ages is envisaged and how its significances are encoded in modern times.

Children's literature and medievalism studies: disciplines at the margins

This book draws together children's literature research with medievalism studies. The latter developed from medieval studies (the study of the literature and history of the Middle Ages) in the late 1970s, when the journal *Studies in Medievalism* was inaugurated. Since this time, the field of medievalism studies has steadily grown, and is now represented in a large and diverse body of publications and at the principal conferences on medieval studies. Distinctions between medieval studies and medievalism studies have been driven, in part, by the sense that medieval studies is the original, whereas medievalism studies is merely a weak, reductive and impoverished imitation of this original. Yet this differentiation vastly undersells the complexity of relations between medieval and modern. Neither medieval studies nor medievalism studies offers unmediated access to the Middle Ages. And whether scholars focus on medieval or medievalist texts, their interpretative and analytical approaches are shaped by their tastes and predilections as much as by disciplinary and cross-disciplinary practices.

Considering the relationship between medieval and medievalism studies, Thomas Prendergast and Stephanie Trigg conclude that 'the long-cherished opposition between medieval and medievalism studies … may turn out to be less about epistemology, as the historical purists would maintain, and more about different kinds of desiring subjects' (2009: 118). These scholars are by no means alone in contesting distinctions between the two. Louise Fradenburg remarks that 'the differences between academic and popular medievalism are of course *made*, and sometimes are made to occlude similarities' (1997: 209); and Davis and Altschul, conceiving of the Middle Ages as an idea rather than a coherent entity, maintain that once seen in this light, 'medieval studies itself becomes a form of constructing the "Middle Ages" and thus takes on the hue of an educated form of medievalism as intellectual creation' (2009: 7–8).[1]

The sometimes testy negotiations between medieval studies and medievalism studies which are suggested by the preceding summary may well strike children's literature scholars as oddly familiar, for the fields of children's literature studies and medievalism studies have much in common. Both emerged in the 1970s from well-established disciplines: respectively, literature and medieval studies. Both occupy somewhat marginal positions in relation to these more traditional areas: children's literature is sometimes regarded, in the words of John Stephens and Roderick McGillis, as the 'immature simple sister to mainstream literature' (2006: 367); and Prendergast and Trigg remark that when medievalism studies emerged 'it was seen by many as hopelessly tertiary: a weak discipline that studied the weak reflections of the Middle Ages' (2009: 117). Both children's literature research and studies of medievalist texts include in their ambit a vast array of textual genres and forms, from popular to literary, and both attract large and growing numbers of students from a variety of disciplinary fields. The very attractiveness of children's literature and medievalism studies to students tends to be regarded by literary scholars and medievalists as a sign of the disintegration of 'traditional' disciplines and their abandonment to mediocrity.

One of the arguments against taking both children's literature research and medievalism studies seriously is that both tend to be regarded as fundamentally unserious and lightweight in comparison with the weighty and labour-intensive scholarly enterprises of literary and medieval studies. Although the illusion that children's books are by nature simple and straightforward is prevalent among those with only a glancing knowledge of such books, producers of fiction for the young and scholars of children's literature know better. Similarly, medievalist texts are as varied and rich with meaning as any field of production, demonstrating the potency of the medieval and its global reach. Both medievalism studies and children's literature studies call on an interdisciplinary array of ideas and reading strategies to inform their investigation of texts. While children's literature scholarship is distinguished by its consciousness of the socialising and pedagogical agendas which permeate textual production for the young, medievalism studies is centrally focused on how medievalist texts and practices make sense of and represent the medieval past to modern audiences.

Louise D'Arcens argues that both medieval and medievalist studies manifest a paradoxical insistence on the alterity of the Middle Ages and, coexisting with this, 'a disavowed desire to rescue the text from that alterity – a forensic impulse to restore it to life, render it knowable, and thereby possess it' (2008: 82). D'Arcens notes a tendency for scholars of medievalism to invoke analogies between medievalist texts and medieval antecedents, thereby treating the Middle Ages as a source of originary validation. Thus, many of the scholars who discuss Brian Helgeland's film *A Knight's Tale* (2001) both disavow the idea that it is possible to retrieve 'the real Middle Ages' and also criticise the film for its lack of adherence to the spirit of the Middle Ages. Although it is generally agreed that the film is not an adaptation of Chaucer's 'The Knight's Tale', it is common for critics to compare it unfavourably with Chaucer's text (D'Arcens 2008: 85–98). Such contradictory impulses are visible, too, in children's literature scholarship dealing with medievalist texts.

Medievalism and children's literature research

Scholars working in the fields of medieval and medievalist studies frequently acknowledge the role of children's texts in inducting the young into the Middle Ages. In her introduction to *Adapting the Arthurian Legends for Children* (2004), for instance, Barbara Tepa Lupack lists a roll call of American writers whose reminiscences of childhood reading linger on their exposure to Arthurian and medieval narratives, including Jane Yolen, Tennessee Williams, Thomas Berger, F. Scott Fitzgerald, Ernest Hemingway and John Steinbeck (xv–xvii). Although the wide reach and influence of medievalist texts for the young is acknowledged, this body of texts is only gradually finding visibility in scholarly collections and at key conferences such as the International Congress on Medieval Studies at Kalamazoo. Stephen Knight's comprehensive studies *Robin Hood: A Mythic Biography* (2003) and *Merlin: Knowledge and Power Through the Ages* (2009) incorporate discussions of children's texts, and Velma Bourgeois Richmond's *Chaucer as Children's Literature: Retellings from the Victorian and Edwardian Eras* (2004) and Lupack's *Adapting the Arthurian Legends for Children* canvass a wide range of retellings of Chaucer and Arthurian narratives. Over the last few years scholarly work in medievalism studies has begun to incorporate discussions of children's literature, including Stephanie Trigg's *Medievalism and the Gothic in Australian Culture* (2006), Tison Pugh and Angela Jane Weisl's *Medievalisms: Making the Past in the Present* (2013), Gail Ashton and Daniel T. Kline's *Medieval Afterlives in Popular Culture* (2013) and Louise D'Arcens and Andrew Lynch's *International Medievalism and Popular Culture* (2014), all of which include chapters on popular or literary texts for the young.

In children's literature scholarship, discussions of medievalist texts manifest tensions which centre on historicist concerns. Adherence to the idea of a 'real Middle Ages' retains a strong hold on the field of children's literature, together with a related anxiety over accuracy and authenticity. This preoccupation with historicism and notions of accuracy is not confined to children's literature but is nevertheless heightened by the fact that children and young people are more or less inexperienced readers with differential perceptions of chronology and historicity; the implication is that they therefore require accuracy and reliability in fictive accounts of the Middle Ages. In discussions of medievalist texts the fiction of scholar-authors such as J. R. R. Tolkien, C. S. Lewis and Kevin Crossley-Holland is often read in the light of their professional expertise as medievalists, so that their novels are attributed with a degree of authority not possessed by non-specialist authors. Similarly, authority is associated with the research involved in writing historical novels; thus, Miriam Youngerman Miller, citing Sheila A. Egoff, praises Cynthia Harnett, Robert Welch, Barbara Leonie Picard, Rosemary Sutcliff, C. Walter Hodges and other authors who have written historical novels set in the Middle Ages because they 'have produced fiction that is every bit as convincing as the modern realistic novel, at the same time describing past societies with the knowledge and integrity of the scholar' (1995: 72).

As Tison Pugh and Angela Jane Weisl note in *Medievalisms*, 'running through much analysis of "medieval" children's literature is the assumption that it should, even as fantasy, teach about the real Middle Ages' (2013: 60). Thus, Rebecca Barnhouse's guide for teachers, *Recasting the Past: The Middle Ages in Young Adult Literature* (2000), castigates Roy Gerrard for the levity with which he treats the Middle Ages in his picture book, *Sir Cedric* (1984): 'Elements of chivalry give the book a medieval flavor, but Gerrard's intent is to have fun, not to present an accurate view of the Middle Ages' (2000: 164). Barnhouse's complaint is symptomatic of her conception of the distinction between narratives which 'capture' the 'real Middle Ages', and those which merely 'use' the Middle Ages for purposes of humour or atmosphere. However, as Helen Young observes, an emphasis on the 'accuracy' of medievalist texts based on the sources of allusions, narratives and representations is of limited usefulness because 'modern texts engage with multiple temporalities, not just the Middle Ages and the present' (2010: 166). Rather than drawing unproblematically on a 'real Middle Ages' for settings, characters and other elements of fiction, children's authors engage with versions of the Middle Ages which are themselves mediated and contingent. Contrary to Barnhouse's insistence that fantasy texts merely 'use' the Middle Ages to entertain their audiences, such texts engage with the afterlife of the past by reimagining ancient stories, and by interpolating spectral visitations and anachronistic intertextual references into their narratives. Moreover, as I will demonstrate throughout this book, the medieval is often treated in quite contradictory ways within texts, testifying to the complexity of modern engagements with the past.

Childhood, the medieval and modernity

Comparisons have often been drawn between childhood and the Middle Ages. Seth Lerer observes that the child was a metaphor for the medieval in the post-medieval world: 'Renaissance and Enlightenment historians saw medieval Europe as a childish time, a kind of cultural formation moment in the history of the West that they, more modern figures, had outgrown' (2008: 13). This perspective of the Middle Ages is aligned with the formulations of periodicity which effected a temporal break between the Middle Ages and the Renaissance, privileging the latter through comparison with the former: maturity against youth; knowledge against ignorance; sophistication against simplicity. To push the comparison further, one might regard the Middle Ages, children's literature and child readers as occupying a 'pre' state: the Middle Ages as premodern, children's literature as that literature which precedes literature proper, and child readers as pre-adults.

Such oppositions, always conceived retrospectively, incorporate hierarchies of value which assume that modernity, literature 'proper' and adulthood constitute normative states or stages from which their 'pre' versions derive meaning. Rather, as Fradenburg argues, past and present, then and now, coexist in individuals as well as across temporalities: 'the intersubjectivity of subjectivity is in part a temporal matter; we all live in many different times; different times live on in us and in our practices' (2009: 88). Similarly, children's texts, like child readers, negotiate across the spaces between adulthood and childhood. Produced by adults, but (unlike other fields of literature) defined in relation to their readership, children's texts embody adults' fears and anxieties, projected onto the imagined childhoods they construct.

The idea that the medieval constitutes modernity's other is resilient in children's literature, manifesting in settings, characters and existents which tend to represent the Middle Ages along two opposing poles of signification: as a romanticised pre-industrial and pre-technological world whose inhabitants lead simple, wholesome lives; or as a primitive time/place permeated by filth, disease and superstition. But medievalisms play out in cultural meanings that go far beyond mere representations or descriptions of the Middle Ages. For instance, medieval settings and narratives often provide a distancing perspective which enables the treatment of contemporary values and practices. Thus, recent historical fiction set in the period of the Third Crusade traverses a topic of consuming contemporary significance: relations between Muslims and Christians (Bradford 2009). Concepts of nationhood, affiliation and gendered identities, too, are frequently approached through medievalist fantasy narratives.

The most obvious category of medievalist texts for the young comprises retellings of medieval stories, including folk tales, Arthurian narratives and heroic literature. Yet even such retellings are far from straightforward in their uses of the medieval, since they involve processes of interpretation and adaptation which embody judgements about medieval stories, about their fitness for contemporary audiences, and about the values they promote. Whether authors translate from Middle English or draw upon previous versions of stories (as in retellings of fairy tales), the language they use is never ideologically neutral, because retold texts, like any others, embody social and cultural relations and rehearse the values and tensions of their times and places of production. In other texts, medievalisms can be more difficult to detect, embedded subtly into narratives, characters and allusions. Fradenburg, for instance, constructs a convincing argument that the film *Babe* possesses a 'recognizably medievalist agenda', celebrating 'love between master and servant'[2] and 'rural life as the scene in which such love might be rediscovered' (1997: 205), and evincing both a distrust of technology (the fax machine which features in the film) and also a canny capacity to exploit its possibilities.

Quite apart from a tendency to adhere to a negative historicist version of a Middle Ages characterised by filth, disease and poverty, medievalist children's texts sometimes advocate social imaginaries with a distinctly regressive tinge. Historical novels involving representations of Islam and Muslim societies, for instance, tend to fall back on oppositions that flatter the European Middle Ages; and in Chapter 4 I discuss an historical novel in which depictions of disability are shaped by stereotypical assumptions about the Muslim Other. In Chapter 3 of this book I consider Richelle Mead's *Vampire Academy* (2007), arguing that the medievalist setting of this novel affords a context for ethnically charged distinctions which privilege whiteness. As these examples suggest, concepts of 'tradition', 'pre-modernity' and 'modernity' are readily subsumed into versions of the medieval which are deployed to underpin distinctions between Europeans and their Others.

This book adopts a capacious approach to medievalisms for the young, considering positive and negative representations of the medieval across the genres of fiction, film and non-fiction, and in relation to various textual modes including animation, fantasy, picture books, gothic novel, paranormal romance, melodrama and comedy.[3] The chapters address what I regard as some of the key concepts underpinning medievalist texts for the young, beginning in Chapter 1 with a consideration of the purposes and functions of the Middle Ages in contemporary texts. As the discipline of history has increasingly scrutinised its assumptions about what constitutes historical knowledge, innovations in historical fiction have translated these debates into metafictional and postmodern approaches to narrative. At the same time, children's literature scholarship continues to manifest an anxious preoccupation with how the past is, or should be, represented to young readers. Chapter 2 draws upon Elizabeth Grosz's and Carolyn Dinshaw's reflections on temporality to explore how the medieval past irrupts in contemporary fiction for the young, woven into recursive narratives and representations which disrupt linear models of time. Chapter 3 takes up concepts of the 'spatial turn' in literary and cultural theory articulated, for instance, by Michel Foucault and David Harvey, investigating how ancient places and artefacts resonate in contemporary texts and encourage negotiations across time and space.

Chapters 4, 5 and 6 pursue depictions of medieval embodiment, commencing in Chapter 4 with a consideration of the non-normative (disabled) bodies which are so prevalent in medievalist texts for the young. In this chapter I call upon theorists of disability such as David T. Mitchell, Sharon L. Snyder and Rosemarie Garland-Thomson. Chapter 5 shifts to a consideration of monstrous identities in fantasy: fairies, vampires, dragons and werewolves, drawing upon the field of monster theory and Jacques Derrida's conception of the 'monstrous *arrivant*' (1995: 386–7), the monstrous figure which ushers in change and futurity. Chapter 6 focuses on animals in medievalist texts in the light of Bruno Latour's version of actor-network theory, exploring the affective and ontological roles played by animals in their relations to humans. Chapter 7 considers one of the most common and least discussed modes of medievalism for the young: comic treatments of the Middle Ages in film, fiction and non-fiction. Theorists of humour and comedy ranging from Henri Bergson to Simon Critchley provide conceptual frameworks within to locate this influential body of texts.

My investigations of medievalisms for the young are informed by my conviction that the medieval is not back there in a remote past, but is rather beside us, entering our present through memory, imagination and invention. My intention in this book is to call upon concepts, theories and reading strategies from children's literature research and medievalism studies in order to analyse contemporary medievalisms for children and young people. I focus not on taxonomies of medievalist texts, but on the literary and cultural functions of the medieval, probing how imaginings of the Middle Ages propose and advocate values, offer models (negative and positive) of human behaviour and sociality, and speculate about future worlds.

1
Thinking about the Middle Ages

The pervasiveness of the Middle Ages in contemporary texts for children and young people, like the proliferation of medievalisms more generally, feeds off a cluster of phenomena: the allure of the past in modern times; the prominence of the visual; the global production and circulation of media texts and digital games; the ready availability of online information about medieval culture and history. The explanatory capacity of these phenomena is, however, limited, since in themselves they do not explain why the medieval is taken up with such enthusiasm by producers and audiences. Medievalist narratives self-evidently engage with the past, while their creators and audiences are enmeshed in the present time in which texts are produced and received. As I will explain, the idea of the *present past* (Robinson 2011) offers a useful way of thinking about how fictions about the past are shaped by the world views and ideologies of the present time of their authors. This chapter considers the conceptualisation of the medieval in relation to the contemporary, the cultural purposes of the medieval in texts for the young, and the historiographical questions that surround these texts and their critical reception.

Negotiations between past and present are central to the pleasures offered by medievalist imaginings for young people, and the cultural work they carry out. For the past is vividly present in contemporary society; as David Lowenthal remarks, 'the past is not dead ...; it is not even sleeping. A mass of memories and records, of relics and replicas, of monuments and memorabilia, lives at the core of our being. And as we remake it, the past remakes us' (1985: xxv). Medievalist texts for the young train audiences to respond to the past by offering them experiences of imagination, empathy and insight at the same time that they play out the socialising agendas which always inform texts for young people. This is true of works of fantasy as much as realist historical narratives. As Helen Young points out, there exists a 'continuum of medievalism which stretches between imaginative and historical' (2010: 179). But texts cannot readily be slotted into positions along this continuum; for instance, imaginative elements may manifest in historical texts, and historically grounded features in imaginative texts. For this reason I work across the diverse genres and forms whose narratives engage with the Middle Ages rather than assuming a taxonomic approach which distinguishes between historical and imaginative approaches. I begin this discussion by considering two key aspects of medievalist texts for the young: their provision of experiences of enchantment; and their strategies of providing distanced treatments of contemporary questions and issues.

Disenchantment and medievalist enchantments in texts for the young

Studies of modernity in recent years have frequently grappled with the legacy of Max Weber's gloomy view, articulated in his 1917 lecture 'Science as a Vocation', that 'the fate of our times is characterized by rationalization and intellectualization and, above all, by the "disenchantment of the world"' (1991: 155). In *As If: Modern Enchantment and the Literary Prehistory of Virtual Reality* (2012), the historian Michael Saler traces the origins and development of the discourses of disenchantment which have informed accounts of modernity since the eighteenth century. He points to the recent historiographic counter-view which argues that far from comprising a zone of disenchantment, Western modernity has increasingly valued experiences and moments of enchantment (Saler 2006, 2012; Chakrabarty 2000; Owen 2004). Saler finds that modern historians commonly adopt an approach which recognises the unresolved ambiguities and ambivalences characteristic of modern enchantment: 'Modern enchantment often depends upon its antinomial other, modern disenchantment, and a specifically modern enchantment might be defined as one that enchants and disenchants simultaneously: one that delights but does not delude' (2006: 702). This view of modern enchantment acknowledges the fluctuating and contradictory impulses which attend modern perspectives of the past, encapsulated in Dipesh Chakrabarty's coinage of the term 'timeknot' (2000: 243), the entanglement which occurs when ancient artefacts or practices reappear in modern times. Chakrabarty draws attention to the effects of such entanglement, which manifests 'the plurality that inheres in the "now," the lack of totality, the constant fragmentariness, that constitutes one's present' (243), and which occasions negotiations between past and present, ancient and modern.

Defining the experience of enchantment in *The Enchantment of Modern Life*, Jane Bennett says that it involves 'a surprising encounter' (2001: 5) with something unexpected which occasions both pleasure and also a sense of the uncanny. Such encounters may involve the slippery negotiations which occur when one species morphs into another, or when a person experiences the unexpected in the everyday, or when elements of the past irrupt in contemporary settings, or when consumer society offers pleasures which are both fugitive and real. Descriptions of enchantment have historically lumped children together with groups regarded as inferior ('primitives', women and the lower classes) because of their susceptibility to enchantment. Moreover, recent discussions frequently treat childhood as the paradigmatic state of enchantment, which Bennett describes as 'a shot in the arm, a fleeting return to childlike excitement about life' (5). Ulrich Beck regards the child as 'the *private type of re-enchantment*', a bulwark against disenchantment and the instability of adult relationships (1992: 118). These allusions to childhood and enchantment are not without their dangers, since they teeter on the edge of treating children as passive subjects of social and cultural processes and forces, of assuming too readily that all childhoods are enchanted, and, in Beck's case, of reverting to nineteenth-century concepts of the salvific child who provides an antidote to the failings of adults.

Nevertheless, studies of enchantment afford a useful lens through which to consider contemporary medievalist texts for children. Saler argues that the emergence of works of fantasy for children during the mid-nineteenth century marks the beginnings of a cultural shift occasioned by 'the spread of secularism, the greater diffusion of economic prosperity, the increase in leisure time, and the irresistible allures of the new mass culture' (2012: 48). This cultural shift is visible in the popularity of fantasy works and traditional tales from the middle of the nineteenth century, exemplified by medievalist fiction like that of George MacDonald, and retellings of fairy tales, including Andrew Lang's influential Fairy Books, published between 1889 and 1910. Coinciding with the Medieval Revival of Thomas Carlyle, John Ruskin and Tennyson's *Idylls of the King*, fantasy for children and young people increasingly called on medievalist tropes, settings and figures.[1]

From the end of the nineteenth century, writers for adults and children have located fantasy narratives in imaginary worlds which, Saler argues, carry out the cultural project of 're-enchanting an allegedly disenchanted world' (2012: 17). Saler identifies two features that, he says, characterise modern imaginary worlds constructed in fiction, film and popular culture: 'First, while they are understood to be explicitly fictional, they are also taken to be real, often to such an extent that they continue to be "inhabited" long after the tale has been told ... Second, they combine fantasy with realism, wild imagination with sober logic' (39). Saler's term 'the ironic imagination' (25) captures the double consciousness of audience responses to these imagined worlds, where fantastic elements are bound up with the mimetic strategies of realism to create highly detailed and believable settings. The paradigmatic example is J. R. R. Tolkien's Middle-earth, which is both an imagined world and also an intricately mapped space based on Tolkien's conception of Englishness.[2] Well before the advent of postmodernism, then, young audiences were positioned to engage with modern forms of enchantment which played with relationships between real and imagined worlds. These narratives invited an ironic and sceptical response, anticipating the self-reflexiveness which characterises the reception of mass culture products and texts.

More recently, new technologies have enabled the persistence of virtual worlds, so that players of medievalist role-playing computer games such as *World of Warcraft*, *Diablo* and *Baldur's Gate* return over and over to online worlds where they engage in continuing projects and campaigns conducted in settings sustained in real time. Film versions of medievalist fantasy, too, cement the impression of worlds 'taken to be real'; Peter Jackson's *Lord of the Rings* films and *Hobbit* trilogy, for instance, are so closely associated with the New Zealand landscapes where these films have been made that New Zealand is often referred to as 'Middle-earth' in tourism guides and promotional material. Such powerful depictions of imagined worlds inevitably carry over to the experience of reading fiction; thus, readers who have viewed films based on J. K. Rowling's 'Harry Potter' novels and Tolkien's fiction can be expected to visualise settings and characters in line with the film versions of these texts. Further, many readers produce texts based on the fiction they love, locating virtual communities where they construct fanfiction, artwork and non-fiction material such as maps, genealogical tables and floor plans. As Arjun Appadurai notes, one of the effects of the global cultural order is that 'fantasy is now social practice; it enters, in a host of ways, into the fabrication of social lives for many people in many societies' (1996: 53). Medievalist fantasy, available to global audiences through film, television and video technologies, comprises just such a social practice in contemporary culture.

Medievalist picture books constitute a prominent site of enchantment, incorporating spectacular and often comical depictions of figures identified with contemporary imaginings of the Middle Ages.[3] One such figure, prominent in picture books and novels, is that of the dragon, which appears in three categories of picture book: (1) those located in contemporary settings where dragons appear as marvellous, strange and mysterious elements in the modern world; (2) texts with medieval settings, in which dragons are predictable and 'normal' elements; and (3) texts which play with the strategies of boundary breaking, metafictional play and self-reflexivity often associated with the postmodern.[4] Picture books in the third of these categories tend to assume experienced readers accustomed to the playful and allusive narratives and stylistics of postmodernism.

Bruce Whatley's *Hunting for Dragons* (2010) fits within the first of the three categories I have identified. A young girl hunts for dragons in the setting of the suburban home where she lives with her older brother and parents. For a helmet she wears a saucepan; her breastplate is a metal colander; her knees are protected by a foam rubber cleaning pad (Figure 1.1). These commonplace items afford a sharp contrast with the *idée fixe* which propels the protagonist's actions: that dragons live in and about her home, and that one day she will catch one with the butterfly net which she carries for the purpose. The girl's parents respond to her imaginings of dragons in a common-sense and placatory style represented only as dialogue, since neither they nor her brother feature in the illustrations except for a glimpse of the protagonist's father in one image.

The central conceit of *Hunting for Dragons* is the gap between the protagonist's imaginings and the real-world existents on which her fantasy is based. When she 'sees' dragons in her father's workshop, her brother's bedroom or the dinner table, the illustrations show both the material objects which drive her fantasy, and how these objects create an illusion of dragons. Thus, the workshop scene shows a dragon-shaped shadow on the wall; in the foreground is the jumble of tools and everyday objects (workman's saw, keys, hammer) which create the shadow. The gap between what the girl imagines and the reality behind her imaginings is, however, complicated by the medievalist references that permeate the domestic setting. The toys in her brother's bedroom

> One day I saw a dragon
> that didn't see me.
> I tried to catch him.

Figure 1.1 Illustration from *Hunting for Dragons* by Bruce Whatley

include a model castle and knight; in the laundry, a jester's hat tumbles out of a wicker basket.

Indeed, the domestic aesthetic can be read as 'medieval', since the house is filled with rustic and hand-wrought items made of wood, metal and natural fabrics. The distinctions between real and imagined are, then, always fluid, and in one instance they collapse altogether. In a scene at the family dinner table, the girl sees a dragon in the food (pork chop, cauliflower, tomatoes, peas, potatoes) on her father's plate. She pounces on this plate with her butterfly net, so that the food splatters her father as he sits at the table. He is dressed in a Tudor doublet and linen shirt, his neatly trimmed beard visible above his collar.

These playful negotiations evoke ontological questions concerning what is real and what is imagined. If the girl's father is 'really' a medieval man, the possibility is open that the dragon, too, is real. In the book's final sequence the girl stands in front of the gothic door that leads to her bedroom (Figure 1.2).

She calls to her parents:

'Mum! Dad! There's a dragon in my bedroom!'
'Yes, dear,' said Mum.
'A huge one, I bet,' said Dad. 'Big and scary.'
But I knew there was definitely a dragon in my room. (2010, unpaged)

The turning page leads to a double spread in which the girl finds the dragon sitting on her bed: 'And he wasn't scary at all'. This illustration is replete with details from previous illustrations: the dragon wears the jester's hat and carries spectacles, keys and saucepan as he balances a ball on his tail. Gathering up these items, this illustration refuses distinctions between real and imagined, undercutting the reassurances of the girl's parents and exposing the unreliability of adult common sense. The faces of the two mirror each other, conjuring up a consuming and ecstatic moment of enchantment during which 'a new circuit

Figure 1.2 Illustration from *Hunting for Dragons* by Bruce Whatley

of intensities forms between material bodies' (Bennett 2001: 104). This scene and the narrative outcome it incorporates positions young readers to experience a kind of sympathetic enchantment.

The enchantment modelled in *Hunting for Dragons* is more complex than the conventional distinction between disenchanted adults whose rationality renders them incapable of seeing dragons, and the enchanted child who can. For the *habitus* of the family home – what Bourdieu refers to as the 'durably installed generative principle of regulated improvisations' (1977: 78) – is itself replete with a set of dispositions, tastes and practices which locate enchantment in the medieval. This delight in the Middle Ages manifests in ordinary items such as clothing and furniture; it spills over into fantasy in the dinner table scene and in the images which precede the girl's encounter with the dragon. These images, showing a castle, a life-size set of armour and a stone-framed gothic door, extravagantly exceed the norms of domestic architecture which apply through preceding illustrations. Combining postmodernist excess with the homeliness of domestic details – a laundry basket, kitchen utensils, a bowl of strawberries – the illustrations sweep up the entire household, adults and children, into a *habitus* whose regulated improvisations combine the real and the imagined. The protagonist's encounter with the dragon is thus situated within a setting that encourages and even advocates medievalist fantasies.

But sites of enchantment are not confined to fantasy texts; rather, historical fiction and even non-fiction texts incorporate imaginings of premodern settings and lives where readers are positioned to align with characters who experience moments of enchantment which momentarily propel them beyond the mundane. In Kevin Crossley-Holland's novel *Gatty's Tale* (2006), for instance, the narrative lingers on an episode of this kind, which occurs when the eponymous protagonist reaches the Church of the Holy Sepulchre in Jerusalem, following her long pilgrimage from the English manor house where she is a servant. Gatty experiences two (related) moments of intense insight and pleasure, one identified with religious belief and the other with an intersubjective experience which transcends religious and cultural difference.

In Jerusalem, Gatty contrives to remain in the Church of the Holy Sepulchre when it is closed to pilgrims at sundown so that she can fulfil a promise she has made to her mistress, Lady Gwyneth, before her death. This episode is introduced by an incident during which Gatty encounters a young Saracen boy who is charged with ensuring that all pilgrims leave the Holy Sepulchre. She persuades him to close his eyes to the fact that she intends to remain in the church. At the end of their exchange, conducted through gestures and the few words they have in common, he purses his lips and blows lightly over her face; imitating his actions, she does the same to him. When she is alone in the heart of the Holy Sepulchre Gatty prays for Lady Gwyneth, and for all those she knows, living and dead; then she begins to sing: 'She sang and she sang' (2006: 315). Gatty's giftedness as a singer is a constant feature of her identity, recognised by her mistress who arranges for her to have lessons in singing and reading. Her singing in the Holy Sepulchre articulates an enhanced sense of self which draws both on her love of singing and also on the advances of knowledge and insight she has gained during the pilgrimage.

The morning after her vigil, her fellow pilgrim Snout asks her what she has sung. Gatty explains that she has sung the psalms she has learned, 'songs without words' and 'a new song' which creates by naming: 'I made steps climb and passages twist, I made darkness blind, and candles waxen. I made light shine. In my song, I created them' (2006: 315). With its echoes of the creation myth of the Book of Genesis, where naming effects creation, Gatty's song gestures to Judaeo-Christian traditions; but her song is also wrought out of experience and affect. Bennett observes that the derivation of the word *enchant*, linked to the French verb *chanter*, suggests that 'to enchant' is to 'surround with song or incantation; hence, to cast a spell with sounds ..., to carry away on a sonorous stream' (2001: 6), much as Gatty's song fills her with a transcendent sense of oneness with her world. To introduce an episode involving a powerful incident of religious experience is to run the risk of alienating contemporary readers who may be ignorant of or hostile to the Christian significances of the setting. The novel negotiates these uncertainties by emphasising the materiality in which religious impulses clothe themselves: the soaring building, which seems 'more like a mantle than armour' (2006: 313), the misty atmospherics of incense and candles, and the bodily actions of singing, sobbing and speaking which constitute Gatty's prayer.

A second kind of enchantment is manifested in Gatty's encounter with the Saracen boy, which she experiences at the time as a strange and unexplained event. This encounter is later explicated by Brother Gabriel, the Hospitaller who has provided accommodation in Jerusalem to Gatty and the other pilgrims. Following Gatty's overnight stay in the Church of the Holy Sepulchre, Brother Gabriel tells her that the Saracen boy's act of blowing on her face signified that he blew verses from the Koran over her to protect and bless her. When Gatty copied his action she performed a Muslim ritual without knowing it, prompted by her desire to reach across the boundaries of race and religion which separated her from the boy. Her action thus instantiates a form of crossing which symbolises her liberation from her previous, reflex conviction about the primacy of Christianity and the infamy of non-Christians. Bennett notes that the enchanting effect of crossing carries 'an ethical potential' (2001: 30); in *Gatty's Tale*, this moment of border-crossing advocates an ethic of respect for and engagement with the beliefs of the other.

These episodes and moments of enchantment connect the medieval with strangeness, difference and transcendence. Young readers of *Hunting for Dragons* are positioned to align with the protagonist as she engages in the playful enterprise of discovering dragons in the safety of the family home, a discovery which links medieval and modern, fantasy and reality. Gatty's out-of-the-world experience during her vigil in the Church of the Holy Sepulchre invites readers, regardless of their religious affiliation, to imagine an experience of transcendence; and her fleeting encounter with the Saracen boy constitutes an enchanted moment as religious and cultural differences fade away.

Medievalisms as distancing strategies

If some medievalist texts for children incorporate experiences of enchantment, others address contemporary questions indirectly, by interpolating such questions into medieval settings. This distancing strategy is evident in dragon picture books set in the Middle Ages, typically represented by way of conventional medievalist schemas populated by stock elements such as castles, maidens, princes, forests and magical elements. In these settings, young protagonists encounter dragons as friends, antagonists or sidekicks. The dragons in such books typically do not devour maidens or lay waste to villages; if they do, such events occur extradiegetically or they are treated comically, as in Robert Munsch and Michael Martchenko's *The Paper Bag Princess* (1980), in which the beautiful princess Elizabeth, who 'lived in a castle and had expensive princess clothes ... was going to marry a prince named Ronald. Unfortunately, a dragon smashed her castle, burned all her clothes with his fiery breath, and carried off Prince Ronald' (1980, unpaged).

The distancing strategies deployed in *The Paper Bag Princess* begin with its medievalist setting, which enables the interrogation of gender binarisms in the contemporary world. Concepts such as female agency, hegemonic masculinity and masculinist regimes of power, weighty ideas for the implied readership, are addressed through a style of medievalism which also nods to the real-world experience of young readers accustomed to narratives (films, fairy tales, fiction) incorporating princesses, princes and romance. Elizabeth anticipates other 1980s female action heroes, being similar in style to Supergirl (1984) and She-Ra, Princess of Power, He-Man's counterpart (1985). Like these powerful female figures, she does not regard marriage as a normal and usual romantic outcome, but models female independence and agency as she escapes cultural norms and the weight of the past.

Following the dragon's depredations Elizabeth, wearing only a paper bag, tricks the dragon into exhausting his energy so that she is able to enter his cave and save Ronald. The dragon represents a second distancing strategy. Stupid and easily fooled, he is an entertaining and comical prop, blearily viewing Elizabeth through his cave door: 'Well, a princess! I love to eat princesses, but I have already eaten a whole castle today. I am a very busy dragon. Come back tomorrow' (1980, unpaged). Posed at the door to his cave, legs crossed and examining his talons, the dragon performs a camped-up version of hyper-femininity which undercuts the pomposity of his language and the power of his fiery breath (Figure 1.3). This camp display anticipates the book's closure, when Elizabeth rescues Ronald from the dragon's cave. Ronald reprimands her for her dishevelled state and demands that Elizabeth should come back when she is 'dressed like a real princess': '"Ronald," said Elizabeth, "your clothes are really pretty and your hair is very neat. You look like a real prince, but you are a toad." They didn't get married after all' (1980, unpaged).

Like the dragon, Prince Ronald is somewhat camp, with his really pretty clothes, his very neat hair, and his extravagant horror at Elizabeth's dishevelled state (Figure 1.4). By implication, the narrative applauds Elizabeth's good judgement in evading the heteronormative closure represented by her projected marriage to Ronald.

Medievalist camp in picture books (and also, notably, in animated films) manifests most often in narratives which use the medieval to produce disjunctions between conventional gender stereotypes and the incongruity encoded in camp displays and performances (Mallan 2009: 160). In effect, the dragon and Prince Ronald function as a composite, and the camp elements of their depiction draw attention to the instability of hegemonic masculinity. At the same time, these representations of camp behaviour implicate the text in what might be regarded as a coded form of homophobia, since the figures of the dragon and Prince Roland valorise traditional forms of masculinity by representing feminine males as comical.

Figure 1.3 Illustration from *The Paper Bag Princess* by Robert Munsch and Michael Martchenko

In other picture books anthropomorphised dragons function as surrogate children, often in narratives where former enemies develop empathetic relations to become friends. In Martin Baynton's *Jane and the Dragon* (1988), for instance, the eponymous protagonist, obliged to spend weary hours practising her stitches, longs to be a knight. She secretly practises swordplay and horsemanship, and when a dragon abducts the prince she rides off to rescue him, dressed in armour and helmet. During the long battle that ensues, both Jane and the dragon have opportunities to kill each other, and when they abandon the battle out of exhaustion, both confess that they are not what they seem: the dragon abducts princes only because of the weight of expectations

Figure 1.4 Illustration from *The Paper Bag Princess* by Robert Munsch and Michael Martchenko

that he should; and Jane is disguised as a knight because her gender precludes her from adventures. Like many other medievalist texts for the young, *Jane and the Dragon* features a protagonist who is exceptional for her time; who, indeed, manifests many of the values and attitudes promoted to young girls in progressive contemporary societies. In picture books featuring dragons, friendships between dragons and human protagonists result from their recognition of the stultifying effects of cultural norms.[5] Jane becomes a knight, negotiating a contract giving her time off to visit the dragon every Saturday; and the dragon lives a peaceful life released from the obligation to attack humans. The medieval in *Jane and the Dragon* thus affords a convenient shorthand for cultural fixity, positioning child readers to respond positively to narratives which show that happiness and friendship are contingent on liberation from outmoded ('medieval') practices.

The figures of Elizabeth and Jane in *The Paper Bag Princess* and *Jane and the Dragon* enact 1980s feminist agendas, promoting female agency and anticipating the 'girl power' discourses of the 1990s. The flattened, formulaic Middle Ages of these picture books affords a background for feminist narratives, catering to young audiences who are assumed to be familiar with similar depictions of the medieval in fiction, cartoons and film. *Gatty's Tale*, in contrast, implies older readers with a more developed sense of historical time, and engages explicitly with the events and politics of the time in which it is set. Yet like *The Paper Bag Princess* and *Jane and the Dragon* this novel too constructs a version of the Middle Ages which enables explorations of contemporary ideas and values. In particular it responds to current anxieties about relationships between Muslim and Christian individuals and cultures. Tracking Gatty's travels from England to Jerusalem, the narrative also tracks the cognitive and affective processes involved in her shift from a reflex distrust of 'Saracens' to empathetic relationships with the Muslim characters she meets during her travels. Historical novels have enjoyed a resurgence over the last two decades precisely because they can both claim distance from the contemporary world, and also address contested questions such as relations between Christian and Muslim people, and the cultural practices whereby modern nations exclude their others.

The differences between the two genres reside not in the 'accuracy' with which they represent the Middle Ages, but rather in how they engage with the medieval and with earlier traditions of medievalism. Picture books like *The Paper Bag Princess* and *Jane and the Dragon* locate their protagonists, Elizabeth and Jane, in medieval settings which offer a safe and light-hearted context in which to treat feminist agendas. In *Gatty's Tale*, the protagonist's progress towards an enhanced appreciation of religious and cultural diversity positions readers to consider the socialising influences which have shaped their perceptions of difference in their own cultural settings. These negotiations between medieval and modern hinge on narrative strategies which simultaneously contrast the medieval with modernity, and encourage readers to align themselves, as reading subjects, with medieval protagonists.

Historiography and medievalist fiction

Imaginings of the medieval are intimately bound up with conceptions of history and historiography. The narrative turn which transformed the discipline of history from the 1970s was ushered in by the work of Hayden White who, reacting against the so-called 'scientific history' of the nineteenth and earlier twentieth centuries, introduced a narrativist conception of history. White drew attention to the extent to which historians select historical events and facts in order to construct history through emplotment, the attribution of relations of cause and effect which produces shapely narratives. Since White, historiography has developed along three lines. The first of these is characterised by empiricist or reconstructionist methods which sustain traditional beliefs in the capacity of history to 'accurately' depict past times and cultures. Most contemporary historians adhere to the second approach, a constructionist orientation whereby they acknowledge their own subjectivities as scholars and adopt a self-critical stance in establishing and deploying conceptual frameworks. The third and most radical direction is taken up by historians such as F. R. Andersmit, Alun Munslow and Keith Jenkins, whose deconstructionist approaches critique historical methods, procedures and protocols. For scholars such as Munslow, history is less a set of tools and practices than a study of the narratives of history as they appear in the sources which historians use and the interpretations they and other historians develop. Munslow argues that 'sources are never transcendent signifiers because they have a pre-figured historical status by being already recounted in chronicles, diaries, legends, memories and interpretations' (1997: 65).

Literary theorists have applied these poststructuralist and postmodern perspectives of history to literary forms including historical fiction and fantasy, responding to the emergence of metafictional and magical realist modes of approaching the past. Although children's literature criticism has incorporated some of these debates into investigations of historical fiction for children, it clings to a preoccupation with questions of accuracy, truth and authenticity to a far greater extent than is the case in historical or literary studies scholarship more generally. The same is not, however, true of contemporary texts for children, many of which deploy narrative and discursive strategies consonant with the approaches of deconstructionist historiography. There is, then, something of a tension between the deconstructive tendencies of much medievalist fiction for the young, and the empirical and reconstructionist approaches which survive in discussions of this fiction, in scholarly discourses and especially in mainstream material (reviews, media reports and so on) dealing with children's texts. It is easy to discern the persistence of empirical approaches to history in the titles of books such as *Historical Fiction for Children: Capturing the Past*, a collection of essays edited by Fiona M. Collins and Judith Graham (2001), where the assumption is that the past exists as something knowable, to be 'captured' through fiction. The title 'Past Continuous: Historical Fiction for Children', used of a conference held at Newcastle University in 2009, evokes the idea of history as a seamless (continuous) succession of periods defined retrospectively as a neat, orderly sequence.

These titles point to the persistence of a set of ideas now highly contentious in the disciplines of history and literature: that the past can be reduced to truths or facts; that it comprises definable periods or sequences of events which can be accessed in the present; and that fiction about the past delivers past times and cultures to contemporary readers. Rather, I would argue, our relationship to the past is dynamic and changing; the past enters the present in unpredictable ways; periodicity is itself a way of narrating the past; and depictions of the past are inevitably inflected by the times and cultures in which they are produced. This last idea is not new, but in children's literature criticism it is strangely yoked with discourses of authenticity and truth.

Texts which narrate the past, whether historical fiction or fantasy, always project what Alan Robinson (calling on the German historian Reinhart Koselleck) refers to as the *present past*, the imagining of the past shaped in relation to the present (2011). Such imaginings of the past are provisional and changing because the human subjects producing them change, learn and revise their understandings of the past. The *present past* often understands the past as the prehistory or precondition of its present, writing the past to accord with teleologies which tend towards the now of the writing subject. Works of fiction also incorporate protagonists who occupy the *past present*, and who seek to predict what is ahead of them; that is, they look to a *past future* without knowing how it will turn out. Whether actual or invented historical figures, they are embedded in past worlds constructed through narrative and thus they project the world views and ideological preoccupations of authors, whether or not authors are conscious of these values and ideas. Readers are positioned to align themselves with protagonists living in the past and to empathetically predict how their futures might turn out.

In modern times the term 'anachronism' is often regarded as problematic in representations of the past — a misstep which draws attention to a lack of fidelity to the reality of past cultures and times. In fact, because we cannot experience the reality of the past our consumption of the past relies on anachronism, a word which need not be pejorative; it derives from the Greek *ana* (not, without) and *chronos* (time). As long ago as 1962 Georg Lukács, one of the first theorists of historical fiction, borrowed the term 'necessary anachronism' from Hegel to refer to the inescapable presentism of writing about the past; Lowenthal, discussing heritage and the past, says that 'we are bound to update the past whenever we engage with it; no matter how much we may feel we owe to or empathize with earlier epochs, we remain people of our own time' (1996: 153).

We cannot, then, directly experience the Middle Ages, which is present to us only in mediated forms such as texts, the built environment, monuments and artefacts. We 'know' the medieval through these texts and objects, but we cannot read or understand them as though we encountered them at the time they were created. This is not to deny the materiality of the past or the power of past texts, their capacity to grab at our emotions and engage our imaginations. It is impossible for us to disentangle our experience of our selves as contemporary subjects from our engagement with the past. Medievalist texts for young people are inescapably anachronistic because their *present past* is redolent with teleologies which tend towards the times of their production. Children's texts call upon aspects of the past in order to make sense of the present and to imagine the future, not to produce 'authentic' versions of past times and cultures.

The case of Catherine

Debates about truth, authenticity and facts are particularly prominent in reviews and discussions of historical fiction for children, and I turn now to Karen Cushman's *Catherine, Called Birdy* (1994) as a test case in order to probe these ideas and to suggest an alternative reading of the novel. *Catherine, Called Birdy* has attracted praise and criticism equally for its 'authenticity' and for its lack thereof. The reissued novel of 2007 incorporates the following snippets from reviews which appear in the paratextual front matter of the book under the heading 'Critical Acclaim for *Catherine, Called Birdy*':

1.
The Horn Book: [Birdy's] diary of the year 1290 is a revealing, amusing, and sometimes horrifying view both of Catherine's thoughts and life in the Middle Ages .... The vivid picture of medieval life presents a seemingly eye-witness view of a culture remote from contemporary beliefs. Fascinating and thought-provoking.

2.
The Kirkus Review: The period has rarely been presented for young people with such authenticity; the exotic details will intrigue readers

while they relate more closely to Birdy's yen for independence and her sensibilities toward the downtrodden. Her tenacity and ebullient naivete are extraordinary.

3.
School Library Journal: Birdy reveals fascinating facts about her time period. A feminist far ahead of her time, she is both believable and lovable ....

4.
The New York Times: Rambunctious ... a first-person scramble through Catherine's 14th year ... [and a] gallant attempt at re-creating the pastoral landscapes and the smoky halls of a vanished era.
(*Catherine, Called Birdy,* 1994 [2007])

Expressions such as 'seemingly eye-witness view' (Excerpt 1), 'has rarely been presented for young people with such authenticity' (Excerpt 2) and 'reveals fascinating facts' (Excerpt 3) disclose a bundle of assumptions: that the figure of Birdy is an 'authentically' medieval young woman; that the narrative delivers the Middle Ages through details and vivid descriptions; that Birdy is like contemporary girls ('a feminist far ahead of her time') but also wholly medieval. In the fourth of these excerpts, the phrase 'gallant attempt', together with the patchiness of the quotation – indicated by ellipses which raise questions as to what has been left out – suggests a more guarded response to the novel than is the case with the other three. In fact, the publishers have delicately stepped around the misgivings of the *New York Times* reviewer, Jane Langton. They have strategically quoted from her review, which includes the following:

> There is a good deal of stinking, vomiting and spitting, and there are fleas in the bedclothes and maggots in the meat. Probably this picture of medieval life is closer to reality than the fairy tale images many children are used to, but sometimes Catherine's wild jokes and confessions are too much like contemporary slapstick. They seem arch rather than true: 'I am near 14 and have never yet seen a hanging. My life is barren.' (Langton 1994: 20)

Langton's review is, then, torn between admiration for the novel's deployment of telling details, and criticism of its language ('arch rather than true'; 'like contemporary slapstick'). Unlike the other three excerpts, it acknowledges, even if implicitly, a distinction between 'the real Middle Ages' and fiction set in the Middle Ages. Langton ends with the following sentence, referring to the two novels which her review addresses, Frances Temple's *The Ramsay Scallop* and *Catherine, Called Birdy*: 'If the two fidgety young protagonists sometimes seem more like invaders from an American high school, with thick sneakers under their long gowns, young readers will probably like them the better for it' (Langton 1994: 20). Here we have a clear recognition of the presentism of historical fiction, its necessary imbrication with the time and culture in which it is produced. This complexity is, however, ironed out for promotional purposes by the publishers of *Catherine, Called Birdy*. The snippets they include are, I suspect, directed to adults – teachers, parents, librarians – who, it is assumed, want historical fiction to educate young readers about history.

Critical approaches to *Catherine, Called Birdy* are similarly divided, often foundering on the illusion that there exists a monolithic and internally consistent 'Middle Ages', and that this 'authentic' Middle Ages can readily be delivered by fiction for the young. To bolster such claims about the Middle Ages, scholars occasionally draw on historical sources such as the Paston Letters (MacLeod 1998; Wilson 2011). Thus, Anne Scott Macleod critiques the depiction of Birdy's resistance to her father when he demands that she should marry a middle-aged suitor for dynastic and business reasons, arguing that this narrative strand does not accord with 'medieval' practices of punishing young women for insubordination as recorded in the Paston Letters, where a daughter who opposes her mother's authority is beaten 'once in the week or twice, sometimes twice in one day' (Macleod 1998: 30). Similarly, in an essay on three novels set in the Middle Ages, Rebecca Barnhouse takes issue with what she refers to as the 'anachronistic fallacies' of these novels which, she says, overemphasise the importance of books and literacy in the Middle Ages. Barnhouse criticises the depiction of Birdy's friend, Perkin the goat boy, who yearns to read, memorises Latin and French words, and plans to run away from the village to become a scholar. According to Barnhouse, Perkin represents a compulsion on Cushman's part to 'promote literacy' (1998: 164), 'providing modern audiences with improbable role models who value books' (165).

These critiques of *Catherine, Called Birdy* collapse when their use of historical evidence is examined. The Paston Letters emanate from a wealthy and influential Norfolk family and were written between 1422 and 1509. *Catherine, Called Birdy* is a fictive diary by a 14-year-old girl living in a small manor house in Lincolnshire during the year 1290.

That is, the Paston Letters were produced a century and a half later than the temporal setting of *Catherine, Called Birdy*, and emanate from a very different place, class location and enunciative position. Letters are produced for an audience and are coloured by the writer's relationship to that audience as well as by her experience, views, values and tastes, so that it cannot be assumed that they present an authoritative account of the entire culture from which they originate. To call on the Paston Letters as evidence of medieval practices a century and a half before they were written is, then, to assume both that the Middle Ages comprises a homogeneous and stable historical period, and that the letters provide an 'authentic' picture of that period.

Similar objections might be made about Barnhouse's criticism, which hinges on Perkin's love of language and learning. Barnhouse approves of the novel's treatment of Birdy's state of literacy but not Perkin's, presumably because of his lowly status as a goat boy. Yet class location is not the only determinant of attitudes to books and learning in any time or culture; the judgement that Perkin is 'an improbable role model' (1998: 372) is based on the assumption that classes and levels of society comprise homogeneous and invariable categories whose members all behave in the same way. Barnhouse's emphasis on what she refers to as 'misconceptions about books and literacy in the Middle Ages' (1998: 364) is sharply at odds with Nicholas Orme's *Medieval Children* (2001), which draws upon multiple forms of historical evidence including unpublished sources such as court records, rolls, chancery proceedings and Middle English manuscripts and artworks as well as published works from Caxton to the present. Orme concludes that 'by 1250, at the latest, the whole of the population [of England] was in contact with writings and literate people, whether or not they were personally literate' (2001: 238–9). Tison Pugh and Angela Jane Weisl observe that 'one need only read Christine de Pizan's *Livre de la Cité des Dames* ... to see that medieval authors were quite aware of gender inequality and the values of education' (2013: 54).

To draw attention to questions of historical evidence, as I have just done, is, however, to acquiesce to the principle that historical fiction should be, as Macleod, says, 'good fiction and good history' (1998: 26). Rather, historical fiction is primarily fiction, and its historical details function to construct the illusion of a world which is viewed through the perspective of the present time of its creation. John Stephens observes that fiction imposes order on history because the 'novelistic requirements of shapeliness, meaningfulness, and especially of closure' tend to 'displace large-scale events ... into stories of personal relationships' (1992: 206). Historical identities and events are represented and interpreted in line with the narratives in which they feature, and are changed to accord with the 'enclosed pattern[s] of causation' (Stephens 1992: 207) which shape these narratives. Rather than the terms 'true', 'real' and 'authentic', which carry a sense of moral as well as historical correctness, I prefer to use terms such as 'plausible', 'believable' and 'credible', which refer not to 'facts' of history but to the writerly strategies deployed to construct past worlds from the *present past* of authors' locations in time. Modes of analysis which pronounce upon the authenticity or otherwise of imaginings of the past often seek to corral the past into fixity. Rather, the past is alive in the present, as unpredictable and active as the writers and audiences who play with its echoes and remnants.

Crucially, arguments about 'authenticity' and 'accuracy' in depictions of the Middle Ages are insufficiently conscious of the effects of the radical changes which have been evident in the discipline of history over the last few decades, or how 'innovations in the historical novel are related to transformations within historiography' (Robinson 2011: 26). Contemporary historical fiction for children does not always or necessarily adhere to the models of seamless realism which informed earlier fiction in this genre. The habits of irony and self-reflexiveness which so pervade postmodern textuality are evident in fiction for children, inflecting the way realist and fantasy narratives contest and play with concepts of reality, history and representation.

Metafiction, narrative, history

Joseph Zornado is, I think, correct in his judgement that Cushman's fiction 'calls attention to the provisional, slippery nature of storytelling, the writing of history, and the nature of the self' (1997: 257), although I am not so convinced by his argument that *Catherine, Called Birdy* comprises a kind of template of Hayden White's formulation of metahistory, or that Cushman 'has at her disposal all of the tools White describes in his *Metahistory*' (1997: 255), since the text does not divulge the author's methods of writing fiction but only the imagined world itself, rendered through narrative and language.

The novel is presented as a journal written by Birdy on the scraps of vellum she scavenges from her father's steward. She expostulates about the tedium of spinning and sewing, and about the suitors her father invites to inspect her. The narrative foregrounds the experience of girls and women at a time when significance was attributed to the doings of men, especially aristocratic men, although this in itself is not new in historical fiction for the young, which has a long tradition of focusing on young protagonists with whom readers are positioned to align themselves. The narrative of *Catherine, Called Birdy* incorporates details of Birdy's training in herbalism at the hands of the servant Morwenna, her experience of tending her mother who is in danger of dying after childbirth and of caring for her baby sister Eleanor: the traditionally female enterprises of herbalism, midwifery, nursing. The novel's deployment of the journal form, too, refers to genres of female textuality practised in domestic settings. The *present past* of *Catherine, Called Birdy* thus imagines the medieval past as the necessary prehistory of the present, purveying a history of girls and women that anticipates the feminist movements which developed from the nineteenth century. Birdy occupies a *past present* whose outcome she cannot anticipate, although readers are positioned to desire the *past future* she desires: romance, freedom, education.

Langton, the *New York Times* reviewer who criticised the novel on the grounds that 'sometimes Catherine's wild jokes and confessions are too much like contemporary slapstick' is right in her view that Birdy's style of address is over the top, but mistaken, I think, in her diagnosis that the novel is flawed because of its departure from the 'truth' of the Middle Ages (she says that the journal entries are 'arch rather than true'). For instance, the following excerpt from Birdy's journal for 9 October 1290 relates her encounter with a good-looking and self-important young man, Rolf, whom her father has invited to inspect Birdy with a view to marriage: 'Corpus bones, I thought. To be wedded to this perfumed prig with his mouth in a knot and a frown always on his face!' (1994: 22). Birdy's language, profane and expressive, interweaves past and present. It deploys the Middle English slang term *corpus bones*, which carries a hint of blasphemy in that it sometimes means 'Christ's bones' (for instance, in Chaucer's 'Pardoner's Tale'). While the syntax and vocabulary of Birdy's language suggest pre-modernity, her opposition to her father's selection of suitors anticipates second-wave feminism and its emphasis on female self-determination. The novel's depiction of Birdy's speech is not 'untrue' but rather points, self-consciously, to the distance between then and now.

Throughout the novel the narrative identifies the dates of journal entries with the saints whose feasts are celebrated on these days and whose stories Birdy reads in her mother's book of saints. Her reflections on these saints incorporate her interpretations of their lives:

16TH DAY OF OCTOBER, Feast of Saint Helwig, who was unlucky in her children. (1994: 31)

19TH DAY OF OCTOBER, Feast of Saint Frileswide, virgin, though why that should make someone a saint I do not know. (1994: 33)

24TH DAY OF OCTOBER, Feast of Saint Maglorius, who chased a dragon out of Jersey. (1994: 37)

26TH DAY OF OCTOBER, Feast of Saints Eata and Bean, which I think is very funny. (1994: 38)

Birdy's summaries of the saints' lives present a self-reflexive and sceptical view of medieval hagiography. This is not to say that scepticism or cynicism are inherently modern; but rather that Birdy's journal proleptically constructs a modern, secular sensibility where these impulses are habitual and where stories of the lives of saints are no more than quaint remnants of a superstitious past. Birdy's puzzlement as to why Saint Frileswide's virginity should endow her with sainthood draws attention to the present-based perspective of the narrative, and hence the gap between the *present past* of the novel's production and its thirteenth-century setting.

The novel ends with a surprising twist. In the space of a day, the middle-aged man Birdy calls Shaggy Beard, to whom her father has promised her as a bride, dies suddenly in a tavern brawl, and her parents decide that Birdy is to marry his son and heir Stephen, who is 'young and clean, loves learning, and is not Shaggy Beard' (1994: 205). Quoting Brian Richardson's *Unlikely Stories*, Robinson notes that 'even when plausible enough within the fictional world, excessively fortuitous encounters clearly show the author's hand' (2011: 43). In *Catherine, Called Birdy*, this combination of events produces a metafictional moment when the *present past* of the narrative meets Birdy's imaginings of a *past future* when she will exercise agency and personal freedom. Reminding readers of the artfulness of narrative, it positions them to consciously advert to the sleight of hand whereby Birdy's dilemma is solved.

The metafictional touches of *Catherine, Called Birdy* are subtle enough for many reviewers and scholars to miss the novel's narrative playfulness. In contrast, Philip Reeve's *Here Lies Arthur* (2007) leaves readers in no doubt as to his project of playing with notions of truth.[6] In his deadpan author's note, Reeve says: '*Here Lies Arthur* is not a historical novel, and in writing it I did not set out to portray "the real King

Arthur"' (2007: unpaged). If *Here Lies Arthur* is not an historical novel, it assumes many of the features of historical fiction, with its evocation of the sixth-century world of Arthur's Britain and its combination of real (or possibly real) and invented characters. In the absence of historical evidence for the existence of Arthur, Merlin, Guinevere and the other Arthurian figures, Reeve is not bound by facts or truths. Backfilling the narrative from the Arthurian traditions that circulated throughout the Middle Ages, the novel comprises an account of how stories, delivered in the right way and at the right time, become truth.

This radical revisioning of the Arthuriad is presented, like Birdy's story, through a first-person account by a girl. Gwyna is an orphan, a disregarded slave in a remote Welsh village pillaged by Arthur and his men at the beginning of the narrative. She has learned to swim by setting fish-traps for her master, and when she tumbles into a river to escape one of Arthur's men, her feat of swimming under water to the safety of the riverbank is observed by Myrddin, Arthur's bard and adviser, the novel's equivalent to Merlin.[7] Gwyna's skill at swimming suggests to Myrddin a strategy for cementing Arthur's pre-eminence as a warlord. Myrddin directs Arthur and his followers to a lake associated with the old pagan gods and promises to call up the spirits of the lake. Gwyna waits on a rocky shelf behind a waterfall until she receives Myrddin's signal, whereupon she discards her clothing, dives into the lake and holds up a sword that Myrddin has bought from a trader. Thus begins the story of how the Lady of the Lake gave the sword Caliburn to Arthur.

So persuasive are Myrddin's stories about Arthur that even Gwyna, who knows that Arthur is only 'a little tyrant in an age of tyrants' (2007: 286), is not immune from the power of invention. She says:

> It started to seem that there were two Arthurs: the hard man who had burned my home, and another one who lived in Myrddin's stories and spent his time hunting magical stags and fighting giants and brigands. I liked the Arthur of the stories better, but some of his bravery and mystery rubbed off on the real man, so that when ... I saw him, I could not help but think of the time he had captured that glass castle in the Irish Sea, or sliced the Black Witch into two halves, like two tubs. (2007: 53–4)

The 'two Arthurs' of Gwyna's experience are the flesh-and-blood Arthur who destroyed the stronghold of Ban, Gwyna's master, when he refused to pay for Arthur's protection; and the Arthur constructed by Myrddin's stories about him. In the opening pages of the novel Gwyna catches a glimpse of the real Arthur, observing his physical strength and his fierceness as he rides ahead of his horsemen. The Arthur of Myrddin's stories occupies legendary spaces replete with magical stags, giants and witches, and performs heroic deeds which elevate him above his rivals. Gwyna's perspective alerts readers to the power of these stories and to their effects: that is, when she sees the real Arthur her perception of him is coloured by Myrddin's stories about his magical deeds, to the extent that he seems to possess an enhanced version of humanness.

The *present past* of *Here Lies Arthur* is informed by a number of historiographical orientations which chime with those of *Catherine, Called Birdy*: both novels privilege the perspectives of the young, female and marginalised; both advocate a wary suspicion about truth, stories and religious beliefs; both create a sense of the contingency of identities, particularly gendered identities, and their malleability. What distinguishes *Here Lies Arthur* is the novel's deconstructive approach to the purposes and functions of stories in political life. The novel was published in 2007, following a period when the role of public relations in British politics was widely criticised. Catherine Butler and Hallie O'Donovan note that at the IBBY (International Board on Books for Young People) conference of 2006, Reeve 'emphasized the role of political "spin" in its genesis, particularly as practised by modern politicians such as Peter Mandelson and Tony Blair' (2012: 58). In essence, Myrddin is a spin doctor: he invents Arthur as a hero, creating audacious and persuasive stories which generate their own reality, producing effects such as war, and the death of individuals caught up in war (as 'collateral damage'). *Here Lies Arthur* advocates resistance to stories which elevate individuals to hero status, and which pit one group (ethnic, gendered) against another. It does so by alerting readers to the constructedness of such stories and to the agendas they promote. At the same time the novel foregrounds the cultural and political import of stories and their capacity to bind communities and individuals together.

The medieval postmodern

Historical novels are by no means the only mode of fiction for the young which take up questions about the relationships between truth and fiction, history and narrative. With their capacity for playing with words, images and form, picture books (and more recently, graphic novels) have often deployed metafictional and experimental strategies that evoke the postmodern, or what Cherie Allan refers to as the postmodernesque (2012).[8] Informed by many of the historiographical transformations which, I argue, have influenced historical narratives for children, these picture books engage with the past through strategies which include parody, metafiction and pastiche. I return to dragon picture books to identify how the medieval enters the postmodern, focusing on David Wiesner's *The Three Pigs* (2001), in which a dragon features prominently.

Yoking together a pastiche of narratives and elements from a variety of genres and times, *The Three Pigs* engages readers in an ontological game incorporating the story of the three pigs, an 'old' story about a dragon, and an assortment of nursery rhymes. At the beginning of the book the three pigs escape from the wolf and find themselves among the scattered pages of the 'three pigs' story. They form a paper aeroplane from these pages, and land first in the saccharine world of a collection of nursery rhymes, and next into a medievalist text populated by a dragon, a king and his eldest son: 'High on a hill there lived a great dragon, who stood guard over a rose made of the purest gold. The king was determined to own this treasure. So he sent his eldest son to slay the dragon and bring back the golden rose' (Wiesner 2001, unpaged).

The story of the dragon interpolated into *The Three Pigs* comprises an amalgam of fairy tale elements, nodding to the Grimm Brothers' story 'The Two Brothers' and to familiar fairy tale scripts involving dragon treasure, eldest sons and impossible tasks.[9] The language of the narrative comprises formulaic phrases ('high on a hill', 'a great dragon', 'made of the purest gold') which echo fairy tale conventions (Figure 1.5). Similarly, the illustrations in this sequence of the book, with their pen-and-ink sepia drawings, evoke stock depictions of dragon stories in which dragons merely perform their conventional roles of guarding treasure and affording occasions where knights demonstrate heroism. In effect, the dragon of *The Three Pigs* contests the stultifying effects of fairy tale formulas and of representations where he is trapped in a web of hackneyed language, derivative images and predictable narratives.

Two of the three pigs, defying the two-dimensional space of the page, climb into the dragon's lair while the third pig persuades him to break out of his sepia-coloured environment into a world of colour and movement, signified by the photo-realistic depiction of the climbing pigs. In the central panel in the lower third of the page the dragon bemusedly observes the pigs who cling to his back as he proceeds from the fairy tale setting to new narrative worlds. Beyond the dragon and his cargo of pigs stands the king's castle, a stock Disney-style structure; the panels on either side bear the static image of the golden rose of the story. The

Thinking about the Middle Ages 37

Figure 1.5 Illustration from *The Three Pigs* by David Wiesner

central opposition of this illustration is that between stasis, exemplified by the style in which the dragon is represented, and action, encoded in the forward movement of the narrative as the three pigs take control over their world.

The next illustration shows the prince and his horse looking about in puzzlement as they find themselves unable to complete their narrative: 'The prince spurred his steed to the mountaintop, drew his sword, and slew the mighty dragon' (Wiesner 2001, unpaged). Having escaped from the story in which he has been trapped, the dragon continues to speak in the archaic register to which he is accustomed: 'Many thanks for rescuing me, O brave and noble swine', to which the third pig replies, 'Don't mention it.' This play with registers reinforces the opposition between representational styles which plays out in the illustrations.

The book's final illustration depicts a re-formed family group, comprising the dragon, the three pigs, and the cat with his fiddle, now

38 *The Middle Ages in Children's Literature*

Figure 1.6 Illustration from *The Three Pigs* by David Wiesner

happily occupying the domestic space of the third pig's house of bricks (Figure 1.6). Two of the pigs enjoy wolf soup, which has been cooked in a soup-pot powered by the dragon's breath; the cat entertains the group with his fiddle-playing, and the third pig perches companionably on the dragon's haunch. The golden rose has been reconfigured as table decoration. The caption above this happy scene might be the formulaic fairy tale ending 'And they all lived happily ever after' except that each letter is out of line with those next to it, producing the effect of a collage of letters glued separately onto the page. The last two letters of 'after' are missing; the third pig holds them as if preparing to add them to the caption.

The dragon, incorporated into the new order, is both ancient and new. Rescued from stories where he occupies no more than an inert element in a formulaic narrative, he has been inducted into a new world, where new stories might be told. Just as the 'happily ever after' ending in this illustration is not complete, so, the narrative implies, all stories are contingent and liable to change. *The Three Pigs* concerns itself not with the truth about dragons, but with how narratives shape ideas about dragons. The dragon, like the medieval, may carry the weight of previous representations and narratives, but it is always susceptible to reinvention and reformulation.

The Middle Ages does not, then, reside in factual details to be 'accurately' realised in fiction for contemporary audiences. Rather, the medieval is always remade and reinvented to accord with the values and practices of the times and places in which it is reconfigured. Medievalist narratives offer modern audiences experiences of enchantment, or distance readers from present-day issues. As Robinson explains (2011), the *present past* orientation of contemporary fiction is inescapably anachronistic, since it cannot but view the past from the perspective of its own time. Moreover, the radical changes which have characterised the discipline of history since the 1960s have inevitably found their way into medievalist fiction (whether in realist or fantasy narratives), transforming and contesting depictions of the past.

2
Temporality and the Medieval

I argued in Chapter 1 that medievalist texts for children afford both experiences of enchantment and also narrative strategies whereby contemporary dilemmas and tensions are addressed indirectly, interpolated into medieval settings. In this chapter I focus on the dynamics between times which are at play in medievalist texts, and on the narrative functions they perform. Reflecting on time and narrative, Paul Ricoeur comes to the conclusion that we do not experience time as a series of disjointed episodes or events but rather as a threefold present which incorporates 'the dialectic of expectation, memory, and attention' (1984: 20), that is, we experience or attend to the present moment in the light of what has happened (memory) and what may be expected to occur in the future (expectation). Time, Ricoeur says, 'becomes human to the extent that it is articulated through a narrative mode' (52). For Ricoeur, then, narrative orders time (in his terms, makes time human), whether in the stories we tell about our own lives, in works of fiction or in the writing of history. One of the strategies whereby narrative orders time is through the deployment of past events, places and objects. Narratives for the young, for instance, are replete with settings, figures and artefacts imbued with ghostly or material traces of the Middle Ages. These elements carry out symbolic functions within narratives; they are often hinges on which a plot turns; and they are potent with political and social ideologies.

In *The Nick of Time* (2004), Elizabeth Grosz explores questions about the movement of time and its implications for investigations of the biological, cultural, historical and political forces which shape human subjects and identities. Focusing on the work of Charles Darwin, Friedrich Nietzsche and Henri Bergson and their insights about ontology, Grosz observes that time is not an entity in itself but erupts into our conscious thought through 'nicks, disruptions or upheavals' (2004: 5) which disturb our immersion in the present. Even when past representations capture features of the real past, time 'ineluctably, relentlessly ... exerts its own active force of aging' (249), so that later interpretations of such representations inevitably recontextualise them. Grosz notes that 'This coexistence of present and past, the ways the past grows and augments itself with every present, the virtual potential the past brings to each present, provides it with a capacity to enrich the present through resonances that are not themselves present' (250). The present does not possess the temporal perspective to know itself, but relies on the past to inform its consciousness of actions, perceptions and reflections, and to suggest how the future might turn out. Grosz's insights chime with Alan Robinson's conception of the *present past* (2011), discussed in Chapter 1, which similarly emphasises how the present invests meaning in the past and understands it in the light of its own experience of the present.

Grosz's discussion of the coexistence of past and present captures something of the mobility of the medieval in contemporary textuality and its purchase on the present. The relationship of premodern to modern is never closed down, never finally enunciated, but is central to studies of medieval and medievalist texts, and debates over this relationship have formed a prominent aspect of scholarly work over the last few decades.[1] These debates have often centred on notions of temporality which pit modernity against the Middle Ages, and one view of the Middle Ages against another. On the one hand, the often-repeated phrase 'hard-edged alterity'[2] insists on the radical differences between premodern and modern, the strangeness of the Middle Ages and its incomprehensibility to modern sensibilities. On the other hand, continuist understandings of the Middle Ages construct grand narratives which focus on the commonalities and connections between past and present, interpreting past texts, artefacts and events in the light of the *now* in which they are read, viewed and examined. Like most binaries, the continuist/alterist opposition collapses under its own weight once subjected to close scrutiny. The past, especially the swathe of time referred to as the Middle Ages, resists the sweeping generalisations which attach to both continuist and alterist positions; and the neatness of periodisation fails to account for the stubborn refusal of ideas, stories, values and practices to confine themselves to particular times and cultures.

In *How Soon Is Now?* (2012), Carolyn Dinshaw approaches notions of time in relation to medieval and medievalist texts, focusing on the temporal theme of asynchrony: 'different time frames or temporal systems colliding in a single moment of *now*' (2012: 5). Dinshaw argues that desires for other times and other ways of being disrupt linear and measurable time schemes. These engagements with time challenge and expand normative temporalities and demonstrate that 'time itself is wondrous, marvellous, full of queer potential' (4). In her focus on texts (medieval and post-medieval) which incorporate asynchrony, Dinshaw maintains that such texts do not merely queer temporality but that they afford queer reading experiences in which the reader's present is shot through with other times, other modes of being. Like Chakrabarty's conception of the timeknot, to which I referred in Chapter 1, and Grosz's insistence on the coexistence of then and now, Dinshaw's approach identifies textual moments and strategies which alert readers to the 'heterogeneity of the present' (104). In line with her emphasis on asynchrony, Dinshaw questions the conventional view that nostalgia consists merely of a 'yearning for an idealized past as escape from a present felt to be dismal and unpromising' (34). Rather, Dinshaw argues, the temporal desire of nostalgia is more contradictory than this, since 'past times interact in complex material ways with present moments' (2011: 230) so that past and present are not definitively distinct from each other.

I turn my attention now to texts which play with time, through the deployment of medieval settings and elements experienced in multi-temporal fantasy, through time-travel narratives where protagonists move between the Middle Ages and the present of the texts' production, through an evocation of virtual time in a medievalist video game, and through the back-and-forward imaginings of Arthurian post-disaster fiction. These deployments of the medieval are significant not so much for what they say about the Middle Ages (as a time of innocence or ignorance, romanticism or barbarity) but rather because they demonstrate the valency of ancient stories and symbols, and their usefulness to the socialising agendas which underpin children's literature. Children's literature is imbued with a powerful consciousness of time, partly because its implied audiences are bounded by age, partly because its narratives typically hinge upon stories of maturation and personal growth which play out over time. Medievalist texts fold these stories into narratives which incorporate a relational dynamic of medieval to modern, complicated by the recursiveness with which the Middle Ages is drawn and redrawn.

The medieval and multi-temporal fantasy

Young people's textual encounters with the past often take the form of multi-temporal narratives in which elements from different times and settings jostle and mix. Such narratives manifest in postmodern texts of the kind I have discussed in Chapter 1, exemplified by David Wiesner's *The Three Pigs*, in which diverse styles and modes of medievalism are combined with metafictional play. Other texts, more focused on action, involve narratives in which protagonists shift across and between times and cultures. The flourishing category of time-slip novels, for instance, includes numerous series in which a central character or group of characters travel to different times and places, positioning readers as tourists or travellers in time and space.[3] In this chapter I focus on two examples of multi-temporal fantasy: Neil Gaiman's *The Graveyard Book* (2008), and Charlie Fletcher's Stoneheart trilogy (*Stoneheart*, 2006; *Ironhand*, 2007; *Silvertongue*, 2008), in which the medieval mixes with representations of other times and cultures in fantasy settings. My focus here is on the interplay (in Grosz's terms, the coexistence) of times wrought through these cultural and historical references, and on the significances attributed to the Middle Ages.

The Graveyard Book traces the trajectory from infancy to adolescence of a child known as Nobody Owens (Bod) whose father, mother and sister are murdered at the beginning of the novel, and who is adopted by the ghostly inhabitants of a graveyard under the guardianship of the vampire Silas and taught by the werewolf Miss Lupescu. The graveyard and its chapel are of medieval origin, but its inhabitants come from various centuries, classes and occupations. Similarly, the city of London, the setting of the Stoneheart trilogy, is replete with traces of the Middle Ages and post-medieval allusions to the medieval in the form of buildings, dragons, gargoyles and statues, alongside contemporary elements of built design and public art. George Chapman, the 12-year-old protagonist, is the victim of bullying at the hands of his fellow students and of Mr Killingbeck, their teacher, during a school excursion to the Natural History Museum. George absconds from the museum and takes out his anger on a stone carving of a dragon's head on the front portico of the museum. He punches the carving with his clenched fist, and knocks it to the ground. This action reawakens old enmities in the realm of 'un-London',[4] whose inhabitants exist in a parallel London invisible to its human, everyday occupants. Both novels combine many of the historical and cultural associations of the gothic: crumbling medieval buildings; Victorian medievalist architecture; a sensibility which encompasses the uncanny and the presence of supernatural forces; an atmosphere characterised by menace and the intimation of danger.

In *The Graveyard Book*, these sinister implications are undercut by the novel's descriptions of Bod's everyday life. Adopted by the ghosts of

Mr and Mrs Owens, buried over three hundred years ago, he resides in their 'lovely little tomb over by the daffodil patch' (2008: 28), and mingles with the graveyard's inhabitants who range from Caius Pompeius, a Roman general who died during the occupation of Britain, to the family of Victorian children, all buried before their tenth birthdays, with whom he plays on summer nights. The democratic organisation of the graveyard, where Caius Pompeius rubs shoulders with the eighteenth-century politician Josiah Worthington and with the vampire Silas, dissipates the temporal distances between characters. At the same time, the narration is filtered through the perspectives of various of the graveyard's inhabitants, so conjuring up voices and value systems from diverse times and social strata. These pasts are present to Bod, the novel's main focalising character, as he interacts with others, and are filtered through his perspective, that of a modern boy making sense of a world constituted by multiple pasts. In *The Graveyard Book* then, the past is not an inert space against which modernity unfolds, but is more akin to Bergson's understanding of the past, which he sees as 'not only the accompanying condition for every present, but also the (virtual) condition for any and every future' (Grosz 2004: 182). The past is, of course, more than virtual to Bod during his tenure as a ward of the graveyard, and in this sense his encounters with his ghostly neighbours render the virtual actual, giving life to the bareness of epitaphs on tombs and mausoleums.

The deepest recesses of the graveyard are occupied by a barrow which, as Caius Pompeius explains to Bod, pre-dates Roman Britain. The spatial location of the barrow might seem to suggest deep history, a site of origins. In keeping with the postmodernist tenor of the novel, however, the ancient past is neither privileged over modernity, nor are its traces reified as precious objects. Caius Pompeius tells Bod about two incidents, each involving a grave-robber: the first took place three hundred years after the death of Caius (that is, around the seventh century); the second, in the nineteenth century. These tiny narratives both end badly for the grave-robbers: in the first, the robber suffers the most abject terror so that his hair instantly turns white; in the second the robber never returns. Sure enough, when Bod and his friend Scarlett investigate the barrow they find the skeleton of the second robber. They also see an apparition, a Pict-like man whose skin is painted with woad. As this ancient figure fades into darkness, they hear the voices of the three-headed monster called the Sleer, which guards the treasures of the barrow (a brooch, a goblet, a knife) as it awaits the return of its master. Accustomed to non-human beings, Bod regards these ghostly and monstrous beings with a degree of detachment, reflecting that the second grave-robber might well have been disappointed to find so little of value in the barrow; in a wry reflection on the depreciation of assets, Bod muses that 'the treasures of ten thousand years ago were not the treasures of today' (2008: 56). Bod's judgement about what counts as valuable is indicative of the novel's treatment of ancient pasts. First, the past is always revisited and revalued, as the stories of the two grave-robbers indicate, but its significances change over time. Second, ancient figures and artefacts are not in themselves objects either of reverence or fear, but accrete meaning insofar as they impinge on the lives and emotions of humans.

The Sleer is not the villain of *The Graveyard Book* but is, rather, a pathetic and lonely figure consigned to 'dust and loneliness' (2008: 250) as it waits for its master to return. The evil forces which killed Bod's family are the Jacks of All Trades, a group of undead assassins engaged in a murderous search for him. Power and danger, it turns out, reside in the margins between living and dead, and Bod is the exceptional child who walks these margins, threatening the power of the Jacks. In order to save Scarlett and himself from death, Bod tricks the Sleer into the belief that the surviving assassin, Jack Frost, is its master, so that Jack is crushed in its monstrous coils. Monstrosity wears many faces in this narrative: whereas the Sleer and the Jacks are trapped in their own incapacity to adapt to changing orders, the vampire Silas and the werewolf Miss Lupescu are members of the Honour Guard which patrol 'the borders of things' (2008: 303); indeed, Miss Lupescu gives up her life to protect humans from the chaos wrought by the Jacks. By positioning readers to align with Bod, whose focalising perspective frames figures and events, the narrative affirms the margins as a space of vitality and innovation. Whereas the Sleer, the Ghouls and the undead Jacks offer negative examples of existence in the margins, Silas and Miss Lupescu model in-between lives and their queer possibilities.

The Graveyard Book treats the past not as a source of transcendent meaning but as a reservoir of knowledge and emotions to be accessed by modern characters alive to its presence in their world. Bod leaves the graveyard at the end of the novel carrying with him both material and also intangible provisions: a passport, a wallet containing money and a leather suitcase filled with necessities, given to him by Silas; and the knowledge, affection and resilience he has gained through his interactions with his ghostly companions. Living with the dead and their memories has endowed Bod with a sense that his emergence into life is predicated on his engagement with the past. Grosz says that time 'can be understood as always doubled' (2004: 250), since at the same time that the past informs the present, the present re-enervates aspects of the past. The narrative of *The Graveyard Book* plays out just such doubleness, as Bod and the occupants of the graveyard construct and reconstruct time through memories, stories and actions.

Like Bod's graveyard, Fletcher's 'un-London' in the Stoneheart trilogy constitutes a multi-temporal setting where traces of the Middle Ages mingle with medievalist and modern identities, buildings and monuments. After George breaks off the carved head of the small dragon outside the Natural History Museum, he finds himself pursued first by a large pterodactyl from the museum's facade, and next by a cluster of salamanders carved on a drainpipe. Here and throughout the trilogy, the everyday city goes about its business oblivious to George's plight as he flees the monstrous figures of un-London. He is saved from the pterodactyl and the salamanders by the Gunner, one of the figures on the Royal Artillery Memorial at Hyde Park Corner, who descends from his plinth and unloads his revolver into the monsters' bodies. The Gunner explains to George that he is a spit, 'the "spit" and image of a human' (*Stoneheart*: 48), whereas the pterodactyl and salamanders are 'taints', 'made to frighten, to be ugly, to leer at you off church roofs and put the shivers up you' (*Stoneheart*: 50). The logic of this distinction pits human against non-human identities. For the gargoyles, like other taints, possess no spark of humanness and are, according to the Gunner, 'hungry for what makes you you, and me me' (*Stoneheart*: 50).[5]

The gargoyles' implacable hatred of humans is grounded in their alignment with the Darkness, whose primeval struggle with Light took place before the world came into existence. This conventional fantasy trope is spatialised in the trilogy's treatment of London, where Darkness lurks in the London Stone,[6] having inhabited it since prehistoric times even as successive waves of humans occupying London have attributed various meanings to the Stone. London is, then, a 'place of power' (*Ironhand*: 159) where 'all pasts are all still there, layered under the skin' (159) and awaiting the moment when they are set free for good or ill. The binary system on which the fantasy is built sweeps the Middle Ages up into its opposition of human (spit) to non-human (taint) beings. At the same time, the Middle Ages offers symbols and settings which attribute high significance to George's transformation from a fatherless boy, bullied by his classmates and teacher, to a confident young man enjoying an enhanced sense of his agency. Crucially, the test of George's courage lies in his capacity to succeed in three duels with the Last Knight of the Cnihtengild, held respectively on the ground, in water and beneath the ground.[7] Although the Last Knight might seem to qualify as a spit, he is in fact a taint because he and his horse are hollow, built of curving sheets of metal. The Last Knight is, then, almost a man but not quite, and this makes him dangerous, since, as the Gunner tells George, 'it's the "almost" that makes 'em so angry' (*Silvertongue*: 347).

This privileging of humanness is sustained through George's final encounter with the Last Knight, who is an Agent of Fate devoid of an inner life and hence susceptible to the encroachment of the Darkness which fills the hollowness within him, transforming him into the Black Knight. It is his lack of imagination and affect that ultimately destroys the Black Knight, when George duels against him on the Impossible Bridge, a fantastic structure suspended over the Thames. By this stage in the narrative George has faced the fear which has blighted his life: that his final angry encounter with his father has in some way led to his father's death. Having resolved this question, George now takes his father's advice that 'sometimes you just had to walk the walk, even when it was the last thing you felt like doing' (*Stoneheart*: 315). He plunges his hand through the Dark Knight's hollowness, exposing the Knight's own emptiness and fear and rendering him powerless. This narrative outcome externalises a subjective shift expressed in relation to George's transition from boy to man: 'He stopped feeling like a lonely boy of thirteen summers. He felt older, much older, almost ancient, and stronger than any one person could ever be' (318). The archaic temporal expression 'boy of thirteen summers' and George's consciousness of himself as 'almost ancient' signify his acquisition of a knightly identity where he sees himself as the heir to a long line of ancestors.

But this reference to the genealogy of heroism associated with the name 'George' aligns George with the demotic and mercantile associations of his family name, Chapman, rather than the aristocratic associations of his given name. Instead of envisaging himself as a member of a knightly order akin to the Cnihtengild, George feels 'the great weight of every earlier George, every Chapman, every mother, every father down the long centuries ..., and they were all somehow standing with him, their shoulders to his' (*Silvertongue*: 318). This sense of what Grosz describes as the doubleness of the past in the present, the 'way the past grows and augments itself with every present' (2004: 250), is at odds with other medievalist allusions in the trilogy, particularly the gargoyles which (with the exception of Spout) are imprinted with the hatred and hostility attributed to their makers. Although they too are taints, dragons are differentially treated: a distinction is made between the City Dragons which guard the boundaries of the City of London, and the Temple Bar Dragon, which stands in front of the Royal Courts of

Justice.[8] The City Dragons are, according to the spit Shackleton,[9] 'mass-produced trash' (*Silvertongue*: 216), readily caught up in the Darkness as it seeks to destroy London. The mindless ferocity of the City Dragons is contrasted with the intelligent purposefulness of the Temple Bar Dragon, which speaks in short bursts of words: 'First. Dragon. Am. I. ... To. Guard. City. Made' (281). This contrast is in part an aesthetic one, between mass-produced and artisan-made medievalisms. Post-medieval artefacts are, it seems, more 'real' when they are handmade and painstakingly wrought than when they are machine-made.

The trilogy's ambivalent treatment of the medieval is evident, too, in its selection of role models and protectors. Most prominent among the spits who guide George in his quest for identity and agency are First World War soldiers whose memorials are dotted about London; in particular, the Gunner from the Royal Artillery Memorial. Other significant spits based on historical figures include William Shakespeare, the Duke of Wellington, Samuel Johnson, Winston Churchill and Ernest Shackleton, while the principal female spits are Boadicea and the allegorical figures of the Queen of America on the Albert Memorial, and the Queen of Time, outside Selfridges. The only medieval historical figure who features in the narrative is Richard the Lionheart. Choleric and imperious, he is comically outmanoeuvred by Boadicea, who reminds him that she was 'Queen and conqueror centuries before you were whelped!' (128).

A curious aspect of the Stoneheart trilogy, then, is the dissonance between its deployment of medieval tropes and schemas, and its treatment of medieval figures, both invented and historical. George's quest for self-actualisation is mapped onto his progress as a warrior: like a hero of medieval romance, he chooses the most arduous of paths, referred to as 'the Hard Way' (*Stoneheart*: 274), and discovers his intrinsic nobility (he possesses the magical power of Making) through tests of his courage. The sequence dealing with the first of George's three duels with the Last Knight of the Cnihtengild is telling in its modulations between high seriousness and parody. The voice of the Last Knight is 'deep and sonorous' (*Ironhand*: 127), and it utters three variations of the sentence: 'Will you stand?' George, hearing these merely as questions about whether he is literally standing or sitting, is unaware that by replying 'Yes' he accepts the Last Knight's challenge, and speculates as to whether the Knight is deaf, or perhaps mad. When George attempts to negotiate with the Knight, or to dissuade him from jousting, the Knight has no capacity to engage in negotiation but is locked into the rituals of the chivalric contest. This incapacity for flexibility is true, as well, of the way the Lionheart is represented in *Silvertongue*, where he is unable to keep up with the rapid pace of events as the spits struggle to prevent the Dark from destroying London, so that his constant interruptions and questions enrage Boadicea and provoke the scorn of other kings and queens who glare at him, 'distinctly unamused' (*Silvertongue*: 230). To be medieval, it seems, is to be trapped, unable to move beyond a rigid adherence to modes of thought and action.

The medievalist elements of the trilogy, which adhere to fantasy conventions based on binary oppositions between good and evil, dark and light, thus jut up awkwardly against their approach to the historical Middle Ages. Other pasts, notably the First World War, are accorded a far higher degree of respect. The Gunner, for instance, is a focalising character through much of *Ironhand*, so that he is attributed with a voice and a perspective on events. It would be naïve to imagine that his perspective unproblematically captures the ethos and values of First World War soldiers, because he represents a contemporary view of what Robinson refers to as the 'usable past' (2011: 6). Specifically, the First World War figures of the Stoneheart trilogy, especially the Gunner, offer a model of heroic behaviour which George emulates, and which the novels advocate as desirable.[10] The historical Middle Ages, in comparison, is not nearly so 'usable', since the medieval is associated in the trilogy with stasis and rigidity, exemplified by the figure of the Lionheart.

The touristic Middle Ages: adventures in time

Of all the texts I discuss in this chapter, fiction involving time travel most explicitly incorporates shifts between modernity and the Middle Ages. Yet, as I will argue, time-travel novels seem to embrace alterist rather than continuist orientations to the medieval. The protagonists of time-travel novels are either modern young people who through accident or magic find themselves in the Middle Ages, or (less often) medieval characters transported to modernity. As Kim Wilson notes (2011), many time-travel novels have a good deal in common with the 'living history' movement which has transformed museums and historical sites from musty collections of artefacts to multi-sensory replications of ancient places and people, often in locations where extensive archaeological investigations have been conducted, such as the Jorvik Centre in York. Medievalist time-travel novels, like much medievalist tourism, are also deeply influenced by nostalgia and its complex combination of emotional effects.

A significant element in medievalist time-travel fiction is the deployment of humour and satirical modes of representation, a topic to which I will return in Chapter 7. Shifts between modernity and the Middle Ages in this fiction often occasion comedic moments, such as an episode at the beginning of Sherryl Jordan's *Wednesday Wizard* (1991), in which Denzil, the apprentice wizard, makes an error which transports him from an English village in 1291 to the MacAllisters' back garden in New Zealand. Here he discovers a 'strange thin pole' from which are suspended various items of clothing. Some he recognises as shirts and skirts, while others appear to be 'very small' (1991: 29). Selecting one of these 'very small' garments, he discovers that it incorporates three holes, and that it stretches readily. He comes to the conclusion that it must be a hat, and pulls it over his head. This comedy of errors comes to a head when 11-year-old Samantha MacAllister discovers Denzil in the back garden and demands: 'Why have you got Theresa's knickers on your head?' (31). The comedic impact of this moment of slapstick relies on two related elements: the strategy of defamiliarisation whereby Theresa's knickers are rendered strange; and the medieval itself, in the person of Denzil. His shock and confusion (he believes at first that he has been transported to heaven and that Samantha is an angel) establishes him as credulous and naïve, and the novel's comedy relies largely on his misapprehensions about the modern world: for instance, his obsession with George Lucas's *Star Wars* films leads him to transform into a mouse so that he can enter the galaxy which, he believes, is concealed inside the MacAllisters' television.

If Denzil is a comic figure because of his ignorance of the modern world, this very ignorance also grounds the novel's longing for a simpler world. I return here to Carolyn Dinshaw's discussion of the limitations of conventional understandings of nostalgia which posit 'a clear, and insurmountable, break between present and past' (2011: 230), such that the medieval stands for a set of practices and values definitively other to those of modernity. In *Wednesday Wizard* Theresa MacAllister's boyfriend Adam suggests that too much modernity is not in Denzil's interests because 'he's seven hundred years behind us' (1991: 133) and will become needlessly confused if he is introduced to modern technologies. Adam says: 'It's bad enough that the kid's using a knife and fork, let alone seeing things that in his world haven't even been invented. Let's keep his life simple' (132). The nostalgia embedded in Adam's attitude hinges on the idea that the simple life of the Middle Ages is at once a desirable state and a melancholy one, since Denzil's simplicity incorporates an unawareness of modern products and inventions which, as a medieval subject, he cannot know and enjoy.

The parallels between Denzil and representations of 'primitive' cultures are unmistakeable. Renato Rosaldo, discussing what he refers to as 'imperial nostalgia' in *Culture and Truth* (1993: 68), argues that when imperialists articulate a regret or longing for the simple lives of colonised peoples prior to or in the early stages of imperialism, they displace their own complicity with imperial domination. Like the 'agents of colonialism' to whom Rosaldo refers (69), Adam and the MacAllisters value in Denzil what they are conscious of having compromised or destroyed. The MacAllisters' attitudes to Denzil are shaped not by hierarchies of race, but rather by a reflex regard for progress and a conviction that the Middle Ages, like romanticised imaginings of pristine 'primitive' cultures, comprises a simple, uncomplicated and homogeneous period. Even as they seek to induct Denzil into modernity the MacAllisters become anxious about the loss of innocence which, they assume, attaches to his preoccupation with modern technologies and media.

As Dinshaw remarks, nostalgia is 'inevitably more temporally complex than the usual deployment of the term allows' (2012: 36). In *The Wednesday Wizard*, the MacAllisters attempt to maintain their belief in a medieval past which is radically other to the present. But in other respects *The Wednesday Wizard* sketches a connection between the Middle Ages and modernity. Thus, Denzil's methods for working out the times and distances he will need to traverse in order to return to the Middle Ages are related to teleologies of scientific development. Adam, a graduate student working in quantum physics, notices that Denzil's calculations rely on a quadrant and on the number of miles a crow flies in an hour. These strategies, Adam explains to Denzil, have been superseded by Einstein's theory of relativity and do not deliver the accuracy required for travel through space and time. Nevertheless, Denzil's methodologies are comprehensible to Adam and provide useful data. The medievalist nostalgia of *The Wednesday Wizard* thus veers between imaginings of the Middle Ages as a time set apart from modernity, and the implication that there exists a continuity from medieval to modern knowledges of science and mathematics.

In *The Wednesday Wizard* much of the action is mediated through the focalising perspective of Denzil as he encounters modernity. In theory this narrative strategy might seem to promise that narrative agency is accorded to a protagonist whose point of view is shaped by past concepts and values. Such a possibility is, however, vitiated in

The Wednesday Wizard by the way Denzil's perspective projects modern imaginings of an abject Middle Ages. Early in the narrative Denzil transforms himself into a rat in order to enter the MacAllisters' home while the family is absent. Like a tourist experiencing the olfactory and visual stimulation offered by the Jorvik Centre,[11] Denzil encounters a cornucopia of smells and visual images:

> There was so much to smell! Strange scented soapy smells, the fragrance of unfamiliar foods, rubber-soled shoes, lino, carpet, plastics, paint – a hundred things he'd never smelled before ... Everything in the kitchen shone: the green painted walls, the creamy cupboards and shelves, the incredible clear glass windows, the strange white cabinets with bright metal strips and cold glossy surfaces, the polished floor, the fantastic glittering machines fixed to the walls. (1991: 59)

Although many of the smells Denzil experiences pertain to products of industrialisation (rubber, lino, carpet, plastics), they do not figure as pungent or 'disgusting' like the smells which modern tourists experience at the Jorvik Centre. Rather, modern smells are listed neutrally, alongside scented soap and unfamiliar food, as 'things he'd never smelled before'. The visual impact of the kitchen is a different matter. Denzil sees this space as a realm of marvels and wonders, suggested by the adjectives 'incredible', 'strange' and 'fantastic', together with the overall emphasis on the reflection of light on surfaces ('shone', 'bright', 'glossy', 'glittering'). The language of Denzil's focalising perspective thus normalises the desirability of the present and its high value to the past, treating Denzil as the outsider whose admiration endorses a glossy and fragrant modernity.

The more conventional narrative direction in medievalist time-travel fantasy involves contemporary protagonists transported into the Middle Ages, exemplified by Theresa Breslin's *Dream Master Nightmare* (2000), Susan Price's *Foiling the Dragon* (1994), Anna Quindlen's *Happily Ever After* (1997) and Charlie Carter's *Battle Boy: Black Prince* (2011). The narrative dynamics of these novels are structured by journeys from modern to medieval and back. In *Foiling the Dragon* and *Happily Ever After*, protagonists travel to the Middle Ages at the beginning of the narrative, returning to modernity at the end, while in *Dream Master Nightmare* the protagonist Cyrus (Cy) Peters inadvertently unleashes his dream of Vikings so that the Middle Ages irrupts spasmodically in contemporary York, manifesting in the sudden appearance of longboats and marauding Viking warriors.

Despite its narrative asynchronicity, which might be expected to manifest in a blending and merging of modern and medieval, *Dream Master Nightmare* takes pains to keep the two separate. This effect relates to the strongly pedagogical orientation of the novel, which functions in part as a guide to medieval York, as though written with an eye to the UK National Curriculum and its requirements for Key Stage 2 history (that is, directed to children around Cy's age), which included the Vikings among its list of topics at the time the novel was published.[12] The novel's action occurs during a week-long excursion to York when Cy and his classmates visit the city's various museums, notably the Jorvik Centre, and take a tour of the city walls. Historical information about the city and the arrival of the Viking longships is dropped into the narrative through the direct speech of guides and the children's teacher. This material is treated as irrefutable, reliant on authorities such as the archaeologists who have researched the history of York, and the history books from which Cy's teacher reads. But the novel's approach calls on touristic strategies to translate 'facts' into narrative. Louise D'Arcens points out that 'living history' tourism relies on the impact of premodern faces, presented in videos, holograms and images on screens and paper (2011: 156–9).[13] The opening lines of *Dream Master Nightmare* introduce just such an encounter as Cy comes face to face with the Saxon princess Hilde. Commencing *in media res*, the narrative aligns readers with Cy's perspective as he struggles to make sense of the place where his dream plays out, tenth-century York where Hilde flees with her grandfather from the marauding Vikings. Seen through Cy's eyes, Hilde is a blue-eyed, flaxen-haired virago; to Hilde, Cy is a swineherd whose lowly status entitles her to order him about. Their odd-couple relationship, ending (predictably enough) in friendship, foregrounds the gaps between their worlds and cultures.

Cy's second encounter with the face of the past occurs when Harald, son of Erik Bloodaxe, bursts through the doorway intent on abducting Hilde. The description of Harald suggests a moment frozen in time, as if Cy stands before one of the 'interactive' faces of York's heritage trail: 'On his head he wore a helmet, a heavy metal helmet with earflaps and a long flat central nose-piece. From within the eye sockets two eyes stared out with murderous intent' (2000: 14). Later, when Cy looks at the York Helmet in the Yorkshire Museum he sees it suddenly inhabited by the face of a Viking warrior: 'The face was lined and hard, chin set with purpose. It was that of a Viking warrior. And from within the eye sockets the eyes, mad with rage, stared out at him' (31–2). Harald and the Viking meld in a warrior face characterised by grim resolve, metonymic of an entire Viking world, 'forbidding, austere, masculinist and violent' (D'Arcens 2011: 157). Interpolated into the narrative of Hilde's resistance to Viking occupation, Cy's focalising perspective privileges the Saxons as plucky, outnumbered citizens fighting the Vikings for land and identity.

This simplistic version of cultural relations in the Middle Ages maps onto Cy's struggle, in the contemporary setting, to contend with the bullying behaviour of three of his classmates. The novel advocates intelligence rather than physical force, skill with language rather than with fists or swords. In the medieval setting Cy saves his own life and distracts Harald from his designs on Hilde by acting as his *skald*,[14] telling stories of his heroic exploits; in the modern setting Cy takes charge of events by acting as narrator in the play his classmates perform for pupils from the local school. Despite the pedagogical orientation of the novel, its depictions of a real-life student excursion to York, and its insistence on the truthfulness of 'living history', the narrative cannot altogether avoid the combination of nostalgia and satire which D'Arcens calls 'comic medieval tourism' (2011: 160), especially in the sequence involving the children's performance of their play.

In this scene Cy time-shifts medieval figures to the present, with the result that Harald and Hilde take over; Harald by abducting Chloe, one of the class bullies, who has taken the role of a Saxon princess, and Hilde by challenging and soundly beating Eddie, another of the bullies. Cy adapts his narration to accord with these extemporaneous events and receives high praise from his teachers for the authenticity of the action and the verisimilitude of Harald's and Hilde's costumes. Harald's action of swinging Chloe over his shoulder satirises stereotypes of Viking behaviour, even as it is read by the adults present as 'ham[ming] it up a bit' (2000: 132). Such postmodern touches point to the impossibility of medieval presence in 'living history' sites and practices: the 'historical' figures, Harald and Hilde, are regarded by Cy's teachers as excessively medieval, extravagantly over the top in their performances of the Middle Ages. This reflexivity undermines the novel's emphasis on historicity and accuracy, according with what D'Arcens describes as 'winking postmodern skepticism' (2011: 156) rather than the more overt historicist and pedagogical orientation of the narrative.

When contemporary protagonists visit the Middle Ages in time-travel novels, their modernity generally endows them with knowledge and resources unknown to their medieval counterparts. In Quindlen's *Happily Ever After*, the protagonist Kate finds herself in a castle where she teaches the maidens how to play baseball; in Price's *Foiling the Dragon*,

Paul Welsh, spirited by the sorceress Zione to the realm of Dragonsheim, staves off the murderous intentions of the realm's resident dragon by bribing him with foil wrapping paper from a gift shop; in Carter's *Battle Boy: Black Prince*, the time-travelling Napoleon Smythe, Battle Boy 005, restores the crown of Philip VI to its owner by calling on the power of his futuristic body armour. In all three novels, distinctions between medieval and modern fold into narratives of individual progress.

Returning to their contemporary or futuristic lives, the protagonists of these novels evince relief as they are restored to lives of agency and freedom. In *Foiling the Dragon*, Paul returns to Birmingham and to the tawdry setting of the yard of the Old Crown, with its detritus of plastic beer kegs, broken crates, litter and filth: 'His eyes filled with tears, he was so glad to see it all again' (Price 1994: 251). At the end of *Happily Ever After*, Kate reflects that 'life in a tower was not all it was cracked up to be' (Quindlen 1997: 64); and in *Battle Boy: Black Prince*, Napoleon Smythe revels in the technological advancement of the world to which he returns. Mildly regretful though they are to leave behind friends they have made in medieval settings, these protagonists conclude that to be medieval is to be hopelessly inadequate or utterly oppressed in comparison with the brave new world of modernity. As Butler and O'Donovan note, time-travel narratives are liable to view the past as 'something alien, where strange and terrible things happen and which can be judged from the safety and comfort of an enlightened present' (2012: 8–9). Time-travel narratives involving the Middle Ages assent to this general orientation to the past, foregrounding the weirdness of the medieval as a marker of its otherness to modernity and testifying to the solidity and reliability of the present.

Virtually medieval

I do not have the scope in this book to do more than gesture to the vast field of video games which constitute a major component of medievalist narratives for the young, except to note that scholars have increasingly turned their attention to these games, considering how and to what ends the medieval is imagined and deployed.[15] Novels featuring medievalist video games include Susan Cooper's *The Boggart* (1993), which I will discuss in Chapter 3, Vivien Vande Velde's *Heir Apparent* (2002), and Catherine Jinks's *Saving Thanehaven* (2014), my focus in this section of the chapter. The interplay of temporalities in video games is complex and has been extensively discussed.[16] Games are, of course, played in real-world time but incorporate their own temporal schemes, such as day–night cycles, or time limits by which actions must be performed. José P. Zagal and Michael Mateas (2010) identify the category of fictive time, which encompasses the narrative elements of games: the temporal progress of a quest; biological cycles including time to rest or to eat; a character's development from youth to maturity. Medievalist games such as *Thanehaven Slayer*, the game on which Jinks's *Saving Thanehaven* is based, call upon many of the tropes of medieval romance and the givens of popular conceptions of the Middle Ages: on the one hand, filth, violence and death; on the other, ethereal imaginings of magic and mystery.

As Alexander Galloway says, video games are 'not just images or stories or play or games but *actions*' (2006: 37). *Saving Thanehaven* mirrors this emphasis on action through a narrative consisting of constant and often frenetic action which occurs almost exclusively inside various gameworlds. The primary world is that of a first-person shooter game,[17] *Thanehaven Slayer*, in which a young knight, Noble, is charged with the quest of rescuing Princess Lorellina from the Fortress of Bone. He carries a sword called Smite, a shape-changing weapon/ animal who, when hungry, attempts to bite Noble. The knight's body adheres to video game norms for this style of character: he has 'huge shoulders and narrow waist', 'chiselled features', 'level ice-blue glower and sun-streaked hair' (2014: 58). Like all such heroes, he is the product of what Ian Bogost refers to as procedural rhetoric, the practice of 'authoring arguments through process' (2008: 125). For video games are, Bogost says, not merely empty and vacuous forms of entertainment but use programming to produce 'rules of behavior, the construction of dynamic models' (125). *Saving Thanehaven* engages readers with a game-like narrative which positions readers to critically examine the rules of behaviour on which the game is built, pertaining to the heroic, masculinity, and chivalry. Whereas characters in games have no interior life to speak of, the novel's strategy of focalising action through Noble's present-tense perspective both parodies video games and affords psychological depth.

The fictive time of the narrative incorporates multiple allusions to medieval romance – or at least to an attenuated and clichéd version of a romance quest involving a hero, a villain (Lord Harrowmage) and an imprisoned princess (Lorellina). The illusion of historical density is conveyed through the medievalist elements which crowd the game's environment, including architecture, home decor, clothing and objects. The temporal scheme of *Thanehaven Slayer* is relentlessly forward-moving, requiring Noble to respond to a series of trials, obstacles and antagonists as he makes his way to Thanehaven. It is when Noble encounters a character called Rufus, a 'beardless, unarmed youth' (5), that the contemporary world intrudes into the medievalist narrative. Although Noble does not recognise Rufus's nefarious intentions until more than half way through the narrative, it is evident to readers from an early stage that Rufus is in fact malware (Ruthlessrufus) masquerading as a character; he is manipulated by the real-life Rufus, who seeks to attack the operating system of the computer onto which *Thanehaven Slayer* has been uploaded, with a view to corrupting this and other games.

Much of the comedic effect of the narrative derives from the dissonance it creates between Noble's resolute performance of the medieval hero, and readers' recognition of the double game Rufus plays. When Noble approaches the drawbridge of Thanehaven he announces his intentions in heroic style, booming: '"I wish to negotiate a truce in good faith and without bias! Not a soul will suffer *any harm* if I am admitted into the presence of Lord Harrowmage!" "Nice one," Rufus says, grinning' (22). But Rufus misrecognises Noble as a programmed and powerless figure. Rather, the medievalist hero turns out to be intelligent and resourceful, so that when he appreciates the extent of Rufus's malevolence he negotiates firewalls and anti-viral software with the assistance of Yestin, a young boy rescued from the wreckage of the spaceship game *Living Hell*. By the end of the novel Noble has restored the computer's operating system and the malware Rufus is in quarantine. Noble's lack of technological know-how turns out, then, to be less significant than his capacity to grapple with the ethics of gameplay in virtual worlds.

Saving Thanehaven hinges upon the play of temporalities, drawing attention to the reductiveness with which the medieval is treated in *Thanehaven Slayer* and, by extension, in the real world in which the game is designed. By constructing Noble as more than merely a medievalist cipher, the novel performs a reclamation of the medieval in game design, attributing Noble with emotions, intelligence and resolve. Video games, according to Bogost, 'make arguments about how social or cultural systems work in the world' (2008: 136). *Saving Thanehaven* plays with notions of the medieval and its deployment in video games, positioning readers to engage critically with representational and rhetorical systems in which the medieval is cast as a field of fixed, controlled and inexorable cultural systems against which modernity defines itself. Reflecting on Rufus's seductive promises of absolute freedom, Noble recognises that freedom is contingent on knowledge and insight: '*How could I have been master of my own destiny, when I never even knew what was going on?*' (2014: 184). What Pugh and Weisl refer to as 'the pleasures of electronic anachronism' (2013: 122) are mediated in *Saving Thanehaven* through a narrative which at once celebrates these pleasures and positions young readers to critically consider how the medieval is used and abused in video game narratives.

The once and future medieval

The texts I have discussed so far in this chapter have demonstrated the effects which flow from asynchrony, the coexistence of different temporal schemes in the 'now' of the present. To conclude, I consider texts whose imaginings of post-disaster worlds evoke pre-industrial societies along a continuum from dystopian to utopian. Post-disaster fiction, set in a future time following a global catastrophe of some kind, typically depicts the present as history and 'uses this temporal relationship as a strategy to foreground dystopian tendencies in present societies' (Bradford et al. 2008: 13).[18] The 'now' of this fiction may, like Lois Lowry's *Gathering Blue* (2000), call on ideas of a premodern world characterised by violence and superstition; or, like Frances Mary Hendry's *Atlantis* (1997), it may evoke an ordered, peaceful polity whose citizens are content with their regulated society. Traces of diverse times and cultures coexist in post-disaster worlds, where medievalist allusions surface alongside remnants and traces of other cultures, texts and practices.

Post-disaster settings are at once strange and familiar, analogous in some ways to the world of their readers but bearing the marks of the catastrophic events which have transformed this world. The medieval is a durable element in such scenarios because it is a flexible and recognisable cultural sign, readily invoked as a distant antecedent of post-disaster futures, either dystopian or utopian. The openness of the medieval to multiple interpretations means that it can signify a range of meanings in any one text. This is the case in Janice Elliott's *The Empty Throne* (1988), in which medievalisms range across Arthurian legend, tribal politics, and a suggestion of an Arcadian pre-industrial natural world. *The Empty Throne* is the sequel of *The King Awakes* (1987), and is one of a cluster of texts featuring the return of Arthur to post-disaster Britain: Ron Langenus's *Merlin's Return* (1993), and Pamela F. Service's *Winter of Magic's Return* (1985), *Tomorrow's Magic* (1987), *Yesterday's Magic* (2008) and *Earth's Magic* (2009).

The world of *The Empty Throne* is populated by groups of survivors who eke out a living in a despoiled landscape, maintaining a continuous struggle for territory and power. This depiction of a lawless and dangerous realm maps onto modern imaginings of medieval Britain during the so-called Dark Ages, especially the post-Roman centuries most commonly associated with the figure of Arthur.[19] The nuclear explosion referred to as the Catastrophe is now several generations back, and the boy protagonist, Red, has thrown in his lot with the Travellers, a group of itinerants modelled loosely on Romani, whose leader, Joss, aims to take control of the British capital city known as Jerusalem, and to install himself on its ancient throne. Another band, led by Haldred the Hunter, contends with the Travellers for ascendancy. In addition groups of cannibals and religious extremists known as Crucifiers prey on survivors. In the Deadlands beyond settlements and roads live Wanderers, individuals with no family or tribal affiliations, and animals and humans known as Outbeasts and Outmen, monstrous beings whose deformations result from nuclear damage and mutation.

In this gloomy and perilous world, the myth of Arthur's return signifies both a source of hope for the restitution of an ordered society and a threat to powerful groups and individuals. Rumours that 'the king awakes and has come to save Britain' (1988: 27) circulate, and in the third chapter of the book a man dressed as a beggar seeks water and oatcake from a widow. His bearing is more 'manly' (27) than that of the other mendicants who come to her door, a word which conveys the masculinist tone of the book's treatment of Arthur, who disguises himself first as a beggar and then as Noman, a Wanderer who wears a black hood with eyeholes. In this guise Arthur/Noman accompanies Red and his family as they travel to Jerusalem, always hovering on the edges of the group so as not to draw attention to himself. Readers are primed to recognise Arthur in Noman when he saves Red from death during a battle with Haldred's Wanderers, a moment which reinforces Arthur's credentials as a warrior. But the Arthur of *The Empty Throne* is not only a warrior; he is, rather, the saviour of the nation. When Red asks 'Why did you come back?', he replies: 'I never really left .... It may be I must stay until Britain is whole again' (116).

The novel's version of Arthur is, then, a strongly nationalistic one, calling on hazy notions of a genealogy reaching back to Celtic origins and embellished with Christian and Druidic symbols. These appeals to antiquity easily trump the claims of the corrupt and ambitious Owen, the High Guardian of what is known as the Sacred Box, the 'Ray Dio' (93) which is ceremoniously produced each day to play a snatch of William Blake's anthem 'Jerusalem': 'And we shall build Jerusalem / In England's green and pleasant land' (94).[20] The radio itself conjures up the mid-twentieth century, prior to the Catastrophe, while the anthem it plays, 'Jerusalem', evokes the stretch of time back to Blake and encompassing the biblical resonances of his poem. The larger meanings of 'Jerusalem' are, however, lost on the High Guardian who, like the priestly caste more generally in *The Empty Throne*, exploits the credulousness of the survivors to bolster his power.

Andrew Lynch observes that 'the apparently compulsive desire to revise and refashion the Arthurian legend for contemporary tastes ... holds within itself a more obscure but possibly more powerful desire – to assert connection, continuity, and the idea of legendariness across national and temporal boundaries' (2014: 228). In *The Empty Throne*, the future time of post-disaster England derives connection and continuity from the past through an amalgamation of symbols and myths centred on Arthur. The novel's climax occurs in Westminster Abbey, the scene of the final battle between the Travellers and Haldred's forces, who are backed by the starving city dwellers known as Scum. In a sign of the loss of memory and tradition caused by the Catastrophe, the Abbey and London are not named in the novel but exist as mere remnants of pre-disaster England, known as the Before-time. Nevertheless, Red's focalising perspective of the Abbey evokes ancient meanings: 'With its high curved roof that seemed to soar nearly out of sight, tall windows, some with bright coloured pictures in the glass, carved wood and avenue of stone pillars, it was like a clearing in a forest' (1988: 148–9). Thus defamiliarised, the Abbey is associated with the natural world, its 'avenue' leading to the building's focal point: the 'wonderful golden chair' (149) at its far end.

Red is marked out as the successor to Arthur, who appears on the throne, clothed in red and holding his sword, which 'shone as though from a light of its own. And it was ruby and gold and emerald from the high sun's rays through the coloured windows' (166). Arthur addresses Haldred with the words 'Let Britain heal' (166) and passes the sword to Red, whose hand-to-hand combat ends in Haldred's death and the inauguration of a new order. In the final moments of the novel, Red works with his mother Bron in an overgrown orchard they have found outside the city walls. The weather has changed: the pitiless sequence of high summer followed by coldest winter which has succeeded the Catastrophe has now given way to the seasonal patterns of the Before-time, in which autumnal weather brings the old apples of the orchard, a sign of a futurity which regathers the past. Arthur has vanished into the absence from which he entered the post-disaster world at the beginning of the novel, leaving behind the promise of a better time founded on the symbols and practices of the Before-time. Referring to Roger Lancelyn Green's assertion that 'there is always something new to be found' in retellings of legends (in Lynch 2014: 232), Lynch notes that this insistence on newness discloses that 'the legendary core of the story is kept unstable and elusive, with almost nothing indispensable to it' (233), while affirming 'the sense of legendariness against the consciousness of modernity's radical alterations' (233). This is exactly how the Arthurian elements of *The Empty Throne* operate: Arthur is defined by the magical qualities of his sword, by his symbolic significance as a sign of Britishness, and, most importantly for this novel, by his action of bequeathing power and authority to Red, the ordinary boy who is destined to lead Britain.

As I have demonstrated in this chapter, narratives which centre upon temporality traverse genres and modes of fiction, ranging across gothic-inspired fantasy, realism and post-disaster fiction, and the blend of historical realism and fantasy which marks out time-travel novels. These texts are always shaped by the preoccupations and anxieties of the times in which they are produced. Tensions between different ways of envisaging relations between premodern and modern surface in textual aporia such as occur in Fletcher's Stoneheart trilogy, where the Middle Ages signifies in various ways: as abject, as loaded with archetypal meanings, or as incommensurable with the present. In *The Graveyard Book* Bod's multi-temporal experience both destabilises narratives of origins, continuity and order, and also endows Bod with insights gained from his close knowledge of past people and cultures. The time-travel narratives I have discussed are imbued with nostalgia (in its complex combination of positive and negative impulses) and, in time-travel texts which take contemporary protagonists to the Middle Ages and back to modernity, a profound sense of the advantages of modernity. Jinks's *Saving Thanehaven* scrutinises the ethics and representational practices of medievalist video games, and the valency of the past for the present; and Arthurian post-disaster fiction, exemplified by *The Empty Throne*, calls on the medieval to provide symbols and traditions which look to future worlds. These texts are all multi-temporal in the relationships they construe between the medieval and the diverse times to which they allude. Calling on fragments, discourses and narratives associated with the Middle Ages, they reassemble these elements for modern audiences, enabling the pleasures of asynchronous reading.

3
Spatiality and the Medieval

In Chapter 2 I considered a selection of medievalist texts in the light of theories of temporality. In practice it is impossible to sever time from space in fictional worlds, because space is represented as existing in time, and because the textual interplay of different times (the asynchrony to which Dinshaw refers) is grounded in places that evoke or symbolise these times. The Middle Ages enters the present through represented and real-world materiality: buildings, monuments, gardens and landscapes which impinge on the consciousness of modern people and cultures. Many medievalist texts incorporate maps and architectural plans which ground characters' movements and locate narratives in relation to territory, nations, urban and rural settings, and buildings. In reading such texts I often find myself flicking back to their maps and plans, plotting events and the movements of characters in fictional space. This back-and-forth movement offers a metaphor for how fiction spatialises narratives, inviting readerly practices which traverse between the here of the reader's present, the there of the narrative, and the other places and times to which the narrative alludes. Time is unthinkable without reference to space, space without reference to time.[1]

Foucault's celebrated summary encapsulates the subordination of space to time in nineteenth-century social theory: 'Space was treated as the dead, the fixed, the undialectical, the immobile. Time, on the contrary, was richness, fecundity, life, dialectic' (1980: 70). The 'spatial turn' which emerged in literary and cultural theory during the second half of the twentieth century responded to dramatic shifts in global geopolitical relations, a growing disillusionment with concepts of time-as-progress, and technological developments which, in Robert Tally's words, have 'served to suppress distance while also augmenting one's sense of place or of displacement' (2012: 14). These cultural and conceptual shifts have influenced critical studies of literature and film, which increasingly focus on questions of place, space and mapping, and on the spatial or geographical dimensions of cultural production.

The spatial turn has been evident, too, in studies of medieval and medievalist texts and cultures. In his introduction to *The Postcolonial Middle Ages* (2000), Jeffrey Cohen reflects on Meridian Hill Park in Washington, and on the hybrid and contested histories which have left their traces in this location: formerly the habitation of Native Americans, a site of civil rights rallies, its design a combination of French and Italian Renaissance styles. Cohen observes that statues of two medieval figures feature prominently in the park: Dante and Joan of Arc, a 'little fragment of the medieval lodged in the heart of the postcolonial' (2). These statues, jostling with other signifiers of the past, exist as material and geographically located elements in an urban space where they manifest a 'surprising affiliation (with each other, with the minority and dominating histories that surround them)' (2). Cohen's analysis begins with a description of Meridian Hill as a place, gradually complicating this description by reflecting on the multiple temporalities (medieval, modern, postmodern) encoded in architecture, statuary and park design.

The spaces and places of medievalist fiction for the young are inescapably hybrid, suggesting the politics and ideologies of different times and cultures. Whether they take the form of historical fiction, contemporary realism, fantasy, or time-travel narratives, texts are shaped by the structures and conventions of the genres within which they work and by the representations of spatiality which characterise these genres. For instance, as I observed in Chapter 2, time-travel fiction tends to treat the Middle Ages as a time-space definitively other to modernity, so that when contemporary protagonists return to the present they experience a sense of relief at having left behind less congenial locations. The genre of the gothic romance employs a very different orientation towards the medieval, in which gloomy and forbidding castles and graveyards project the interior struggles of protagonists oppressed by prohibited desires.

The medieval churches, castles, city walls and monuments which feature in many contemporary texts for the young point to a European Middle Ages familiar to readers for whom ancient buildings and structures, or their modern replicas and copies constructed as heritage, are literally part of the landscape. Texts produced in nations which do not have their own Middle Ages, including the former settler societies of the United States, Canada, Australia and New Zealand, frequently incorporate historical and mythological deployments of the medieval, sometimes, as in Susan Cooper's *The Boggart* (1993) and *The Boggart and the Monster* (1997), foregrounding the implications of geographical and cultural shifts between the Old World and the New. In the contemporary global marketplace, young audiences around the world access the medieval in texts from Europe and the New World, through literary cartography which conjures up the gothic ambience of Hogwarts, the misty forests of fantasy, the weird pre-modernity of the Horrible Histories franchise. Whether created in Britain or in its former colonies, medievalist texts are always inflected by the cultures which produce them, and are received differentially by readers in widely dispersed national and cultural settings.

The manor house in texts for the young

Inhabited and visited by protagonists in texts for the young, medieval settings conjure up past lives and cultures, often incorporating ghostly or magical presences. Of the buildings which feature in children's texts, the manor house is one of the most pervasive, particularly (but not exclusively) in canonical British texts including Rudyard Kipling's *Puck of Pook's Hill* (1906), Edith Nesbit's *The Wouldbegoods,* the second of the Bastable novels (1899–1904), and Lucy M. Boston's Green Knowe sequence (1954–76).[2] Writing on the discourses of imperialism which inform these texts, Daphne Kutzer (2000) remarks on the genealogical work carried out by settings such as the Moat House, in Nesbit's *The Wouldbegoods* (1901). The novel's description of the Moat House foregrounds historical depth and longevity: 'There has been a house [where the Moat House stands] since Saxon times. It is a manor, and a manor goes on having a house on it whatever happens' (1901: 21). Spending their summer holidays at the Moat House, the Bastable children play out fantasies of exploration and combat. As Kutzer observes, the novel's references to the Roman occupation of Britain and the Saxon invasions of the fifth century normalise Britain's imperial project and its military enterprises, introduced through episodes when the Bastables encounter soldiers enlisted to fight in the Boer War.

In the words of the novel's narrator, Oswald Bastable, 'The Moat House was burned down once or twice in ancient centuries – I don't remember which – but they always built a new one' (21). The past, like the Moat House, is always capable of reinvention in the novel's present: the young Bastables take on the roles of Chaucer's pilgrims, basing their costumes on the illustrations in J. R. Green's *A Short History of the English*

People (1893); they plant 'antiquities' about the Moat House to be discovered by the visiting Maidstone Society of Antiquaries; they conduct a siege of the Roman ruins near the house, using bows and arrows. To the Bastable children, then, the Moat House and its outbuildings, orchards and gardens invite imaginative play, much of it based on their exposure to medievalist tropes, texts and narratives. While the Moat House's antiquity renders it unfashionable – its owner 'likes new houses, so he built a big one with conservatories and a stable with a clock in a turret on the top' (21) – the children delight in its difference from their smart house in Blackheath, which is 'replete with every modern convenience' (3). The first chapter of *The Wouldbegoods* opens at the Blackheath house, where the Bastables, with an excess of time on their hands, simulate scenes from Kipling's *The Jungle Book*. They improvise a waterfall and an array of wild animals, terrifying Daisy, their young visitor, and ruining the stuffed animals and skins they have 'borrowed' from the house.

The Bastables are dispatched to the country, so they are told, until they have 'grown into better children' (19); their return to the Blackheath house is described in the final chapter of *The Wouldbegoods*. Their sojourn in the Moat House during the summer holidays thus locates them in a liminal state where they are relatively free from the tedious requirements of city life: cleanliness, tidiness and punctuality. Like the children's games discussed by the anthropologist Victor Turner in *From Ritual to Theatre* (1982), the Bastables' ludic activities incorporate forms of liminality which involve disorderliness, enabling them to let off steam after experiencing a surfeit of order. As Turner observes, only certain kinds of children's games can be regarded as liminal, since purposeful games such as those pertaining to organised sport are typically ordered, rule-bound and regarded as preparation for life. The Bastables' games, in contrast, constitute an escape from the everyday. Their experience of liminality hinges upon the antiquity of the Moat House, which is itself a space and time apart, being away from the city and immune from the regular routines of the school year.

Oswald associates the Moat House with a glamorised past, a 'dear old adventurous time' (259) of heroism and adventure. This romantic medievalism is enlisted to celebrate the valour of British forces and specifically the soldiers who march past the Moat House, and who are preparing to fight in the Boer War.[3] The captain, in Oswald's eyes, is 'like a Viking. Very tall and fair, with moustaches very long, and bright blue eyes' (1901: 46). Enchanted by the medievalist aura surrounding the captain, Oswald divulges his desire to emulate him: 'I should like to be a soldier. It is better than going to the best schools, and to Oxford afterwards, even if it is Balliol you go to' (1901: 45). The narrative, however, casts a cool eye on Oswald's ardour, exposing the limitations of his knowledge and experience: 'Oswald wanted to go to South Africa for a bugler, but father would not let him. And it is true that Oswald does not yet know how to bugle, though he can play the infantry "advance", and the "charge" and the "halt" on a penny whistle' (1901: 45). As Barbara Wall (1991) observes, Nesbit's invention of Oswald Bastable is directed towards child readers capable of recognising and enjoying his many malapropisms, misjudgements and lapses of understanding. Oswald's view of a romantic Middle Ages, like his firm belief in his own acumen, is thus undercut by his comical fallibility.

Whereas the Moat House is the backdrop to the Bastables' medievalist fantasies, the Middle Ages in Boston's Green Knowe series interacts with modernity as young protagonists living in Green Knowe encounter ghostly children who have also occupied the manor house between the twelfth and the twentieth centuries. The present time of these protagonists is, in Grosz's terms, 'riven by memory' (2004: 251) as their access to the past enlivens and shapes their actions and decisions. In the final book of the series, *The Stones of Green Knowe*, the narrative turns to the building of the manor, seen through the eyes of Roger, the middle son of the Norman lord of the manor, Osmund d'Aulneaux. Roger's grandfather is Norman but his beloved grandmother is Saxon. The novel's view of Englishness is, then, built on the combination of Saxon and Norman ancestry embodied by Roger, and enhanced by references to older magics, exemplified by the ancient stone chairs, the Stones, which stand in a grove near the manor house. When Roger sits on one of the Stones he travels forwards in time; similarly, later inhabitants of the house travel backwards in time to meet Roger and see Green Knowe.

Like the Moat House, Green Knowe represents an England constructed and reconstructed over time. The opening chapters of the narrative are devoted to a close description of the building of the house, a stone structure, with windows and a chimney, erected over the foundation of the Saxon hall at the centre of the manor. Roger d'Aulneaux is to receive Green Knowe as his inheritance; his older brother Bernard will inherit his mother's lands in Normandy, and his younger brother Edgar will have a small estate nearby. The narrative positions readers to align themselves with Roger, the focalising protagonist, and to engage with the delight and excitement he experiences as he observes the building take shape. Later in the novel, when Roger time-travels to the year 1800, in the place where the manor house stood he comes across a large and ornate building made of brick: '[Roger] found that the walls were made of blocks of what felt to the touch like coarse earthenware. "A house made like a jug!" he thought contemptuously' (1976: 85). He is relieved to discover that 'his' house has survived, and that a red brick facade has been erected over the Norman house, which is itself built upon the Saxon hall. Readers are positioned to agree with Roger's judgements about the aesthetics and durability of the Georgian additions which have supplanted the old manor. Sure enough, when Roger time-shifts to the 1950s, where he meets his remote descendant Tolly Oldknow, he discovers that the old house has survived while most of its Georgian carapace has burned down. Restored to its medieval beginnings, with its 'steep tiled roof, its high-gabled ends, its stone windows' (115), Green Knowe comprises a potent symbol of nationhood, defined by the blend of Stone Age, Saxon and Norman influences which shape the house and its surroundings. The novel's account of its history leaves readers in no doubt that authentic, deep Englishness resides in the medieval past, not in the nouveau-riche accretions represented by the Georgian refashioning of the house.

In *The Wouldbegoods* and *The Stones of Green Knowe*, the Saxons and Normans who establish manor houses are the precursors of the British children who later occupy these houses. Whereas the Moat House offers the Bastables a medievalist time-out from the everyday world of school and city life, Green Knowe functions as a site where Roger and the children who succeed him form identities and establish systems of belief and values. The survival of Green Knowe is thus imbricated with familial and personal affiliations, figured through the relationships forged between the children who inhabit the house. At the end of *The Stones of Green Knowe*, Roger, transported into the 1950s, witnesses what he regards as an assault on his own identity and that of Green Knowe itself. He watches helplessly as the Stones are wrested from their grove, grabbed by tractors and cranes, and taken to the local museum, where, Tolly tells him, 'old things are kept' (132). Roger's objection, 'But they were in their own place' (132), rejects memorialisation, insisting that ancient objects are robbed of meaning when displaced. At the core of this rejection is a contrast between stasis and movement. In the local museum, the Stones will be merely ancient artefacts, still and mute, viewed behind glass. In their grove near Green Knowe, they function as engines whereby the past enters the present, and the present the past, within the narrative dynamic of the Green Knowe series. When the Stones are removed from their place, they are stripped of their power to enable these relationships across time.

68 *The Middle Ages in Children's Literature*

Perhaps the most unlikely manifestation of the English manor house in contemporary fiction for young adults occurs in Meg Rosoff's *How I Live Now* (2004). In this novel, the first-person narrator Daisy travels from her home in Manhattan to stay with her English aunt (the sister of her dead mother) and four cousins at their home in the English countryside. Although the novel is silent on the medieval origins of the house and the history of the family who live there, Daisy's description is laced with references to its antiquity:

> [The house is] made out of big chunks of yellowish stone, and has a steep roof, and is shaped like an L around a big courtyard with fat pebbles set in the ground. The short part of the L has a wide arched doorway and it used to be the stable, but now it's the kitchen and it's huge, with zigzag brick floors and big windows all across the front ... Behind the house and up some stone steps is a square garden surrounded by high brick walls and in there are tons of flowers blooming already all in shades of white. In one corner there's a stone angel about the size of a child, very worn, with folded wings and Piper told me it was a child who lived in the house hundreds of years ago and is buried in the garden. (2004: 8–9)

These details of the house's stone walls and steep roof, its white garden, courtyard, statuary and huge kitchen, evoke manor houses from *The Wouldbegoods* to *The Stones of Green Knowe* as well as historical houses such as Sissinghurst, with its famous white garden. Like many other fictive visitors to manor houses, Daisy is needy and neglected: her mother died when she was born, her stepmother dislikes her, and she is anorexic. The medievalist associations of the manor house inflect Daisy's struggle to make sense of her transition from the New World to the Old. In the first instance, her assumptions about the staidness of life in the English countryside are overturned when she discovers that her cousins enjoy freedom from adult supervision unknown to her as a 15-year-old from New York City, that her 14-year-old cousin Edmond drives the family's jeep and is a chain-smoker, and that her Aunt Penn, who 'always has Important Work To do Related To The Peace Process' (9), is about to depart for Oslo to deliver a lecture on peace negotiations, leaving Daisy and her cousins (from 16-year-old Osbert to 9-year-old Piper) to their own devices.

In itself, the cousins' independence from adults follows a pattern common in fiction for the young, directing attention to the subject-formation of children and young people. In *How I Live Now* this scenario is complicated, first, by Daisy's romantic and sexual relationship with Edmond. Second, Britain is invaded by an unidentified enemy army and during the dystopian regime which ensues communication and transport are disrupted, the house is sequestered for troop accommodation and the cousins are dispersed to different locations. Prior to this enforced separation, however, Daisy and her cousins enjoy an idyllic summer, shielded from the war by the beauty of the manor house and the bounty of its garden and farm. Indeed, the absence of vehicles and the cessation of industry create the illusion of an older, pre-industrial England where 'all [the birds] did was lay eggs and sing and try to avoid getting eaten by foxes' (50). In this context, Daisy and Edmond's relationship is rendered 'natural', as if its two impediments, their first-cousin relationship, and modern prohibitions against under-age sex, are obviated not only by the exceptional circumstances in which they find themselves but also by their sense of living 'as if' in the past time of the manor house's origins.

The global warfare which has swept the world soon disrupts this idyllic existence; the cousins are separated, and when, months later, Daisy and Piper reach Gateshead Farm, where Edmond and Isaac were billeted, they discover that the civilians who took refuge there have been massacred, and that the two boys are nowhere to be found. Daisy's influential father arranges for her to return to New York where she passes the next five years prior to her return to her cousins' home, when she is liberated from what she terms the 'limbo' (161) of her life in New York City, where she merely fills in time while waiting for the borders between the United States and Britain to reopen. Since Aunt Penn's death has been confirmed, her cousins have returned to the manor house estate, which they have restored to self-sufficiency, a 'natural way for them to live' (169). Edmond's psychic distress at the violence he has witnessed and his sense of having been abandoned by Daisy has manifested in self-harming and muteness, and in the final pages of the novel Daisy talks him back into health, working with him in his self-imposed task of regenerating the walled white garden. The house and its garden and farm now suggest an alternative (medievalist) paradigm of communitarian life which, as in many dystopian texts for young people, rejects capitalist economies in favour of pre-industrial models of production and consumption.[4]

The novel's account of the causes and effects of the global war is displaced by the narrative of Daisy and Edmond's romance, its disruption and its ultimate restoration. As Edmond recovers, he educates Daisy in the ancient names of the plants which grow in the walled garden:

'Corylus avellana. Hazelnuts. *Rubus fruticosus.* Blackberries. *Agaricus campestris.* Field mushroom'. The incantational power of these names, along with 'hard work and the feel of old tools' (184), suggest that the maintenance of ancient practices and languages offers an antidote to the dangers and traumas of the modern (post-disaster) world. The new world which Daisy and Edmond forge from the ruins of modernity relies on its maintenance of a *hortus conclusus* sequestered from the larger society.

The manor houses of these novels are intensely and self-consciously European and English: the 'commons and osier beds and orchards' (Boston 1976: 124) of Green Knowe, like the farm with 'barns and oast-houses and stables' (Nesbit 1901: 21) which lies beyond the Moat House, and the barn, old stable and orchard of *How I Live Now* evoke histories of English agrarian economics and jurisdiction.[5] All three houses function inter alia as places of refuge. At the Moat House the Bastables are released from the demands of school and family; and protagonists in the Green Knowe series are often neglected by or at odds with their parents, finding solace in the house itself and in the grandmother figures (Mrs Oldknow and Roger's Saxon grandmother) who feature in all except one of the books.[6] Daisy, too, finds in her cousins' home a refuge from conflict with her father and stepmother. In the Green Knowe series, family and nation are homologous: as Roger was the first heir apparent of Green Knowe, so Tolly is his modern counterpart, an English boy in Roger's mould. Daisy's return from New York in *How I Live Now* can be read as both escape and also restitution: abandoning the New World for the Old, she returns to her mother's home. The antiquity of the manor houses of the Green Knowe series and *How I Live Now* is folded into versions of personal and national identity which depend upon tradition, continuity and endurance.

The Wouldbegoods and *How I Live Now*, for all their contrasts of style, narrative approach and genre, have in common an orientation which maintains distinctions between premodern and modern, investing the Middle Ages with romanticised significances which keep the medieval in its place. The protagonists of these novels inhabit their own time and space while calling on the symbolic resonances of ancient buildings, artefacts and gardens. Of the three texts I have considered in this section, *The Stones of Green Knowe* most radically represents asynchronous engagements between and across times because of its powerful sense of the co-presence of child protagonists in the ancient buildings, gardens and woods of Green Knowe. Roger's forays into other times are always defined by visual depictions of Green Knowe and its environs – the laying of the hearthstone in Norman times; his view of the red brick cladding of Georgian times; a glimpse of the Saxon invasion which preceded that of the Normans. The 'persistence of the past in the present' (Grosz 2004: 25) is thus grounded in spatiality. This interplay of space and time invites reading practices that negotiate across diverse historical times and recognise affective bonds which transcend difference.

Gothic spaces, modern narratives

The term 'gothic' in its many permutations of meaning is haunted by the Middle Ages. Fred Botting notes that the word calls up 'feudal associations, medieval styles of architecture and a notoriously fierce Germanic tribe' (2014: 2), and that gothic texts always engage with a medieval past shaped by the times and cultures in which they are produced. Used to define the architectural style prevalent in Europe between the twelfth and fifteenth centuries, 'gothic' refers to the constellation of features that characterise this style, such as the pointed arch, stonework tracery in windows, the use of buttresses to shore up buildings. From the perspective of the Enlightenment, the Middle Ages and its architecture represented a barbaric and superstitious 'Gothic' past against which Enlightenment rationalism defined itself, but by the eighteenth century, with the advent of the Gothic Revival, the medieval was back in fashion, giving rise to the gothic novel, in which psychological and psychic disturbances are projected through settings such as ruined abbeys and castles, graveyards and isolated mansions. The word 'gothic', and the diverse cultural forms and practices which claim a gothic legacy, are always, as Botting says, 'implicated in an ongoing political struggle over meanings' (2014: 40). Contemporary texts refer recursively to the medieval and post-medieval associations of the gothic, often in hybrid and reflexive forms.

In this section I focus on spatial dimensions of gothic medievalism, beginning with Walt Disney's interpretation of gothic architecture in the animated film *The Hunchback of Notre Dame* (1996). The film's medievalist flavour is introduced first through its soundtrack as the bells of the cathedral toll, layered with the Gregorian chant of the Tridentine Mass. The soundtrack accompanies a hazy view of the gothic towers of Notre-Dame cathedral, depicted in romantic blues, creams and pinks with shafts of light piercing the sky. Then a conventionally Disney element is added to the mix: the voices of a massed choir accompanied by a lush orchestral score dominated by strings and percussion. Finally the angle of vision drops to the streets of Paris against the track of the song

'The Bells of Notre Dame', a jaunty number with piano accordion backing which accompanies a tour of the neighbourhood, including a resident emptying a chamber-pot from a window onto the cobbled street below, a boy fishing from a bridge over the Seine, a baker placing loaves in front of his shop. These fluctuating evocations of place, from the lofty to the demotic, incorporate Notre-Dame and Paris into a Disney aesthetic whose settings function, as Martha Bayless says, as 'inviting play spaces in which personal stories can be enacted' (2012: 39).

Gothic cathedrals of the Middle Ages were godly buildings whose towers, soaring stonework and stained glass comprised 'a semblance of the Heavenly Jerusalem' (Scott 2011: 110). The interior of Notre-Dame in *The Hunchback* comprises two main settings: the devotional spaces of its nave and side chapels; and the tower to which Quasimodo has been consigned by the evil judge Frollo, and where he performs his role as a bell-ringer. Disney's Notre-Dame is a non-denominational space in which religious sentiment is realised through images carefully oriented to audiences who might be alienated by too-overt signifiers of Catholicism such as the cathedral's high altar, its narrative paintings of the lives of saints, its many statues. The statue of the Virgin Mary is the focus of the scene where the gypsy Esmeralda seeks sanctuary in the cathedral; but Esmeralda's song 'God Help the Outcasts' appeals to Mary's own outsider status ('Still I see your face and wonder / Were you once an outcast too?') rather than to an invocation of Mary's status as mother of Jesus. Avoiding religiously charged elements, the film restricts its depiction of the cathedral's interior to gothic arches, ribbed vaults, candelabra and stained glass, rendered, in line with the colour palette of the opening moments of the film, in hazy blues, purples and pinks. This misty evocation of the medieval has the effect of displacing reference to the real by subsuming it within a romantic setting which prepares viewers for the narrative of Quasimodo's self-actualisation. Viewers are positioned to imagine a positive future for Quasimodo, much as castle settings tend towards narratives of female transformation.

Bayless observes that the personal stories enacted in Disney's castles (both filmically and in Disney-themed parks throughout the world) typically incorporate modes of female identity-formation: 'personal, family-focused, transformative' (40). The gothic cathedral in Disney's *Hunchback* is, in contrast, a masculine space, the territory of the archdeacon and his monks, and the home of Quasimodo. In this film Quasimodo is a confused young man who derives freedom and progress from his platonic love for Esmeralda and liberation from his evil surrogate father, Frollo.[7] Indeed, Quasimodo's living quarters evoke the bedroom of a reclusive, nerdish contemporary boy, incorporating bed, food supplies, and an entertainment area in the form of a table-top model of Notre-Dame and Paris which Quasimodo has carved, and to which he adds figures based on those he observes in the square below. When Esmeralda visits Quasimodo in the bell tower she admires his quarters: 'You're a surprising person, Quasimodo, not to mention lucky. All this room to yourself!' (1996). Victor, Hugo and Laverne, the three gargoyles, function as wise-cracking buddies, reverting to stone before everyone other than Quasimodo.

Lacking confidence and convinced that he is a monster, Quasimodo must be inducted into sociality in order to gain a sense of self-worth; that is, he must abandon the material and psychological isolation of the bell tower for the social spaces of the world outside the cathedral. Here the film's treatment of the Middle Ages is strikingly unstable. When Quasimodo takes the risky step of leaving the bell tower to participate in the Feast of Fools in the cathedral square, he is crowned King and applauded by the populace. But the mood of the crowd quickly changes to disgust and the citizens of Paris hurl vegetables at Quasimodo, so that he retreats to his isolation in the bell tower. At the end of the film, following Frollo's death, Esmeralda draws Quasimodo outside Notre-Dame to face the people, who stand silently gazing at his face. A little girl comes forward and touches his face, whereupon the two embrace. The girl functions as the catalyst for Quasimodo's introduction to sociality, leading him into the crowd. She is not an individuated figure but plays out the trope of childhood innocence which is a prominent aspect of Disney's representations of children, childhood, and the Disney enterprise. Nevertheless, the setting of the cathedral square is also that of the earlier scene in which the crowd treats Quasimodo with cruelty, so that the film's closure seems to offer only a provisional incorporation into the social world.

Disney's *Hunchback* seems, too, to swerve between alternative orientations towards the gothic. The architecture of Notre-Dame, rendered as a romantic vision of soaring spaces and soft colours, suggests the admiration for gothic architecture which, according to Botting, manifests in eighteenth-century conceptions of the sublime as 'sacred nature, glimpsed in sublime settings and evoked by old poetry and buildings' (2014: 38). The death of Frollo suggests a less benign deployment of the gothic. Struggling with Quasimodo on the balcony of the bell tower, Frollo clings to the head of a gargoyle, which cracks just as he is about to attack Esmeralda. In this moment the gargoyle comes to life and roars at Frollo, breaking off and sending him to his death. In one sense the gargoyle's action may be interpreted as a protective gesture, saving the lives of Quasimodo and Esmeralda. Read as an intimation of ancient anger or evil, the gargoyle is metonymic of the gothic as a site of 'savage and primitive energies, archaic and immature' (Botting 2014: 4).

Ambivalent attitudes to the gothic also colour Robert Westall's *Ghost Abbey* (1988) and his novella *The Stones of Muncaster Cathedral* (1991). In *Ghost Abbey* the protagonist, 13-year-old Maggi Adams, mourns the loss of her mother, who died of heart failure two years previously, leaving Maggi to care for Baz and Gaz, her unruly twin brothers, and her depressed and aimless father. When George Adams receives an invitation to act as foreman in the restoration of an abbey in Cheshire, Maggi welcomes a change of place which, she thinks, might provide the family with a more positive orientation to life. Their car trip from Teesside to Northwich in Cheshire involves a journey from life in an urban terrace to the rural location of the Abbey, set in a vast treed park. This is also a journey from the banal modernity of the Teesside setting, with its corner shop, identical houses and inquisitive neighbours, to the multi-temporality of the Abbey, which bears the signs of many generations of occupants and owners.

The Abbey's antiquity and its dilapidated charm seem to offer an antidote to the rootlessness of the Adams family, which derives in part from their unresolved grief and in part from a more general malaise vividly articulated by the unthinking destructiveness of Baz and Gaz. As David Harvey notes, the postmodern condition is marked by the 'volatility and ephemerality of fashions, products, production techniques, labour processes, ideas and ideologies, values and established practices' (1990: 286) so that individuals and groups search for 'secure moorings in a shifting world' (302). This postmodern dilemma[8] is played out in an episode when Maggi and her father, having arrived in Northwich, visit E. M. Morris, Estate Agents, who hold the Abbey keys. Here they encounter Mr Morris, one of the firm's partners, who views the Abbey as a 'mouldering old heap' (1988: 23) ripe for demolition. The Abbey's park, Morris says, would 'take a nice little estate of executive bungalows' (24) for which, however, planning permission is not yet available. George Adams, rejecting Morris's offer of a site foreman's position overseeing the development of just such a 'nice little estate', says, 'I'd sooner shovel pig-manure' (26).

The testy exchange between the two men plays on the contrast between George Adams's bluff north-east dialect and Mr Morris's urbanity, but the more fundamental opposition centres on their views of the value of the past. To Mr Morris, the worth of the Abbey resides in its utility as a site where potential buyers of 'four-bedroomed executive detached bungalows' (24) might be titillated by lurid stories about the nun who 'was in love with the last abbot, and he got her in the family way and gave her the sailor's farewell, so she hanged herself' (25). Maggi's father, in contrast, regards the Abbey as a repository of traditions of craftsmanship and a sign of continuity which offers him a sense of purpose as he embarks on his project of repairing the Abbey's roof.

To Maggi, the Abbey represents a mix of pleasure and fear. To her delight she discovers a garden fragrant with the scent of old roses; but she reads the interior of the Abbey in the light of gothic horror films, so that a door 'pointed at the top, and with huge rusting hinges' seems to come 'straight out of a Dracula movie' (99). The house is alive with the ghosts and voices of its former inhabitants, including a cavalier sniper whose death Maggi observes when she enters a state of dreaming or hallucination involving the siege of the Abbey during the English Civil War in 1644. On other occasions she hears plainchant sung by 'one of those voices ... when you couldn't tell if the singer was a deep-voiced woman, or a shrill man' (115). Maggi sees the cavalier as he stands at the window of a room on the second floor of the Abbey; and she follows the singer's voice from one part of the building to another, from rose garden to corridor, kitchen to rose garden. Her experiences, visual and auditory, and the emotional and psychological states they induce are thus plotted in relation to the novel's cartographic account of the Abbey's physical spaces, and the temporalities evoked by these spaces.

As Botting notes, gothic horror fiction of the late eighteenth century deploys monastic settings as a proxy for anti-Catholicism, but locates all manner of institutions, 'including aristocracy, church and family, as its broader object of criticism' (2014: 71). The 1980s gothic of *Ghost Abbey* disparages not the clerical caste but the nouveau riche, exemplified by Mr Morris and his aspirational clients, who are attracted by executive bungalows with a touch of the medieval about them. Its harshest criticism is, however, reserved for the laissez-faire practices of Jack Timmins, who supervises the young men, clients of a job-creation scheme, who have been detailed to work at the Abbey. The narrative incorporates a comparison between George Adams and Jack Timmins, privileging the former through its parodic treatment of Jack Timmins's advocacy on behalf of his young charges: when Adams complains about the lack of commitment demonstrated by the job-creation boys, Timmins defends them on the grounds that they are 'exploited by the capitalist system' (1988: 88). Maggi's focalising perspective further undermines Timmins's standing: 'You could see he thought he was good with children; and you could see he would be really terrible, the sort they took the mickey out of' (86).

As if these cues were not enough to demonstrate the novel's preference for hard work and discipline over welfare-state leniency towards unemployed youth, the narrative constructs the Abbey as a character that articulates its own severe judgement on the job-creation boys, particularly their ringleader, Stuttwick. Maggi hears a bell ringing on the old bell-board in the kitchen and identifies it by its label on the bell-board, 'GARDEN DOOR' (154). This bell is, however, no longer connected to the wiring system which formerly linked it to the bell-board, so that it is the house itself that speaks to Maggi through the bell, directing her to the garden door which leads to a balustraded terrace. Here she discovers Stuttwick, resentful because he has been sacked from the job-creation programme, taking a hammer to the sandstone balustrade, which now lies in pieces. He tells her that he intends to destroy the Abbey and, eventually, to burn it down. When Maggi dares him to destroy the coat of arms over the door, with its supporting dragons, Stuttwick climbs to a ledge from which he intends to demolish the coat of arms. Maggi sees a crack in the ledge and realises that Stuttwick is about to fall, but cannot find her voice to call out to him. He plunges to the ground below, sustaining injuries which ultimately result in his paralysis. In this melodramatic episode the Abbey seems to exert an uncanny power over Maggi, impelling her to challenge Stuttwick to destroy the coat of arms, and preventing her from coming to his assistance, so that he is punished for his destruction of the house's fabric.

It is when the plaster ceiling of one of the Abbey's corridors collapses that Maggi notices a blackened beam, 'all dents and dimples, as if someone had tried to smooth it with an axe or knife' (208), and embellished with carvings of vines and grapes. This turns out to be the roof beam of the medieval refectory, a discovery which establishes the Abbey's origins and immediately transforms it from a 'mouldering old heap' (23) to an authentic medieval building, eligible for listing by the Society for the Protection of Ancient Buildings, and saved from the demolition so fervently desired by the estate agent Mr Morris. Despite her fear of the house's malevolent energy, Maggi comes to the conclusion that dwellings always imprison their occupants. As the family embark on their return trip to Teesside, Maggi compares their home with the Abbey: 'The Abbey was a wild dangerous monster. And 17 Brannen Street was a monster that *bored* you to death' (214). Choosing danger over boredom, Maggi and her family return to the Abbey; but this narrative closure also places them in harm's way.

Like many gothic novels, *Ghost Abbey* focuses on a young woman whose experience of the uncanny evokes fear and dread. Maggi is a motherless girl who has been thrust into the role of housekeeper and surrogate mother to her brothers. During the family's sojourn at the Abbey her father develops a romantic relationship with Catriona Macfarlane, the owner of the Abbey, and Maggi observes the progress of this relationship with mixed feelings. It is, then, tempting to interpret the uncanny events at the Abbey as projections of Maggi's nascent sexuality, her relationship with her father, her resentment of the maternal responsibilities which have been thrust upon her. But this is only part of the story. The value of the Abbey and its very survival hinge upon its medieval origins, which have been concealed by post-medieval accretions and additions; but the building's status as heritage introduces new regulatory regimes: 'The place was no longer theirs. It belonged now to loud-voiced men with posh accents and expensive Range Rovers' (210). Nonetheless, the apparent quietism of the Abbey in the face of archaeological investigations, red tape and television crews does not, in Maggi's view, alter its malevolence: 'The house was quiet now, because it was getting what it wanted. But it was still dangerous' (212).

The gothic sensibility of *Ghost Abbey* is, then, as ambivalent as its treatment of the medieval past. The figure of Maggi reflects twentieth-century concerns about the rigidity of gendered expectations of girls; at the same time, her experience of the Abbey's uncanny malevolence casts her as the persecuted hysteric of gothic romance. The Abbey is attributed with the mystery and dread common to ancient settings in gothic fiction, but is susceptible to the taming and commodifying effects which occur when premodern sites are transformed into heritage.

Westall's *The Stones of Muncaster Cathedral* falls within the category of texts described by Clive Bloom as gothic horror, characterised by its archaic references, narrow emotional range, the ghostly presence of the dead. While *Ghost Abbey* centres on Maggi's consciousness, *The Stones of Muncaster Cathedral* is focused solidly on the masculine: the first-person narrator is a steeplejack, Joe Clarke, who tells the story of a repair job he carries out on the south-west tower of Muncaster Cathedral; and the narrative turns on the figure of Jacopo of Milan, the master mason who rebuilt the tower in 1538, three centuries after the cathedral itself was completed.

Joe Clarke's narration establishes him as a common-sense, opinionated character who, unlike Maggi in *Ghost Abbey*, searches for rational explanations for the uncanny as it manifests in and around the tower. As the narrative proceeds, such explanations become increasingly untenable, disrupting religious and scientific ideas. When Joe and his co-worker Billy drive wedges into the stone to support their ladders, they hear a sound which reminds Joe of 'a little kid crying out in pain, a little kid lost and frightened' (1991: 15). The motif of lost children permeates the narrative: Joe's own son Kevin manifests a violent compulsion to climb the tower; two small boys are found dead in its vicinity. Finally, Joe discovers the source of the evil which permeates the tower: during its building Jacopo has abducted, raped and killed small boys whose bodies he has secreted in hollow niches set into each level of the stairway. Jacopo himself has been buried alive beneath a gargoyle which bears his likeness, and he remains mysteriously alive:

> And there he squatted, as a man might squat on a primitive privy. Stuffed inside the stone, as he had stuffed his victims. Alive, buried alive, I'd have guessed. For he wasn't a skeleton, as his victims had become skeletons. He was much worse than any skeleton. He was alive as a turnip in the ground is alive. Half skeleton, and half obscene bulging turnip, with a great thick root running down between his skeleton legs into the stone. A root thicker than a man's ... (106)

The ellipsis suggests but does not name the sexual crimes for which Jacopo has been punished by the townsfolk of Muncaster. The narrative deflects this horror narrative through a final sequence in which Joe Clarke escapes from the collapsing tower and eludes the gargoyle which leaps from the steeple 'like a black misshapen cricket ball, bowled by the biggest fast bowler the world had ever seen' (110).

Clive Bloom comments that in horror narratives 'the body, its fluids, passages, and surfaces, is the registration for horror's symbolic significance' (2012: 220). In *The Stones of Muncaster Cathedral* it is the monstrous body of Jacopo of Milan which haunts Joe Clarke and his companions, bringing to the foreground the presence of death in the mundane setting of a modern city where workmen like Joe pursue their occupations and enjoy family lives. The story of Jacopo of Milan *almost* provides a rational explanation for the death of contemporary young boys and the dangerous fragility of the south-west tower of the cathedral. At the end of the novel, Joe decides that he will 'stick to chimneys in future' (112). This decision points to his sense that ancient buildings retain something of the motivations and intentions of their makers, so that 'you can only carve a decent gargoyle if you believe in real devils, and we don't now' (12). In *Ghost Abbey* and *The Stones of Muncaster*

Cathedral, medieval buildings are more than merely stone, wood and glass. The signs of their makers, inscribed on stones and beams, are symbolic of the stories and identities entangled in the lengthy processes of making and remaking. Westall's novels, like Disney's *The Hunchback of Notre Dame*, call on medieval settings to reinvent the past for modern sensibilities.

Transnational medievalisms

As I argued in Chapter 2, medievalist texts are strikingly asynchronous in the interplay and coexistence of times which inform their treatment of relations between medieval and modern. Similarly, the medieval recursively inhabits modern spaces; as Jeffrey Cohen's discussion of Meridian Hill Park suggests, national and civic histories and meanings are conveyed through buildings and monuments which carry traces of the Middle Ages. The enthusiasm for the Middle Ages which permeated British architecture, art, design and literature from the late eighteenth century shaped literature for the young during its emergence as a field of cultural production, and manifested in national literatures far removed from Europe. Thus, when Anne Shirley and her friends seek to locate romance in the waterways and woodlands of Prince Edward Island in L. M. Montgomery's *Anne of Green Gables* (1908), they turn to Tennyson's *Idylls of the King* and in particular to the poem 'Lancelot and Elaine', with which they are familiar because it is prescribed reading in the schools of Prince Edward Island: 'the fair lily maid and Lancelot and Guinevere and King Arthur had become very real people to them, and Anne was devoured by secret regret that she had not been born in Camelot' (1987: 186). Anne's fantasy of being Elaine, acted out when she lies on a flat-bottomed boat which her friends push out onto the water, comes to grief when the boat begins to leak and Anne is obliged to cling to a bridge pile until she is rescued by Gilbert Blythe.

This episode comically undercuts the romanticism of Anne and her friends by emphasising the gap between Tennyson's medievalism and the girls' imperfect performance of it: thus, blackest samite is rendered by an old black shawl discarded by Diana's mother; in the absence of a white lily, Anne holds a blue iris; and for a cloth-of-gold coverlet she makes do with 'an old piano scarf of yellow Japanese *crêpe*' (187). Anne's failure to perform 'Lancelot and Elaine' goes some way to persuade her that 'it is no use trying to be romantic in Avonlea' (191). Rather, Gilbert's intervention, prefiguring Anne's later romance and marriage, advocates the more conventional outcome of normative heterosexuality. The

Middle Ages, filtered through Tennyson's poem, constitutes an ethereal, dreamy ideal against which Montgomery proposes a local and Canadian version of romance grounded in the materiality of the landscape and the social setting of Prince Edward Island.

The gothic settings of paranormal romance, too, take up transnational medievalisms which deploy references to the European Middle Ages. Richelle Mead's *Vampire Academy* (2007), the first in a six-book series, opens in Portland, Oregon, where the two protagonists, the *moroi* (vampire) Lissa and her *dhampir*[9] guardian Rose, have lived for two years following their abscondment from St Vladimir's Academy, a school for vampires and their guardians. Living in Portland, Lissa and Rose attend a local college where they share a house with humans. When they are abducted and forcibly returned to the Academy, their journey from human to vampire sociality is coded through a contrast between the suburban Portland setting and the medievalist trappings of the Academy, which is located in rural Montana, surrounded by forests and ringed by mountains. The Academy functions as a world apart, a remnant of Europe: 'This school wasn't as old as the ones back in Europe, but it had been built in the same style. The buildings boasted elaborate, almost churchlike architecture, with high peaks and stone carvings. Wrought iron gates enclosed small gardens and doorways here and there' (2007: 14).

Built 'in the same style' as 'the ones back in Europe', the Academy is in America but is protected from modernity, surrounded by magical wards which are impassable to those not entitled to enter. Inside the walls, the hierarchies of the Academy are encoded spatially: the *moroi*, dominated by members of the 12 royal families, occupy dormitories which are out of bounds to *dhampir*; and the two groups attend different classes. Feeders – humans who provide blood to the *moroi* – occupy the lowest rung of inhabitants, being relegated to the feeding room where the *moroi* consume their blood. The hierarchies of the Academy are expressed in terms of ethnic differences. The *moroi* are fair-skinned and slim and their eyes are blue or green; Lissa is often described as possessing an angelic appearance which distinguishes her sharply from Rose, whose mother is a *dhampir* of Scottish ancestry and whose father is Turkish. Rose is conscious that she stands out from the *moroi*: 'Among the slim and small-chested Moroi girls, certain features – meaning my larger breasts and more defined hips – stood out' (51). Anxieties about miscegenation dominate *Vampire Academy*. Rose's reflex belief in the valency of racial purity is explained in the most matter-of-fact terms: 'Since Moroi usually wanted to have and raise Moroi children, you didn't find a lot of long-term Moroi–dhampir romances ... But plenty of young Moroi men liked fooling around with dhampir women ...' (80). If 'Moroi' were to be replaced by 'European' in this excerpt, Rose might be describing relations between Europeans and their non-European others in colonial contexts. The racialised overtones of these distinctions are explained in relation to antiquity, order and ritual; the *moroi*, Rose observes, are 'big on tradition; nothing ever changed with them' (14). The figure of the tenth-century Vladimir the Great, after whom the school is named, is celebrated as the progenitor of the *moroi* through a lineage represented as pure and eternal. Thus mapped onto imaginings of a static, ordered and rigid Middle Ages, the concepts of ethnic purity and racialised hierarchies are rendered unremarkable and normal, built into the design of the Academy and its relationship to its environs.

While *Vampire Academy* deploys elements of medievalism to bolster its privileging of whiteness, the novel *Marked* (2007),[10] by P. C. and Kristin Cast, aligns medievalism with Native American traditions. The novel's first-person narrator, Zoey, is marked by a vampire (*vampyre* in this series)[11] and directed to attend the House of Night, a training school for vampires. Her Native American ancestry manifests in her close relationship with her Cherokee grandmother, her 'high cheekbones, long, strong nose, and wide mouth' (2007: 10) and her instinctive access to 'ancient Cherokee magic' (38). Like St Vladimir's Academy, the House of Night is located in middle America, in the suburbs of Tulsa, Oklahoma. The gothic lineaments of the school setting, 'like something out of a creepy dream' (69), incorporate stone buildings surrounded by oaks and lit by candles. The Full Moon Ritual which Zoey attends following her enrolment in the House of Night incorporates a melange of medievalist, Native American and popular culture symbols: a pentagram is traced on Zoey's forehead; the participants turn to face the four directions in the manner of Native American rituals; the wise woman Neferet wears a silk dress adorned with crystals.

In *Vampire Academy* and *Marked*, medievalist elements import gravitas to architectural forms and motifs which emphasise contrasts between vampire culture and the novels' everyday American settings. Both novels deploy the Middle Ages to bolster racialised ideologies: *Vampire Academy* constructs race-based hierarchies by implying that they adhere to traditional 'medieval' practices, while *Marked* combines medievalist and Native American symbols and tropes to claim for Zoey a deep and ancient spirituality. In both novels, the reductive logic of their treatment of the medieval enables a similar reductiveness in regard to race: the unquestioned privileging of whiteness in *Vampire Academy*, and

Zoey's 'Cherokee princess' identity, which relies on the appropriation of qualities associated with Native American culture.[12] More generally, the medievalist settings and tropes of these novels serve to distinguish the vampire world from an American modernity depicted as rootless and shallow.

Although the narratives of paranormal fantasy novels rarely refer explicitly to the transnationalism of their deployment of gothic elements, fiction for younger readers often engages with physical or fantastic travel between Europe and the New World. The narratives of Elizabeth Winthrop's *The Castle in the Attic* (1985) and *The Battle for the Castle* (1993) centre on the model castle, made in England, which the protagonist, William, receives from the family's English housekeeper, Mrs Phillips, before she leaves William's home in New York to return to England. The fantasy sequences of both novels involve episodes during which William, reduced to the size of the model knights in the castle, engages in quests and adventures. These sequences are sandwiched between accounts of William's everyday life in New York, and his achievements in the fantasy realm enable him to face down his real-world insecurities and dilemmas. The castle and the world beyond it are based on British buildings and landscapes whose differences from the American setting are unmarked in the narration and in William's focalising perspective. When William encounters the dragon which constitutes his first test in *The Castle in the Attic*, he bolsters his courage by playing on his recorder 'The Battle Hymn of the Republic', which turns out to exert a magical power over the dragon.

In contrast, Susan Cooper's *The Boggart* directly addresses the transnational aspects of its protagonists' experience as they travel between Toronto and Castle Keep on Lismore Island in the Western Highlands of Scotland. When Devon MacDevon, the owner of Castle Keep, dies without an heir he bequeaths the castle to the family of his late sister, who emigrated to Canada, married an Estonian migrant and lived in Toronto. Twelve-year-old Emily Volnik, her brother Jessup and their parents travel to Lismore Island to claim the castle, but realise that they cannot afford its upkeep. Before they put the castle on the market the family select some items of furniture which they ship to Toronto, among them a roll-top desk in which Castle Keep's boggart[13] has taken up residence. The boggart is, however, cruelly out of place in Toronto, and eventually Jessup and his friends devise a technological strategy to enable the boggart's return to Castle Keep, which has been purchased by Mr Maconochie, MacDevon's lawyer. The novel's omniscient narration is supplemented by focalisation through the perspectives of Emily, the

Scottish boy Tommy Cameron, and the boggart, so enabling comparisons between ancient and contemporary, spirit and human.

The geographies of the novel switch between Castle Keep and the bustling city of Toronto and are in part informed by oppositions between city and country, expressed in terms which evoke Raymond Williams's distinction between the 'knowable community' (1973: 165) of rural society and the more diffuse and anonymous spaces of urban life. To Tommy Cameron, whose mother runs the village store, Castle Keep carries local and tribal meanings as the home of the last MacDevon. It is also a regular part of Tommy's routine of delivering groceries and mail to the island, so that he has grown familiar with the boggart, who loves to play tricks on children. The Volnik children, taken aback by the castle's isolation and antiquity, are at first somewhat inclined to assume that they themselves have a purchase on modernity: Emily expresses surprise that computers exist in Scotland, whereupon Tommy retorts, 'This is Scotland you're in, not the primeval swamp' (1993: 37). These tussles over identity and standing are intensified by Tommy's sense that Emily and Jessup are undeserving inheritors, lacking his deep attachment to Castle Keep and Devon MacDevon. Tommy's and Jessup's common enthusiasm for computers overcomes their initial hostilities and leads to the novel's resolution.

The boggart's journey to Toronto introduces an ancient spirit to a world which has 'driven out the Old Things and buried the Wild Magic deep under layers of reason and time' (67). When he sits in on a history lesson, having tucked himself inside the collar of Jessup's sweatshirt, he finds the teacher's account of Roman Britain inaccurate; when he is transported to an ice hockey match in the same collar, he marvels at the protective padding worn by the young players, which reminds him of the padding worn by medieval knights preparing for a joust. When, however, the ice hockey game begins, he realises that this game is indeed a joust, 'just as passionate and just as dangerous, even though conducted by children' (75). The comedy of this and similar moments derives from the text's playful evocation of the unexpected and aleatory effects of transnational medievalism, in which temporal, cultural and geographical differences are simultaneously invoked and subverted.

At last the boggart's interventions into the lives of the Volniks take on dangerous dimensions, as the psychiatrist Dr Stigmore arrives at the diagnosis of psychokinesis, associated with Emily's puberty, and seeks to persuade her parents that she should be placed in hospital under observation. If science (or, rather, parapsychology) proves incapable of explaining Wild Magic, new technologies serve the children's purposes by shrinking distance and time. Jessup and his friends manage to insert the boggart into a game they have devised and to save the game to a disk which they send to Tommy, who then plays the game and so sets the boggart free. Discovering a new family of children at Castle Keep, and a puppy to tease, he resumes his regime of household pranks, 'contented, at home' (196), in his proper place.

In *The Condition of Postmodernity*, Harvey reaches the conclusion that 'if it is true that time is always memorialized not as flow, but as memories of experienced places and spaces, then history must indeed give way to poetry, time to space, as the fundamental material of social expression' (1990: 218). The medievalist texts I have considered in this chapter invest spatiality with associations and significances which evoke the medieval in rich and varied ways. Whether 'actually' medieval, like Roger d'Aulneaux's home in *The Stones of Green Knowe* and Castle Keep in *The Boggart*, or post-medieval imitations like the gothic-styled schools of *Vampire Academy* and *Marked*, medieval(ist) spaces are always narrativised in the light of their resonances in modernity. Harvey's formulation of history 'giving way' to poetry is true of how texts for the young create a poetics of the past by investing medievalist spaces with a proliferation of meanings, ancient and new.

4
Disabilities in Medievalist Fiction

Children's experiences of engaging with the Middle Ages are often bound up with practices of bodily enactment. From small girls wearing fairy dresses to participants exhibiting their skills in jousting competitions, it seems that consumers seek to capture the Middle Ages through clothing, furniture, home decorations and jewellery which echo or replicate medieval design and aesthetics. Medievalist online games, too, commonly require that players select avatars which function as virtual 'other selves', travelling through medieval-coded towns and across landscapes to undertake quests, often in company with other players formed into armies or questing companies.

When contemporary audiences consume medievalist fiction and film, they encounter imagined bodies inflected with *present past* constructions of the medieval and are positioned to align themselves with characters most of whom possess white, gendered, able bodies. However, medievalist texts frequently incorporate other kinds of body, those that do not conform to a normative perspective. Julia Mickenberg and Philip Nel complain that books for younger readers rarely address 'the facts of disability, depression, and mental illness' (2011: 465). Medievalist fiction and film for the young, in comparison, is replete with disabled bodies, in historical fiction and various modes of fantasy. Moreover, it is common in medievalist texts for characters with disabilities to function as protagonists.[1] This narrative feature is far less pronounced in texts located in contemporary times; Elizabeth A. Wheeler notes that 'while children's literature has a long history of disabled characters as best friends and inspirational figures, the disabled protagonist is something almost entirely new' (2013: 336).

A ready explanation for this tendency as it manifests in medievalist fantasy and historical fiction is that producers of texts adhere to the widely held view that during the Middle Ages disabled bodies were more numerous and more visible than is the case in contemporary Western societies. The reasons advanced to support such an assumption might well include the practice of judicial mutilation; the fact that conditions such as cleft palate and scoliosis, and diseases such as leprosy, were untreatable; the dangers to life and limb present in medieval workplaces and homes; and the effects of war. Jacques Le Goff sums up this dismal view: 'the Middle Ages were full of the maimed, hunchbacks, people with goitres, the lame, and the paralysed' (1988: 240). The historian Irina Metzler refers to Le Goff's generalisations as 'historiographical cliches' (2013: 203), along with the widely held supposition that disabilities were commonly understood during the Middle Ages as markers of sinfulness and signs of divine displeasure.

Rather, recent scholarship on medieval bodies and on disability in the Middle Ages has emphasised the variability and diversity of medical, religious and literary discourses; Joshua Eyler concludes that 'there were many lenses through which medieval societies viewed disability' (2010: 3).[2] It is certainly the case that modern conceptions of disability do not align with medieval understandings of bodily difference, as Eyler observes. Just as historians have rendered visible other populations formerly largely invisible in medieval documents and literature, including peasants and children, so a much more nuanced account of the lives of disabled medieval people has been enabled through research which scrutinises a wide range of sources. Metzler observes that 'the story of medieval disabled persons [can] be unearthed from texts pertaining to legal history, from philosophical treatises, from works of literature and from social and economic sources' (2013: 6). The complex histories of medieval disability which emerge from such research are, however, generally at odds with modern assumptions about the Middle Ages.

The prevalence of disabled bodies in medievalist texts for the young almost certainly stems, in part, from the overgeneralising perspectives I have sketched: that disabled bodies were commonplace in the Middle Ages; and that intolerance for disability was widespread. But these facts do not entirely explain why medievalist texts for the young so noticeably and frequently incorporate disabled bodies, a topic to which I will return later. In this chapter I draw on recent work in the field of disability studies to examine treatments of disabled bodies in film and fiction. In Chapter 5 I will extend my discussion to the broader topic of monstrous bodies and medievalisms.

David T. Mitchell and Sharon L. Snyder use the concept of the 'narrative prosthesis' to argue that disability in fiction 'inaugurates the act of interpretation' (2000: 6), setting in train the need for an explanation to account for the existence of disability and its place in the narrative world. Like a literal prosthesis, the textual prosthesis of disability draws attention to the uncomfortable difference of disability and in this very act of drawing attention runs the risk of reinforcing a normative version of what it is to be human. According to Mitchell and Snyder, 'narratives turn signs of cultural deviance into textually marked bodies' (54). Ato Quayson offers a supplement to the notion of the narrative prosthesis, advancing the concept of 'aesthetic nervousness' (2007: 15), which manifests at a primary level in interactions between disabled and able-bodied characters – or, in Rosemarie Garland-Thomson's useful coinage, normates[3] – and in 'tensions refracted across other levels of the text such as the disposition of symbols and motifs, the overall narrative or dramatic perspective, the constitution and reversals of plot structure, and so on' (15). Quayson's discussion of aesthetic nervousness suggests strategies for identifying signs of textual unease regarding disabled bodies and their representations.

'Most of you': Prosthesis, narrative, nervousness

The DreamWorks animated film *How to Train Your Dragon* (2010)[4] invites analysis along the lines outlined by Mitchell and Snyder because of the high profile it accords to acquired disabilities and to the physical prostheses developed and worn by three of the film's main characters: the prosthetic left leg and right arm of Gobber the blacksmith; the replacement tail fin which the young protagonist Hiccup devises for the injured dragon Toothless; and the prosthesis which Gobber fashions, at the end of the film, to replace Hiccup's foot and lower shin. *How to Train Your Dragon* is set in the Viking village of Berk, which is beset by dragon attacks, and its narrative follows the progress of Hiccup, the son of the village chieftain Stoick the Vast, as he reluctantly trains to become a dragon-slayer. Hiccup's voice provides the voice-over commentary, depicting Berk through a *present past* perspective in which Hiccup presents as a nerdish contemporary boy, commenting ironically on the village's unforgiving climate, 'twelve days north of Hopeless, and a few degrees south of Freezing to Death' (2010).

The film's three prostheses replace body parts destroyed in warfare between Vikings and dragons, and all three are designed to enable disabled bodies to replicate the physical capabilities of able bodies. These prostheses perform distinct metaphorical functions within the narrative, and the ways in which they are represented betray tensions between the film's narrative and some of the psychosocial implications suggested by depictions of disability.

Viking bodies in *How to Train Your Dragon* are highly spectacular; for instance, Gobber is presented as an immense figure sporting a horned helmet, a luxuriant blond moustache and eyebrows so bushy that they occupy half of his forehead. The over-the-top quality of the film's CGI figuration suggests a self-reflexive and parodic inflexion which accords with Hiccup's narration. The prosthesis Gobber wears on his arm is similarly spectacular; he has ingeniously invented a variety of interchangeable attachments, including a hammer, a set of tongs, a beer tankard. This prosthesis, prominently featured in episodes featuring Gobber, invites audiences to imagine the cause of his disability, which thus functions as a narrative prosthesis, propelling the action of the film towards the moment when he discloses the reason for his missing hand and leg. His explanation is presented analeptically, through the story he tells the young dragon-slayer trainees: '… and with one twist [the dragon] took my hand and swallowed it whole. And I saw the look on his face. I was delicious. He must have passed the word, because it wasn't a month before another one of them took my leg' (2010). The trainees respond excitedly to Gobber's story, but it is the young braggart Snotlout who seeks to use it to his own advantage, swearing that he will avenge Gobber: 'I'll chop off the legs of every dragon I fight, with my face' (2010). This rhetorical flourish does not, however, achieve the results Snotlout seeks, which are to impress Astrid, the sole girl trainee, and to elevate his status within the group. Gobber is unmoved by Snotlout's zeal, pointing out that it would make much more sense to destroy a dragon's wings and tail, since 'a downed dragon is a dead dragon' (2010). In this scene Gobber's refusal to accede to Snotlout's gambit builds on the anti-heroic tone of his story, in which the deliciousness of his flesh is cited as the reason why dragons have consumed his limbs. That is, his body, like the 'dynamic entities' to which Mitchell and Snyder refer, resists the 'cultural scripts' (2000: 49) assigned to it.

Gobber's disability is linked in a less marked way to a story of loss and diminution which suggests a degree of aesthetic nervousness. After the dragons' first raid on Berk, Stoick calls on his warriors to join him in a raid on their lairs before the ice sets in. His men are reluctant, but when Stoick threatens that those who do not go on the raid will endure the ignominy of looking after Hiccup, they volunteer immediately. Gobber, however, is left to train the recruits, including Hiccup, rather than joining the warriors. The film averts its attention from this plot element, focusing instead on Gobber's role as trainer of the motley group of initiates. Given that the other warriors have chosen to expose themselves to danger rather than carrying out the task of looking after Hiccup, the fact that Stoick confers this task on Gobber is a clear sign of his exclusion from the warrior group, a sign which is glossed over by the drama and comedy of the training sequences. Nor does the film address Gobber's reaction to his exclusion, which is displaced by the emotionality attributed to Stoick as he laments Hiccup's lack of 'Viking' qualities and his own inability to form a close relationship with his son.

Hiccup is responsible for Toothless's disability by wounding him with a missile from an improvised catapult, which injures the dragon's tail fin so that he can no longer fly. Bérubé observes that in some texts, unlikely as it seems, 'exceptionality is rendered as a disability' (2005: 569), referring to the 1941 animated film *Dumbo*, in which Dumbo's disability (his over-large ears) turns out to be his key advantage. In *How to Train Your Dragon*, Hiccup's disability stems precisely from his exceptionality. Against the tide of Berk's history, which is built on relentless conflict between villagers and dragons, Hiccup and Toothless form a friendship based on trust. The prosthesis which Hiccup devises for Toothless thus hinges upon Hiccup's exceptionality as a Viking boy who loves to invent and who is open to emotional engagement with the despised Other.

Hiccup's difference from other Vikings is rendered specular by his disability – that is, his loss of a limb – when, at the end of the film, he and Toothless destroy the Red Death dragon which has for centuries tyrannised the dragons of Berk. As Hiccup and Toothless plunge to earth they are caught up in the fireball which issues from the Red Death's throat, and when Stoick reaches Toothless he discovers his son, injured and unconscious, tucked inside the dragon's wings. Stoick apologises to the dragon for misjudging him: 'You brought him back alive! ... Thank you for saving my son.' Gobber alerts Stoick to Hiccup's disability: 'Well, you know, most of him' (2010).

Gobber's 'most of him' refers in a literal sense to Hiccup's missing limb. But it also takes up a leitmotif which is deployed throughout the film to signify Hiccup's identity as a nonconformist Viking. Initially, he aspires to fight dragons because 'my life will get infinitely better. I might even get a date.' When Gobber points out to Hiccup that his physical weakness and clumsiness render this unlikely, Hiccup demonstrates the catapult he has invented to launch missiles, but it misfires, narrowly missing Gobber and smashing into a Viking. Gobber says, 'Now this right here is what I'm talking about .... Hiccup, if you ever want to get out there to fight dragons, you need to stop all this', gesturing towards

Hiccup, who responds, 'But you just pointed to all of me!' Gobber shouts at him: 'Yes, that's it! Stop being all of you' (2010). The 'all of you' to which Gobber refers incorporates Hiccup's un-Viking-like nerdishness and his propensity for imagination and invention.

A similar exchange occurs after Hiccup abandons his plan to fight dragons because his encounters with Toothless have radically altered his perspective. Ordering Hiccup to join Gobber's dragon-slaying classes, Stoick presents him with an axe, saying: 'When you carry this axe, you carry all of us with you, which means you walk like us, you talk like us, you think like us. No more of ... this,' at which Stoick gestures towards Hiccup. Hiccup responds: 'You just gestured to all of me', but his objection is lost in Stoick's demand that Hiccup accept the role of dragon-slayer: 'Deal?' (2010). To Stoick, the self is reducible to the body; as he regards his own body as the ideal Viking dragon-slaying machine, so he intends that Hiccup should aspire to the same state. Hiccup, however, is all too conscious that his is not the kind of Viking identity desired by Stoick.

The 'all of him/most of him' leitmotif reappears at the end of the film, when Hiccup, recovered, leaves his house and discovers that Berk is now a transformed polity where dragons and villagers cohabit and the former trainee dragon-slayers fly on the backs of their pet dragons. Gesturing expansively towards Hiccup, Stoick says, 'Turns out all we needed was a little more of this.' Hiccup responds, 'You just gestured to all of me', and Gobber adds wryly, 'Well, most of you' (2010). Hiccup's absent limb, for which Gobber has developed an ingenious spring-loaded prosthesis, carries a double signification: his prosthesis is the sign of an exceptionality now attributed with value; and it draws attention to Hiccup's disability while insisting that he can do everything that an able-bodied Viking can do. The same is true of Toothless, for whom Gobber has devised a bright red tail fin which shows up prominently against his black body.

The film falters again when it depicts Hiccup's recognition of his disability. This sequence is set in his family home, with Hiccup gradually awaking from a recuperative sleep. Rather than focusing on Hiccup, the audience is distracted by the excitable behaviour of Toothless, who frolics and leaps like a happy dog whose owner has at last returned home. The moment when Hiccup peels back his bedclothes to see that his lower leg and foot are missing is quickly overtaken by the next sequence in which he tries out his prosthesis, leaning on Toothless as he moves towards the door leading to the outside world. This sequence occurs three minutes before the film ends, raising questions about Hiccup's emotional state but displacing such questions onto the visual display of the finale, in which Hiccup and his friends swoop about in the sky over Berk, riding their dragons. The prostheses in *How to Train Your Dragon* thus draw attention to the disabled bodies for which they are designed, bodies which, in the words of Mitchell and Snyder, 'call stories into being' by demanding 'a process of explanatory compensation' (2000: 53). The disabilities and prostheses in this film also function as complex metaphors, signifying loss and diminution as well as exceptionality, imagination and reconciliation.

Unorthodox bodies

The disabled bodies of *How to Train Your Dragon* set in train narratives which involve violent conflict between humans and their others. In many other medievalist texts disability functions as 'a deterministic vehicle of characterization' (Mitchell and Snyder 2000: 50). This is especially the case in texts which involve retellings of or allusions to folk tales and traditional narratives. As Garland-Thomson observes, 'medical treatment, surgical normalization, prenatal testing, and selective abortion' (2009: 164) have eliminated many bodies which would in earlier times have been treated as freaks, so that 'people who look like dwarfs, giants, and monsters draw stares because they are unfamiliar as flesh and too familiar as narrative' (2009: 167). The too-familiar narratives to which Garland-Thomson refers include those which incorporate characters distinguished by the shape of their bodies and who are labelled as 'hunchbacks'. These unorthodox bodies have historically been interpreted through discourses of religion, magic or medicine, and have been narrativised in stories in which unsightly crones are transformed into beautiful maidens, as in various versions of the 'loathly lady' script, or in which fairies intervene to change unusual bodies into conventional ones, often with unexpected consequences,[5] or where the disabled body functions as a metaphor for deviance.

Garland-Thomas observes that what is lost in these stories is 'a sense of the particular lives and looks of the people whose shapes have across history given rise to these stories' (167). Many medievalist texts merely rehearse well-worn cultural narratives, such as those surrounding Constance the pilgrim in Laura Amy Schlitz's *Good Masters! Sweet Ladies!* (2007), structured as a series of monologues by the child inhabitants of an English village in the thirteenth century. The village comprises a social system complete in itself, in which systems of power and authority revolve around the lord of the manor. In addition to the inhabitants of the village, the narrative features three peripatetic figures – a beggar, a runaway, a pilgrim – who enter the village en route for other destinations. The pilgrim, Constance, is on her way to Saint Winifred's well:

> I am a pilgrim to Winifred's well,
> For Saint Winifred's well will heal me.
> When I come back, I will have no need
> Of a heavy cloak to conceal me.
> Though I was born crookbacked, crippled and fell,
> I will be cured at Saint Winifred's well. (20)

Constance then narrates the story of Saint Winifred along conventional hagiographic lines, involving the miraculous restoration of the saint's head after it is cut off by the evil Caradog, and the eruption of a health-giving spring at the site where her blood was spilt. The marginal notes accompanying this narrative explain that Constance's impulse to hide her body behind a cloak is 'entirely reasonable. In the Middle Ages, a deformity was considered a sign of God's displeasure' (2007: 20), and that since Caradog dies immediately after his horrible crime, 'there is little doubt about where he'll spend the afterlife' (21). The light-hearted tone of this reference to the afterlife constructs a *present past* orientation informed by the sanguine supposition that life in the Middle Ages was dominated by religious beliefs and practices superseded in the modern world.

The explanatory page on medieval pilgrimages which follows Constance's story sharply distinguishes medieval from modern: 'medieval people did not share our need to understand the world scientifically' (23), where '*our* need' suggests the untroubled assumption that the narrative addresses a universalised readership aligned with the narrator's perspective. In opposition to 'our' regard for scientific explanations of illness or disability, 'they' ('medieval people') had recourse only to 'faith cures' (23) such as the mineral springs at the shrine of Saint Winifred, or 'the hodgepodge of astrology and folk medicine practiced by medieval doctors' (23). The book's treatment of Constance thus situates itself in relation to two binaries: between science and superstition, and between modern and medieval. This univocal view of the Middle Ages is, however, contradicted in other stories in *Good Masters! Sweet Ladies!* featuring characters whose exceptionality signals that they are more 'like us' than Constance: Edgar the falconer's son, who refuses to hand over the sparrowhawk he has trained to Simon, the knight's son, because Simon is unlikely to care for the bird as Edgar has; Lowdy the varlet's daughter, who secretly provides sustenance to Pask, the runaway; Petronella the merchant's daughter, who forms a fragile friendship with the Jewish boy Jacob, the moneylender's son, a friendship proscribed by the norms of the village. In the case of Constance, the intersection of disability and religious belief seems to suggest a degree of aesthetic nervousness which troubles the *present past* orientation of much of *Good Masters! Sweet Ladies!* Constance is the most pitiable figure in the collection precisely because of the rigidity with which she maintains her belief in the efficacy of the healing waters of Saint Winifred's shrine:

> For a hunchback's life is a life of scorn.
> I have known more sorrow than tears can tell.
> There are times when I wish I had never been born,
> But I will be healed at Saint Winifred's well. (21)

In light of its narrative insistence on the gullibility of medieval people, the text here positions readers to assent to the sense of pathos which surrounds Constance, whose physical body constitutes a metaphor for her imaginative and psychological fixity. This narrative insistence on reducing Constance to an essentialised category (that of 'the hunchback') struggles against the book's depiction of dissident and independent subjects, suggesting that her disability, together with her misplaced confidence in the healing power of Saint Winifred's well, locate her as definitively different from modern subjects; in Quayson's terms, as 'the interface with otherness' (2007: 39). In Robert Byrd's illustration accompanying the story of Constance, a group of pilgrims walk towards Saint Winifred's well. Their bodies and clothing differentiate them by age, class, occupation. Constance, bent over and shrouded with a cloak, is defined by her disability; nor does her story, unlike the others in the collection, afford any familial or social context for her character, so that she is attributed with no identity other than that of 'the hunchback'.

Similarly, the character of Quasimodo in the Disney version of *The Hunchback of Notre Dame* is readily mapped onto models of disability which emphasise powerlessness and lack of agency. As I noted in Chapter 3, the figure of Quasimodo concurs with that of the confused and alienated teenage boy common in narratives for the young. Martin F. Norden argues that the film's depiction of Quasimodo wavers between a number of 'disability-related stereotypes' (2013: 169), including the childlike figure dependent on able-bodied adults, the 'sweet innocent', the 'comic adventurer', the 'obsessive avenger' (169) and the animal-like figure capable of scaling the walls and towers of Notre-Dame while carrying Esmeralda and her goat, Djali.

One of the innovations introduced in the Disney *Hunchback* is that Quasimodo is not deaf, enabling dialogue and a sequence in which (voiced by Tom Hulce) he sings Alan Menken and Stephen Schwartz's 'Heaven's Light', which expresses his love for Esmeralda: 'I dare to dream that she / Might even care for me' (1996). The disparity between Hulce's expressive tenor voice and the film's depiction of Quasimodo's face suggests another reading. Close-ups of his face during the song enforce a metaphorical approach to disability in which Quasimodo's body functions as a prison, playing out the common stereotype of the disabled person 'trapped in his body'. His eyes, deep blue and soulful, look out from the twisted contours of his face, just as the beauty of Hulce's voice seems out of place in Quasimodo's body. This disjuncture of form and content leads to the inevitable narrative outcome in which Quasimodo realises that Esmeralda will never love him, and in a gesture of self-sacrifice he joins the hands of Esmeralda and her suitor Phoebus in the film's final moments. This bodily performance of abnegation is where the film's narrative has led from the beginning: Quasimodo is disqualified from the possibility of an intersubjective relationship by reason of his disability.

Disney's Quasimodo bears traces of Victor Hugo's gothic imagining of a body described by David Punter as 'the quintessence of disability' (2000: 44), but its visual model is Charles Laughton's performance of Quasimodo in William Dieterle's 1939 film. Allison Craven argues that whereas Laughton's performance of disability signifies 'the alterity of medieval humanity, subject to nature's punishments for sin' (2012: 229), Disney's Quasimodo is 'rewritten as a melodrama of a young man's insecurities and coming of age' (229). Nevertheless, the end of the film, in which Quasimodo leaves Notre-Dame to join the people of Paris in the cathedral square, does not provide the closure one might expect in a conventional coming of age story. As I noted in Chapter 3, the cathedral square, which comprises a liminal space between Notre-Dame and the larger geographical entity of Paris, is also the site where the people of Paris mocked and abused Quasimodo at the Feast of Fools. No matter how strenuously Disney deploys the figure of Quasimodo to construct a world in which disability is no obstacle to happiness, three factors work against such a narrative outcome: first, the recent episode of his cruel treatment at the hands of Parisians; second, his loss of Esmeralda; third, the obduracy of his difference. In the Disney pantheon of characters, the most desirable asset is beauty, conventionally rewarded through heteronormative romance. In the scenes in *The Hunchback* featuring Quasimodo and Phoebus, the latter exposes Quasimodo's incapacity to measure up: square-jawed, tall, blonde and non-disabled, Phoebus represents the iconic masculine identity to which Quasimodo can never aspire. In the end, then, the Disney fiction of a world in which all are equal proves to be illusory, and Quasimodo reverts to a sign of medieval alterity.

The texts I have discussed so far in this section, *Good Masters! Sweet Ladies!* and Disney's *Hunchback of Notre Dame*, feature disabled bodies whose difference is explained by their pastness, their location in the Middle Ages. Unlike non-disabled bodies in these texts, they cannot be swept up into a *present past* imagining of exceptional figures who are 'like us', because their unorthodox bodies are uncomfortably reminiscent of typologies of disability which are 'too familiar as narrative' (Garland-Thomson 2009: 167) to allow for novel or transformative possibilities. It is, then, surprising to find that a book published in 1970, Rosemary Sutcliff's novel *The Witch's Brat*, takes a very different approach. A disabled boy, Lovel, is the novel's protagonist, unlike the more usual pattern of treating disabled characters as figures secondary to able-bodied main characters. Moreover, the novel treats Lovel as an agential and complex protagonist whose identity is not defined in relation to what Garland-Thomson refers to as the normate, the 'veiled subject position of cultural self, the figure outlined by the array of deviant others whose marked bodies shore up the normate's boundaries' (1997: 8). Rather, the narration of *The Witch's Brat*, focalised in large part through Lovel's perspective, treats as normal and usual his experience of the world rather than filtering the novel's depiction of disability from outside, as is the case, for instance, in the depiction of Constance in *Good Masters! Sweet Ladies!*[6]

The narrative of *The Witch's Brat* is structured by Lovel's progress from a fugitive disabled boy to the respected Infirmarer of St Bartholomew's hospital in London. Lovel is cast out of his village because of his disability and because his grandmother, the witch of the book's title, has died and he can no longer depend on her protection. He finds refuge in a Benedictine abbey at Winchester where he proves himself as a herbalist and bonesetter, eventually moving to London to work with Rahere, who founded St Bartholomew's hospital in 1123.[7] Incidents and settings are deployed to structure a narrative principally concerned with Lovel's identity formation as a subject whose disability shapes his perceptions and his sense of self. Like the open-ended narratives to which Mitchell and Snyder refer, *The Witch's Brat* destabilises the 'sedimented cultural meanings that accrue around ideas of bodily "deviance"' (2000: 48) by foregrounding the lack of fit between Lovel's awareness of his selfhood, and the deterministic perspectives which pervade village culture.

This lack of fit is implied in the novel's first description of Lovel as he walks towards the village:

> He was built crooked, with a hunched shoulder and a twisted leg that made him walk lop-sided like a bird with a broken wing. His bony face under the thatch of dusty dark hair was quick and eager and wanted to be friendly; but nobody had ever bothered to notice his face; unless perhaps it was his grandmother ... (1970: 1)

The other (metaphorical) face at issue is that of the village, which is 'the same village that he had known all his life, but it had put on a stranger's face' (4) following his grandmother's death. When the villagers drive him out and pelt him with stones, he looks back to see frightened faces that are 'all mouths and eyes' (7), a vision which thereafter haunts him in nightmares. The imagery of faces functions as shorthand for the over-determination of disability, and its misrecognition as a sign of deviance. Lovel's face is invisible to the villagers because they see only his hunched shoulder and twisted leg, and because they feared his grandmother even as they sought her ministrations. To the villagers, Lovel's disabled body signifies a malice which they read as his capacity to cause illnesses in animals and humans. For his part, Lovel's recurring nightmare of faces that are all mouths and eyes is symbolic of the power of those interpretations, and their effects on his sense of self.

Sutcliff's depiction of Lovel's progress does not 'remove the unsightly from view', but rather 'reinstitute[s] its discomforting presence' (Mitchell and Snyder 2000: 8) through episodes which remind readers of cultural attitudes towards disabled people. In the abbey where he finds refuge, Lovel overhears the Infirmarer, Brother Eustace, pronounce him 'good as useless' (20), evoking in Lovel a 'cold grey misery' (21) which oppresses him. When Rahere, the King's jongleur, visits the abbey, his encounter with Lovel functions both as a catalyst for change and also as a countervailing mode of representation, modifying the novel's depiction of Lovel as a docile subject, eager to avoid conflict and please those in authority. In contravention of the steward's directions that he should keep out of sight, Lovel dares to enter the guest chamber where Rahere is lodged. Rahere asks, 'What do they call you?', to which Lovel replies, 'Humpy, most times' (33). Rahere's response destabilises the normalcy of this cruel nickname, routinely used by Lovel's fellow servants: 'What pitiful lack of invention' (33). Again, when Lovel explains that he carries out odd jobs around the abbey because this is all he is capable of, Rahere picks away at Lovel's internalised sense of uselessness:

> [Lovel] was not complaining, just trying to tell the truth. 'I'm not much use for anything else, you see,' he added by way of explanation.
> 'Did someone tell you that?' Rahere said. Lovel stood and rubbed one foot over the other, remembering the morning when he had woken from his dream and heard Brother Peter and Brother Eustace talking. 'They thought I was still asleep,' he said.
> 'And they were mistaken.' The King's Jongleur sat and looked at him consideringly, with his head a little on one side. Then he said, 'I have the oddest feeling that they were mistaken about the other thing, too.' (34)

This stretch of dialogue deftly undermines the systemic discrimination against Lovel, carried out through language and cultural practices: the name by which he is called; low expectations of his ability; work practices which solidify his inferior status in the abbey. Sutcliff's treatment of Lovel anticipates foundational ideas in disability studies, exposing the collective representation of disability as 'an exclusionary and oppressive system rather than the natural and appropriate order of things' (Garland-Thomson 2005: 523). A notable aspect of Sutcliff's treatment of Lovel's disability is her attention to the intersectionality of discourses and influences: the discrimination he experiences relates to his disability, his poverty, his relationship to a woman regarded as a witch, his lack of protectors or support.

The Witch's Brat works as a *Bildungsroman*, plotting Lovel's formation as a person by presenting key moments and events in a time span from youth to adulthood, from his eviction from his village as a boy of 11 to his life as a cleric and Infirmarer at Saint Bartholomew's. More specifically, the novel focuses on the disabled subject and the interplay between an interior life and the world outside. For the most part the narrative's events and actions occur in religious institutions, and here Sutcliff's treatment of the intersections of religion and disability presents a sharp contrast to the more schematic approach of *Good Masters! Sweet Ladies!* Having demonstrated his skills of herbalism and healing at the abbey, Lovel receives an invitation from the Abbot to take his vows as a Benedictine monk. His decision to accept this invitation is a pragmatic one: as a disabled boy with no source of income he cannot afford to undertake an apprenticeship to a physician, so that joining a religious order enables him to follow his preferred profession. More broadly, the novel treats the abbey and, later, Saint Bartholomew's, in relation to the systems of power and human relationships which shape Lovel's progress, rather than to doctrinal or theological positions. Just as disability does not exist in isolation from other fields of experience, so religion in *The Witch's Brat* has no purchase on the meanings attributed to disability.

As a narrative prosthesis, Lovel's disability is not resolved through a 'quick fix' (Mitchell and Snyder 2000: 8) which renders it invisible, cured of its capacity to unsettle. When an injured labourer challenges Lovel to cure his own shoulder before 'making hay' (91) with the labourer's dislocated shoulder, Lovel doubts his capacity to ameliorate psychological as well as physical suffering. The narrative resolves this dilemma through an episode which, I think, betrays a degree of aesthetic nervousness, evident in the tight control with which the narrative perspective is managed. A 16-year-old boy, Nick Redpoll, works as a rouseabout, as Lovel did at the abbey. Having fallen from scaffolding on a building site, Nick has injured his knee, which has stiffened to the extent that he cannot walk without a crutch, so destroying his hope of pursuing a career as a stonemason. Lovel treats the injury with massage, splints and rest, and eventually the boy regains mobility and can return to work. Throughout this sequence Nick is the object of narrative, always interpreted and explained through Lovel's focalising perspective or a style of narration which gives the impression that the narrator is close to and intimately conscious of characters' emotions and desires. In effect, the figure of Nick, with his acquired (and treatable) disability, functions as a sign of the *Bildungsroman*'s resolution. Nick recalls the difficult process of his treatment: 'When the pain was bad and that, I says to myself, "It's Brother Lovel, with a game leg of his own, and that humpy shoulder and all, and *he knows"* – and so I hangs on' (125). The use of the word 'humpy', formerly a cruel nickname and now expressive of Nick's admiration, plots Lovel's progress from boy to man, attributing to him an insight and sympathy which result from his experience of disability.

If the novel's treatment of Lovel veers towards the hagiographic as the end of the narrative approaches, it is nevertheless the case that Sutcliff's representation of disability is incomparably more subtle and complex than that of more recent medievalist texts including *The Hunchback of Notre Dame* and *Good Masters! Sweet Ladies!* As Mitchell and Snyder note, 'the history of disability, like the history of any socially produced constituency, proves surprisingly uneven and multifaceted' (2000: 43). The medieval setting, with its distancing effects, enables a *Bildungsroman* of the disabled subject whose *present past* orientation addresses questions as alive now as at the time of the novel's production.

Disability and difference

It is perhaps not altogether surprising that many historical narratives involving medieval boy protagonists incorporate characters with disabilities. Such fiction often involves settings of war or conflict; illness and injuries are common; and medieval life is commonly represented as endemically violent. Contemporary novels, which tend to contest or disrupt notions of hegemonic masculinity, typically present ambivalent perspectives of military action, filtered through the focalisation of boy protagonists caught up in conflicts where they experience misgivings about the morality of war and its associated practices. In such narratives, a disability may constitute a prosthetic which removes a character from physical combat so that he sees events differently from those in the thick of battle. Nevertheless, such removal from action carries its own dangers of marginalisation or derision by those of the warrior caste.

Elizabeth Laird's *Crusade* (2008) sets its narrative at the time of the Third Crusade (1189–92), locating its young protagonist among the Christian and Muslim forces gathering in Palestine. This novel deploys medieval settings to address a topic of high contemporary significance: relations between Christians and Muslims. The third-person narration of *Crusade* is filtered through two focalising characters: a Muslim boy, Salim, and a Christian boy, Adam, who encounter each other in Palestine. Salim, lame in one leg, is the son of Adil, a merchant in Acre, while Adam, orphaned following the death of his mother, is employed to care for the dogs of his baron, Guy de Martel.

In *Crusade*, Salim's disability is introduced at the very beginning of the novel, on a hot day in the city of Acre: 'In the great customs house behind the harbour, Salim sat on a bulging bale of cotton, moodily swinging his one good leg' (2008: 3). The combination of 'moodily' and 'one good leg' performs two narrative functions: it invites questions about the nature of Salim's disability, and it posits the possibility of a connection between his disability and his psychological state. This narrator-focalised account of Salim shifts, in the sequence which follows, to focalisation through Salim's perspective, some of which is rendered through free indirect thought: '*I can slip off home if Ali's not around to stop me*, Salim told himself. *I'll tell Mama I've got a headache*' (5). By referring to Salim's motivation here (he proposes to use an invented headache as a means of gaining his mother's sympathy) the narrative establishes Salim as a fallible character, possibly manipulative or at least calculating. The narrator-focalised description which follows reminds readers of Salim's disability: he is described as limping and as hobbling, and, in a telling sentence, as behaving evasively: 'He sidled round to the far arcade and slipped out through the gate, then set off, walking as quickly as his short left leg would let him' (6).

Thus present in the narrative as a marked and specular element, Salim's disability is suffused with meanings, so that it exemplifies what Mitchell and Snyder refer to as 'the *materiality of metaphor*' (2000: 48, emphasis in original). Readers are positioned, first, to speculate about the origins of his disability, then to consider the extent to which his 'short left leg' gains him sympathy or enables him to evade his father's attention. Moreover, the novel's treatment of Muslim culture is bound up with its representation of family dynamics: Salim's relationship with his father, with his older brother, Ali, with his mother, at an historical juncture when the city of Acre is caught up in the volatile politics of the Crusades.[8] Salim's disability is embedded in the novel's representation of Muslim culture, and it is this intersectionality which so complicates its metaphorical import. When representations of Salim are compared to those of the other focalising character, Adam, a very different frame of reference is evident. Adam is treated as a straightforward figure whose motivations are evident; in comparison, Salim is accorded more complexity and his behaviour is often depicted as strategic, intended to win him sympathy or advantage. When he returns to his home and encounters his mother, for example, he 'put his head affectingly on one side' (2008: 10) before telling her of his fictive headache.

This contrast between the two characters, and the novel's representation of Salim's behaviour, fold its treatment of his disability into an all-too-familiar constellation of representations of the Muslim Other: subtle, indirect, devious. Clare Barker remarks that disability functions as 'a signifier of diverse states of marginality, a universally legible symbol for disenfranchisement and otherness' (2011: 18). More than this, disability trumps other forms of marginalisation, so that in the world of *Crusade*, where whiteness and Christianity are normative modes of being, Salim's disability renders him doubly othered: a Muslim boy with brown skin, whose disability is 'coded as inferior or deviant' (18).

Quayson's typology of disability representations in *Aesthetic Nervousness* includes examples of fictional characters who exemplify 'the intersection of disability, imperialism, and the projection of otherness' (2007: 38). The beginning of *Crusade* casts Salim in this role; but the novel's treatment of his disability is unstable. Called by Adil to bring mint tea to a Jewish doctor who visits the family's home, Salim carries the tray to the room where his father sits with Dr Musa:

> He hated it when people noticed his limp for the first time. He felt the doctor's eyes on him as he approached, and looked up, setting his face in a repressive frown. But there was only interest in the doctor's eyes, and none of the expected pity or contempt. (2008: 13)

To this point, the novel's treatment of Salim's unreliability has dissuaded implied readers from aligning themselves with him; here, an insight is offered into his self-consciousness in front of the doctor, whose response to Salim introduces a shift in perspective. One of the principal functions of the narrative prosthesis, according to Mitchell and Snyder, is to 'return one to an acceptable degree of difference' (2000: 7). Dr Musa is the catalyst in this reorientation, taking Salim on as an apprentice at his father's request and acting as a father-surrogate who is sharply contrasted with Salim's father Adil. Wounded by the alacrity with which Adil hands him over to Dr Musa, Salim sees his father in a new light: 'He saw with disgust that his father was almost cringing with gratitude in front of the doctor, and felt a wave of shame and anger' (2008: 23). By attributing disgust to Salim, the narrative suggests that the boy now observes Adil's behaviour as a spectator, even a non-Muslim spectator; but the description also conveys the impression that his father's attitude is indeed disgusting.

Simi Linton remarks that 'the medicalization of disability casts human variation as deviance from the norm, as pathological condition, as deficit, and significantly, as an individual burden and personal tragedy' (1998: 11). Salim's left leg is always envisioned in this way in *Crusade*, setting up the narrative expectation that Salim will 'rise above' his disability; all seems to depend on him. In such a conceptual scheme, the false logic of normativity escapes attention, since it is assumed that because Salim cannot be cured he must find a way to draw closer to the norm of the able body. As I have argued, Salim is, however, doubly marginalised, being both disabled and Muslim. While the first of these states is recuperable provided that Salim can attain 'an acceptable degree of difference' (Mitchell and Snyder 2000: 7), he is fixed in his Muslim identity.

The remainder of the narrative traces Salim's psychological development, focusing on the two aspects which define him: his disability and his religious and cultural affiliation. At first he essays strategies which have previously achieved positive results: Salim 'put on the suffering expression that had always roused his mother's sympathy and exaggerated his limp' (43). But Dr Musa is not so readily manipulated: 'You don't fool me, young man .... I know you can walk perfectly well' (43). Embarrassed by this admonition, Salim does not call on Dr Musa's help when he injures his 'good' foot, but struggles along despite the pain he experiences. The doctor, recognising the genuineness of Salim's discomfort, praises him for his fortitude. Mitchell and Snyder argue that 'in stories about characters with disabilities, an underlying issue is always whether the disability is the foundation of character itself' (2000: 6). It seems that in *Crusade* Salim is liberated from his disability when he moves from an environment (the family home) in which his lame leg defines his character, to one where he must develop a revised identity that more closely approximates to normalcy.

In line with this narrative emphasis, the action next shifts to the setting of Saladin's army where Dr Musa, with Salim as his assistant, is recruited to serve as a physician and surgeon. Here, the doctor's knowledge and skill are valued, and Salim finds that he too is attributed with prestige as Dr Musa's apprentice, preparing salves and grinding seeds. Indeed, his disability is redefined as a strategic advantage when Saladin enlists Salim as a spy, charged with reporting on the Crusader camp; as one of Saladin's advisers remarks, 'Who would suspect him of anything? A cripple too' (2008: 148–9). Saladin himself attributes Salim's close observation of the Crusaders to his perspective as a boy: 'I've had dozens of men reporting on the camp but none has given me so much detail. It takes the eyes of a boy. Information, intelligence, that's what's required' (149).

Salim's disability thus carries shifting significances, offering him immunity from the dangers encountered by warriors; a useful disguise as Saladin's spy; safe conduct through Saladin's camp and that of the Crusaders. While he longs to join Saladin's armed forces, with their fine horses and glamorous appearance, he ruefully accepts his difference from the normative toughness and physicality of soldiers. Nevertheless, he is drawn into the ambit of Dr Musa's prestige and associated with the magnanimous behaviour of Saladin, who sends Dr Musa and Salim to the Crusader camp to minister to the wounded. Finally, in return for Dr Musa's ministry to Saladin and his men, Salim gains safe conduct for his family from the besieged city of Acre, where he finds his parents and little sister starving and bereft of resources. When he runs the gamut of Saracen guards, his limp identifies him to the soldiers as 'Adil's lame son' (267); but his disability is quickly subsumed in his new identity as the dutiful boy saving his family from certain death.

As the narrative draws to its close, Salim's disability fades from view. He is no longer described as hobbling, limping, or sidling; rather, his parents defer to him now that he has committed himself to following Dr Musa's example by training as a physician and surgeon. The novel's Epilogue, set more than a decade on from the Siege of Acre, depicts Salim as a respected doctor who lives in a large house in Damascus with his wife and young daughters. When memories of his time in Saladin's army and his friendship with the English boy Adam flood Salim's mind, he rides out on one of the horses he keeps in his stable. No longer stigmatised as 'a cripple', Salim is incorporated into mainstream life, so that the narrative prosthesis of his disability tends towards a state of equilibrium which, however, depends entirely on his own investment in making up the deficit of his difference.

As to the other reason for his marginalisation, his adherence to Islam, equilibrium is not so readily achieved. The closure of the novel sketches a distinction between Salim, firmly committed to his religious faith and cultural norms, and Adam, a *present past* figure who returns to England newly sceptical about the morality of the Crusades, the demonisation of Muslims, and the religious practices of Christianity. The comparison between Salim and Adam feeds into a larger opposition between two Middle Ages: an Islamic world characterised by cultural and religious fixity, and a pluralistic England where individuals enjoy agency and self-determination. Salim's disability can, then, be read as a metaphor for his adherence to Islam. The ending of the novel steps away from a 'happily ever after' conclusion to linger on a hint of discontent. Perhaps Salim's memories of Adam and his habit of riding out on his horse, 'happy to be on his own' (390), signify his dissatisfaction with a life represented as a benign form of entrapment.

Face to face

Texts for the young are overwhelmingly directed to implied readers whose appearance identifies them as normates, to use Garland-Thomson's term. Faces are frequently described in these texts, sometimes through third-person narration, sometimes through devices such as self-description by first-person narrators or focalising protagonists who observe themselves in a mirror or window. The faces of protagonists in fiction for the young are predominantly 'normal'; narrative perspectives may intimate that such faces are more attractive than their owners believe, but when protagonists are represented as ordinary or even plain, narrative resolutions commonly provide reassuring messages about the transformative power of self-actualisation and of intersubjective relationships.

In *Staring: How We Look,* Garland-Thomson discusses what she describes as 'scenes of staring' (2009: 96), a series of case studies which identifies how and why humans stare at one another. In narrative, the faces which disclose characters' emotions or conceal them generally adhere to cultural norms that determine which faces are regarded as acceptable, which are outside the pale. Garland-Thomson notes that 'the unexpected face confounds us, presses us – and thus makes us stare' (103). Realistic narratives for the young, including historical fiction, rarely incorporate faces that exhibit such unexpectedness.

Avi's historical novel *Crispin: At the Edge of the World* (2006), the sequel to *Crispin: The Cross of Lead* (2002), is such an exceptional text: one of its protagonists is a girl, Troth, who has a cleft palate. The novel is set in England and Brittany around 1377, and the narrative follows the progress of 13-year-old Crispin, Troth, and a man known as Bear, as they search for safety and the possibility of a new life. Crispin and Bear encounter Troth when they find shelter in the forest with the wise woman Aude, who ministers to Bear, wounded by an arrow. In Crispin's first encounters with Troth she conceals her mouth by drawing her long hair over the bottom part of her face, a self-protective action which signals her lived experience of discrimination. When he sees Troth's face, Crispin's first-person narration calls on his memory of growing up in the village of Stromfield, where it was said that 'if, before a babe was born, the Devil came and touched the mother's swollen belly, the babe's limb or hand or face – like Troth's – would bear the Devil's evil mark' (2006: 36). Readers are positioned to weigh Crispin's explanation against that of Aude, who took Troth in after she was abandoned by her father: that 'men fear most what they understand least. Ignorance ... makes fear' (47).

The narrative prosthesis of Troth's unorthodox face is clearly not susceptible to a 'quick fix' (Mitchell and Snyder 2000: 8) which might restore her to 'normality'. Rather, the narrative arc of *Crispin: At the Edge of the World* tracks the evolution of Crispin's and Troth's friendship, and the shifts in belief and attitude consequent upon this friendship. The first negotiations between the two are encoded in a sequence involving staring. Crispin watches Troth, curled up next to the sleeping Aude. When she awakes, Troth stares at Crispin, who returns her stare: 'When I returned the look she pulled her hair across her face in that gesture that hid her disfigurement – her Devil's mark. Our eyes held' (41). There follows a stretch of dialogue in which Crispin establishes that Troth can speak, though with difficulty, and that she can hear. He asks her if she is a Christian, to which she makes no response, and to test whether she is a witch he makes a sign of the cross with his fingers, to which she also makes no response. Together with Aude, Troth has nursed Bear through fever and injury, and Crispin now thanks her: 'May Jesus ... grant you a blessing for being kind to my friend' (42). Troth's response is to fix her gaze on him: 'But this time, she shifted her hair so it was no longer covering her disfigured mouth: as if she wanted me to see, *dared* me to see' (42–3). Garland-Thomson refers to the work of the theologian Martin Buber and the philosopher Emmanuel Levinas, both of whom write on what is implied and symbolised by face-to-face interactions. While Buber offers 'a theology of the face' (2009: 100), Levinas focuses on the effects of the face on its viewer: 'The immanent "visitation of the face" incurs an obligation, an "epiphany" commanding one to serve the other' (100). The face-to-face gaze of Crispin and Troth suggests just such a reciprocal relationship, which plays out over the course of the narrative as each supports the other.

Nevertheless, Crispin's developing friendship with Troth is tempered by his anxiety over her adherence to a pagan religion, so that he fears that his association with her and Aude may constitute sin. When Aude is killed by villagers who believe her to be responsible for the death of a mother and new-born child, Crispin recognises the power of religious fanaticism, and seeks Troth's forgiveness for his 'unworthy thoughts', pledging to 'be a brother to you for all my days ...' (2006: 81). Troth's response is to take his hand and 'set her broken mouth to it in a kiss. My heart swelled. I thought: though broken, a mouth cannot bestow such a forgiving blessing and be evil' (81).

As this exchange demonstrates, Troth's disability functions, in part, as a vehicle for Crispin's psychological and cognitive development as he progresses from an unreasoned reliance on harsh and punitive versions of Christianity to a more independent and compassionate stance. Because the narrative is filtered through Crispin's perspective, readers see Troth in relation to his subjectivity; however, the self–other negotiations incorporated into the narrative construct a sense of Troth's selfhood distinct from Crispin's. By the end of the novel, Aude and Bear have both died, leaving Crispin and Troth alone in the world. It is Troth who spurs Crispin on to look for a society where they will be self-determining subjects: 'And so it was that Troth and I ... were guided by what Bear had told us: that freedom is not merely to be, but to choose' (231).

At the beginning of this chapter I speculated that disabilities feature more frequently in medievalist narratives than those featuring contemporary settings and protagonists partly because these texts reflect the exaggerated view of misery and filth which pervade depictions of the Middle Ages. There is, however, another explanation, which hinges upon the distance of the medieval from our own time. In Chapter 7, 'The Laughable Middle Ages' I observe that the Middle Ages is vastly over-represented in humorous texts, both fiction and non-fiction, and I advance the explanation that medieval figures and cultures are 'safely out of reach, incapable of outrage or indignation, devoid of defenders and apologists'. Children's texts are, on the whole, conscious of the ethical questions surrounding representations of cultural Others, and these questions arise, too, in representations of disability. Whereas disability in the Middle Ages can safely be treated as consequential upon historically inflected events and practices, representations of contemporary disability are more fraught because they are located in fictive worlds relatable to our own. Perhaps medievalist texts, at a remove from modernity, offer a less perilous context in which to represent disabilities.

5
Monstrous Bodies, Medievalist Inflexions

As the previous chapter has shown, representations of disability are both prevalent in medievalist texts for the young and also prone to what Mitchell and Snyder describe as 'overheated symbolic imagery' (2000: 16) which treats disabled characters metaphorically rather than as complex figures who relate in multiple ways to their cultural and political environments. Disability studies and monster studies have in common a focus on bodies and on physical difference. Kevin Stagg argues that where they depart from each other is in the ends to which they are put: disability studies has moved beyond medical models to focus on how disability functions as a social category, whereas monster studies tends to 'evade the specific social context of physical difference' (2006: 20), concentrating on the symbolic and ideational functions of monsters. Nevertheless, as Garland-Thomson notes, many of the monstrous figures we encounter in literature and film 'are elaborations on infrequent, yet regularly occurring, actual human beings' (2009: 166).

In his introduction to *Monster Theory*, Jeffrey Cohen remarks that the monster is an embodiment of 'a certain cultural moment – of a time, a feeling, and a place' (Cohen 1996: 4). Marina Levina and Diem-My Bui observe that the monsters haunting fiction and film today 'have allowed us to deal with the profound acceleration in changing symbolic, economic, and technological systems' (2013: 1). The twenty-first century texts I discuss in this chapter respond to cultural anxieties which hinge on rapid and unpredictable change exemplified by economic crises, social unrest, mobile populations, and constant technological developments. The potency of monstrous figures in texts for the young is heightened by the fact that these texts are directed to audiences who themselves experience the bodily and psychological changes of puberty and young adulthood, and who occupy a liminal space between child and adult. Jacques Derrida argues that the future is 'necessarily monstrous: the figure of the future, that is, that which can only be surprising, that for which we are not prepared...is heralded by species of monsters... All experience open to the future is prepared or prepares itself to welcome the monstrous *arrivant*' (1995: 386–7). If the future is not monstrous, Derrida says, it is merely a predictable, safe and imaginable replica of today. Medievalist monsters such as dragons, werewolves, vampires and fairies (that is, the malevolent and murderous fairies of the urban fairy genre) are poised between past and future: they refer back to their medieval precursors, and forward to a future in which change is inevitable and unpredictable.

Monsters not only inhabit the spaces between past and future, but they also represent change by destabilising cultural norms; Cohen notes that their 'externally incoherent bodies resist attempts to include them in any systematic structuration', endowing them with 'power to evade and to undermine' (1996: 6). In texts for the young, however, this potential for destabilisation is often offset by tension and ambivalence. It is not only texts incorporating disabled bodies which manifest 'aesthetic nervousness' (Quayson 2007: 15); monstrous figures and the narratives in which they feature frequently jostle against the socialising agendas of fiction and films for young audiences. In Chapter 3 I discussed the gothic spaces of schools for vampires in *Vampire Academy* and *Marked*, showing how the medieval is deployed to support racialised representations of vampire society which privilege whiteness (in *Vampire Academy*), and (in *Marked*) claim access to a commodified and shallow version of Native American culture. These regressive depictions clearly do not destabilise cultural norms, but rather valorise colonial conceptions of a hierarchy of races.

In this chapter I consider the roles played by medievalist monsters, focusing on what these narratives suggest about social change in the twenty-first century; on monstrous figurations of change, narrative responses to them, and imaginings of future worlds with or without monsters. Derrida's invocation of the *arrivant* captures the uncertainty and the incomprehensibility of change, which cannot be analysed except in retrospect, and for which one cannot be altogether prepared. As Nicholas Royle notes, Derrida's preoccupation with the monstrous *arrivant* is 'intimately connected with what is normal, with normality and normalization' (2003: 111). The monsters depicted in the books I discuss address questions of belonging: how and to what extent monstrous *arrivants* find hospitality. The monster, according to Derrida, invites us to 'make it part of the household and have it assume the habits, to make us assume new habits' (1995: 386). The dragons, vampires, werewolves and fairies I discuss in this chapter complicate ideas about what counts as human, functioning as harbingers of futurity.

Mildly monstrous: urban fairies and human girls

Some monsters are more monstrous than others; the fairies of Young Adult paranormal romance tend to occupy the lower end of the continuum. Contemporary representations of fairies call on the extensive body of fairy art and literature produced, almost entirely by men,[1] during the long nineteenth century, and on Victorian imaginings of a medieval world inhabited by fairies and a credulous and superstitious human population.[2] Victorian artworks and fictions comprise an expression of what Isaiah Berlin termed the 'counter-Enlightenment', a movement which opposed the Enlightenment's emphasis on rationality and order, and which argued for 'relativist and historicist views of human society, human knowledge and human nature' (Bown 2001: 16).

In the first decades of the twenty-first century, fairy narratives are again prominent both in popular fantasy and art for general audiences, and also in cultural production for children and young people. Contemporary fairy narratives for the young are largely the province of women artists and writers, with the notable exceptions of Terry Pratchett and Eoin Colfer, whose treatments of fairies generally take on parodic and carnivalesque forms. YA fairy fantasy began to emerge in the 1990s with Neil Gaiman's *Stardust* (1999) and Holly Black's *Tithe* (2002) and 'The Spiderwick Chronicles'; authors writing in this field include Maggie Stiefvater, Melissa Marr, Malinda Lo, Lisa Mantchev, Aprilynne Pyke, Cyn Balog, Lesley Livingston and Holly Black. The subgenre of fairy romance has found a ready market in part because of readers' exposure to fairy narratives and products as young girls, in part because of its appeal to female readers already primed for supernatural romance from their familiarity with other genres such as vampire and werewolf fantasy.[3]

Fairy romance directed to YA female readers typically features narratives in which human girls discover their fairy connections (often linked to dead mothers) and access fairy worlds where they either become romantically involved with fairies or human–fairy hybrids, or undergo a transformation from human to fairy. These girls always possess 'the sight', a gift inherited from mothers or grandmothers and through them traditions of female knowledge or witchcraft. In some fairy romances the otherness of fairies manifests in duplicity, magic or *glamour*, a word whose etymology combines learning with the occult.[4] In other texts fairies take on more sinister shapes, as malevolent figures, assassins and child-stealers. Writing of medieval romance, Helen Cooper notes that 'fairies lie outside normal morality, especially where sex is concerned' (2004: 214), and similarly many of the fairies of YA romance are inhabitants of an amoral or anarchic fairy realm. The narratives of urban fairy romance are commonly shaped by conflict between human and fairy codes and practices, and centre upon romantic relations between human girls and male fairies.

Counter-Enlightenment representations of fairies reacted against the Enlightenment's insistence on the perfectibility of human nature and the inexorability of progress. Contemporary fairy romance responds, rather, to the secularism of Western cultures and the fragmentation of identities in postmodernity. But fairies in YA fantasy are more than they seem. In their more monstrous guises they incorporate 'fear, desire, anxiety, and fantasy' (Cohen 1996: 4); but they are also conventionally represented as miniature humans; and in fairy romance they often assume human likeness. They are, moreover, ancient beings endowed with the lure of the past and associated with a mythologised Middle Ages when humans and spirit beings coexisted. The texts on which I focus here are Melissa Marr's *Wicked Lovely* (2007) and Maggie Stiefvater's *Lament* (2008), both of which incorporate fairies in romantic triangles where female protagonists must choose between human and fairy or human/fairy lovers.

Like most female protagonists in fairy romance, Aislinn in *Wicked Lovely* and Deirdre in *Lament* begin their narrative trajectories as vulnerable and insecure characters. Both are stalked by powerful fairy figures: Aislinn by Keenan, the Summer King, who seeks a human girl as his queen; Deirdre by Luke, a soul-less *gallowglass* who acts as the Fairy Queen's assassin and has been set the task of killing Deirdre.[5] Aislinn is the only human to see and hear the fairies who frequent her neighbourhood, and Deirdre is a cloverhand; the four-leafed clovers which appear wherever she goes signal her capacity to see fairies where other humans do not. The respective grandmothers of Deirdre and Aislinn possess insight about fairy practices and are anxious about the dangers their granddaughters might face if they should fall in love with fairies. This emphasis on the knowledge of grandmothers privileges ancient traditions over a rootless and shallow modernity while emphasising the powerful attraction wielded by fairy suitors.

As the protagonists' names suggest, the fantasy elements of these novels are heavily based on Irish and Scottish Gaelic traditions: in

Lament several of the chapters are introduced by epigraphs comprising verses from Irish songs; and in *Wicked Lovely* each chapter is preceded by an excerpt from a folklorist such as Andrew Lang, Thomas Keightley and Jane Wilde. The effect of these references is to add weight and authority to the narratives they punctuate. Enlightenment scholars and antiquarians sought to codify and describe the 'consoling fictions for the common people' (Bown 2001: 5) represented by fairies. One of the peculiarities of YA fairy fantasy, then, is that it calls on Enlightenment scholarship while insisting that human knowledge systems are incapable of comprehending fairy practices and traditions.

The fairies of *Lament* and *Wicked Lovely* conform to many of the representational conventions which shape their depiction in medieval romance: they exist outside conventional moral frameworks and their behaviour is unpredictable and sometimes capriciously violent. They often affect glamours which enable them to pass as humans, and their preternatural beauty functions as a snare or trap. By filtering events and characters through the perspectives of human protagonists – Deirdre is the first-person narrator of *Lament* and Aislinn the principal focaliser of *Wicked Lovely* – the two novels position readers to engage with the emotional and psychological experiences of human characters attracted to dangerous fairies. Keenan, the Summer King in *Wicked Lovely*, is 'too beautiful to touch, walking with a swagger that said he knew exactly how attractive he was' (2007: 9); in *Lament* Deirdre describes Luke as 'lean as a wolf, with pale blond hair and eyes even paler. And sexy' (2008: 10). Keenan's and Luke's too-perfect bodies are monstrous because they are both like and also unlike human bodies.

The novels' lingering descriptions of Keenan's and Luke's desirable bodies, and of the romantic imaginings they inspire in female protagonists, struggle with accounts of their histories of violence, murder and emotional manipulation. While these grim allusions are swept aside by romance conventions which foreground sexuality and female desire, no such conventions ameliorate representations of the Fairy Queens who are cast as the true monsters of the two novels. Their status as monsters is instantiated in their cruelty towards Keenan and Luke, a narrative emphasis which constructs these characters as victims, so deflecting attention from their own cruel deeds and inviting sympathetic responses from implied readers.

In *Wicked Lovely*, Keenan has selected Aislinn for the role of Summer Queen following a long line of human girls over nine centuries. If Aislinn, like previous girls Keenan has entrapped, turns out not to be 'the one', his malevolent mother Beira, the Winter Queen, will destroy summer altogether, maintaining her control over the dystopian world of the fairies.[6] Humans are, then, in thrall to the fairy realm without realising it, in an uncanny version of climate change. When Keenan visits his mother Beira in her frost-shrouded home, readers see her through his focalising perspective as a 'mockery of a mortal epitome of motherhood' (2007: 38). Just as Keenan's beauty is altogether too much, so Beira's performance of motherhood is excessive: her touch produces ice which gradually permeates Keenan's body, causing horrible pain until he loses consciousness. At the same time she affects the glamour of a middle-class human mother: 'a modest floral dress, frilly apron, and single strand of pearls', her hair caught up in what she calls 'a chignon' (38). This demonstration of gratuitous violence, perpetrated on the helpless Keenan, distracts attention from Keenan's own manipulative practices, inviting readers into a kind of voyeuristic or even sadistic pleasure exacerbated by Keenan's pointless longing for a sign of maternal feeling from Beira, who has offered no evidence of such feelings.

At the end of *Wicked Lovely*, Aislinn rescues Keenan from torture at Beira's hands. Together Aislinn and Keenan kill Beira by piercing her with sunlight so that her body disintegrates. The violence of this episode, unlike the far more explicit description of Keenan's ordeal, is underplayed, treated as inevitable and, indeed, necessary. A moment of regret on Keenan's part is quickly set aside: 'He'd once hoped that they'd not come to this place, that they'd find a way to coexist. They hadn't, but he didn't regret it' (314). Aislinn's intervention seems to foreground her agency, while drawing her into the violence endemic to the fairy world; having become fairy, she agrees to assume the role of Summer Queen as 'a job' (286), while she maintains her primary relationship with her mortal partner Seth, attends college and conducts a conventional human life from which she enters the fairy world when her duties require.[7]

In *Lament* the gallowglass Luke is similarly tortured by the Fairy Queen, who has transformed his soul into a dove, imprisoned in a door-less birdcage. Luke is dragged, tortured and bleeding, before the Queen, who offers him a final opportunity for immortality: 'One last chance, Luke Dillon. Tell me you will love me, and I'll spare you' (2008: 314). When it is clear that the Queen has lost her ascendancy over her realm, the fairy hordes tear her to pieces, and her bloodstained crown is placed on the head of her successor, Eleanor. This violent scene is succeeded by a sequence during which Deirdre restores Luke's soul to his body and he joins the *Daoine Sidhe*, fairy nobility. Luke's transformation is immediate: 'He was so alive, his eyes so bright, his face so light, that I realized I didn't know anything about him. He grinned at me, this strange, young, wild thing, and he kissed me, hard' (325). The contrast between the Fairy Queen's dismemberment and Luke's restoration to youth and beauty hinges upon the meanings attributed to the monstrous figures of bad-boy fairy and malevolent hag.[8]

The Fairy Queen figure as it is represented in *Wicked Lovely* and *Lament* combines two strands of signification: motherhood and aging bodies. Human mothers in these novels are represented as absent or problematic: Aislinn discovers towards the end of the novel that Keenan stalked her mother Moira as his putative Summer Queen, resulting in Moira's suicide; Deirdre's mother is overbearing, seeking to control every moment of her daughter's life. The Fairy Queens of the two novels embody exaggerated and melodramatic versions of dysfunctional human mothers; they are, moreover, immensely old although they are capable of adopting the glamours of young women.

Disgust for aging bodies is written into the novels' depictions of human and fairy females. When Deirdre visits her grandmother in hospital the building smells of 'antiseptic and old people' (2008: 178); responding to her friend Sara who describes her own grandmother, Deirdre says, 'Makes you afraid to get old, doesn't it?', to which Sara replies, 'And ugly. Like, when I get too ugly to wear a mini-skirt, just shoot me' (243). In the fairy world Deirdre sees through the Fairy Queen's glamour: 'She was one of those beautiful girls that made you despise looking in a mirror ... Then her eyelids flicked open and two ancient eyes stared back at me. I was repulsed; it was as if I'd peeked in a baby carriage and found a snake looking back at me' (2008: 300). In *Wicked Lovely*, Beira is always guarded by three hags, 'withered things – looking like the mere husks of women' (2007: 51), toothless, with sunken cheeks, 'haggard and glassy-eyed' (250). These depictions of disgusting, withered bodies are set against reminders of Deirdre and Aislinn's youth, paving the way for the assassination episodes of both novels, which thematise the destruction of ancient, powerful females by younger queens.

If, as Derrida says, the future is monstrous because it embodies 'that for which we are not prepared' (Royle 2003: 110), the Fairy Queens of *Lament* and *Wicked Lovely* evoke disgust not only because they are ancient, but also because they were once young. Glamours which sustain the illusion of youth cannot conceal the inevitability of aging, the spectre of decay. Derrida says that cultural change occurs when the monstrous *arrivant* is welcomed into human life: 'All experience open to the future is prepared or prepares itself to welcome the monstrous *arrivant*, to welcome it, that is, to accord hospitality to that which is absolutely foreign or strange' (1995: 387). Rather, *Lament* and *Wicked Lovely* keep the monstrous at bay, limiting readers' horizons to the present and the immediate future of romance narratives. The desirable bad boys, Keenan and Luke, violent and manipulative as they are, constitute monsters whom human girls might imagine as edgy and dangerous partners. The ancient hags, Beira and the Fairy Queen, are killed by young characters because they have no place in fictional worlds in which aging bodies are beyond the pale, altogether too monstrous to survive.

'Be me a little': Bringing the vampire home

In urban fairy romance, the closer fairies are to human, either through ancestry or romance, the more comprehensible and sympathetic they are. In other genres of fantasy, human monsters represent what Foucault refers to as a double violation: 'What makes a human monster a monster is not just its exceptionality relative to the species form; it is the disturbance it brings to juridical regularities (whether it is a question of marriage laws, canons of baptism, or rules of inheritance)' (1997: 51). Combining 'the impossible and the forbidden' (51), the human monster is haunted by what is regarded as unnatural, and by what is defined as illegal.

The YA vampire romances which have proliferated since the success of Stephenie Meyer's Twilight series[9] are generally structured by the deferral of romantic and/or sexual outcomes between protagonists, and by the agonistic relationship which 'good' vampires such as Edward Cullen evince towards their vampirism. Notwithstanding this emphasis on the psychological and affective aspects of romance between humans and vampires, the Twilight series, like other paranormal romances, can readily be analysed in relation to postmodernity, global identities, and the swirling currents of postfeminism. But the body of critical work focusing on YA and other vampire fiction is so extensive that I do not intend to cover ground already overworked. Instead, I consider a text which directly addresses the cultural and legal contexts and practices which complicate the life of the human monster and those who associate with her/him. In John Ajvide Lindqvist's *Let the Right One In* (2007),[10] the vampire, Eli, like the human monsters to whom Foucault alludes, must negotiate the disturbance which her/his monstrosity presents to legal and bureaucratic systems.

Let the Right One In departs in two obvious ways from the YA vampire romance. First, while the novel incorporates many instances of the uncanny, it eschews the medievalist elements common in gothic romance: castles, decayed monasteries, ancient graveyards, religious icons. Second, the vampire in the novel takes the form of a 12-year-old child, Eli. At the level of setting and plot, then, the novel appears to bypass the vampire's connections to the past; the setting is the mundane suburb of Blackeberg in the outskirts of Stockholm, and the plot traces Eli's project of surviving as a vampire in the 1980s. The medieval is, however, subtly present in imagery and intertextual allusions which avoid the formulaic and predictable tropes of conventional vampire romance.

The narrative of *Let the Right One In* centres upon change, time and mutability. The novel opens with an account of the establishment of Blackeberg in the 1950s, when apartment blocks, cinema and shopping centre were built and the metro opened, and it identifies the suburb's lack of a past as its defining feature:

> Only one thing was missing. A past. At school the children didn't get to do any special projects about Blackeberg's history because there wasn't one. That is to say, there was something about an old mill. A tobacco king. Some strange old buildings down by the water. But that was a long time ago and without any connection to the present. Where the three-storeyed apartment buildings now stood there had been only forest before. (2007: 10)

As the narrative goes on to demonstrate, what happened in the past is, on the contrary, full of connections to the present and shapes the stories characters tell themselves and others in order to make sense of their lived experience.

The action of the novel is set in 1981, three decades after Blackeberg's establishment, when the past moves in to Blackeberg in the form of a man and girl, assumed to be father and daughter, who shift into an apartment building. Readers learn early in the novel that the girl, Eli, is a vampire and the man, Håkan, is not her father but a paedophilic ex-teacher who procures a supply of blood for her by killing people and draining their bodies. Later, it transpires that Eli was once a boy castrated in the distant past, when s/he was made a vampire. The main focus of the novel is the development of an emotional and psychic bond between Eli and Oskar, the bullied and insecure boy who lives in the apartment next to Eli and Håkan.

The past enters the present in myriad ways in *Let the Right One In*. Håkan, a well-read and intelligent man, is impelled by his devotion to Eli to kill the weak – young boys, elderly men – whose blood he drains. As he performs these gruesome duties he speculates about which level of Dante's hell he might be consigned to by King Minos; or he catches sight of a little girl skipping through the forest and tells himself that she is too young to die. The words 'Keep going, little one. Don't stop to play in the forest' (24) come to his mind, an interdiction reminiscent of 'Little Red Riding Hood'. The forest features prominently as a site where bodies are discovered,[11] but it also carries other significances of enchantment: the epigraph to Part Two of the novel refers to the *skogsrå*, glossed as 'a beautiful but sinister forest spirit' (112) who steals men's hearts and thereafter never lets them escape. Oskar's bedroom walls are decorated with photographic wallpaper depicting a forest with broad tree-trunks and green leaves in which Oskar imagines beautiful or threatening figures.

Such intimations of fantastic and enchanted pasts and places are out of step with the banal lives of the characters who feature as representative citizens of Blackeberg: the young bullies who torture Oskar, a group of underemployed men who meet to drink and play cards, the glue-sniffing boys who gather in the basement of Oskar's apartment block. The boredom and anomie associated with these boys and men are set against the friendship which develops between Oskar and Eli, which traverses the radical difference between human and non-human. This difference is symbolised by the contrast between Oskar's ethnically Swedish appearance (blond and blue-eyed) and Eli's dark hair and large dark eyes. Indeed, Eli might be taken for a Gypsy, with her unkempt appearance, her habit of storing up money and jewellery, and her propensity for stealth and secrecy. When adults in the novel see Eli, scantily dressed and barefoot in the cold, their first instinct is to precipitate processes whereby she is taken into care, since as an unregulated minor she presents a threat to practices of control and surveillance.[12] At the local hospital, where Eli persuades Maud, the receptionist, to allow her to visit Håkan after he is apprehended, Maud becomes fixated on alerting child protection authorities: 'the welfare people would have to be brought in' (318). Foucault's categories of the human monster and the 'individual to be corrected' (1997: 52) mingle in the figure of the child vampire whose appearance locates her outside the aegis of the stable, middle-class nuclear family in which, as Foucault notes, the child is placed 'at the center of the parental group' (53), the focus of regulatory practices.

Boundaries between human and non-human are mapped onto divisions between ethnic groups in 1980s Sweden. At the beginning of the novel Håkan kills a boy walking through the forest and drains his body in order to supply Eli with blood. Immediately the newspapers refer to this killing as 'a ritual murder'. The term 'ritual' evokes dread because it suggests that another murder will be perpetrated, since 'a ritual is something that is repeated' (113). But 'ritual' also suggests those continuities whereby ancient practices are sustained through performances incorporated in rites and ceremonies. These meanings coalesce in imaginings of outsiders who might conveniently be blamed for the murder.

The killing is followed by reports of a drug seizure, the 'largest ... ever recorded in Sweden', involving five Lebanese men smuggling heroin. But this is not their only, or even their worst crime: they are said to have 'taken advantage of the extensive Swedish social welfare system during the time they were smuggling heroin' (114). This story very quickly leads to speculations about Muslims: 'It seemed plausible enough, weren't blood rituals common in those Arab countries? Muslims. Sent their kids off with plastic crosses or whatever it was they wore around their necks. Small children working as mine removers. You heard about that. Brutal people. Iran, Iraq. The Lebanese' (114).

The narrative positions readers as observers of the discursive slippages whereby a story about Lebanese drug smugglers segues into speculations about a Muslim murderer. The lexical chain which stretches from the drug smugglers to 'those Arab countries', 'Muslims', 'Iran, Iraq' and returns to 'the Lebanese', lumps together nations, ethnicities and religions under the signs 'Muslim' and 'brutal people', drawing attention to the motivations of racial hatred which drive this language and are expressed by it. Imaginings of 'blood rituals', hazily associated with 'those Arab countries', consign Islam to a barbaric past, in a rhetorical trope common in Western references to Islam, particularly since the September 11 attacks on the United States.[13] The figure of the 'ritual killer' proleptically justifies these suspicions, calling on hazy conceptions of Muslim barbarism. But when the police release a sketch of the murderer, it becomes clear that the citizens of Blackeberg can take no comfort from these racialised assumptions. The face they see is that of 'a normal Swede' (114), someone who looks like many men in the western suburbs of Stockholm. The novel's trenchant critique of anti-Muslim sentiments centres on how the circulation of myths about 'those Arab countries', 'Muslims' and 'the Lebanese' create and maintain boundaries between 'normal Swedes' and those who do not conform to narrow and exclusive standards of normality.

It is in its treatment of the developing relationship between Oskar and Eli that the novel most effectively troubles boundaries: between past and present, Swedish and other, male and female, ancient and modern. The two are attracted to each other initially by loneliness: Eli has led a peripatetic existence on the fringes of society, while Oskar, who lives with his overprotective mother, has no friends and is the target of bullies who force him to carry out demeaning actions such as squealing like a pig. When they first meet, Eli warns Oskar that the boundary between them is too wide to be bridged: 'I can't be friends with you. Just so you know' (53). It is because of an act of tenderness by Oskar that Eli disobeys the interdiction against friendship which has kept her safe from discovery: at the moment when she prepares to bite him on the neck he strokes her face, disrupting her intention of feeding on him and affording her a sudden insight into the possibility of intimacy. Like Derrida's monstrous *arrivant*, Eli is welcomed into a relationship in which Oskar offers hospitality 'to that which is absolutely foreign or strange' (1995: 387).

The book's title alludes to Morrissey's song 'Let the right one slip in' and to the tradition that vampires cannot enter human habitations without being invited. This imagery constitutes a metaphor for the intersubjective bond which develops between Oskar and Eli, and which opens each up to the other. When the two discuss the ethics of killing people, Oskar acknowledges his fantasies of killing those who torment him. Eli tells Oskar that what they have in common is the desire to live:

[Eli]   'If you could wish someone dead and they died. Wouldn't you do it then?'
[Oskar]   'Sure.'
[Eli]   'Sure you would. And that would be for your own enjoyment. Your revenge. I do it because I have to. There is no other way.'
[Oskar]   'But it's only because ... they hurt me, because they tease me, because I ...'
[Eli]   'Because you want to *live*. Just like me.'
         Eli held out his arms, laid them against Oskar's cheeks, brought his face closer.
[Eli]   'Be me a little.' (2007: 433–4)

Eli's plea, 'Be me a little', points to the possibility of an empathy which transcends temporality, species and sexual difference. As if to induct Oskar into his vampirism, Eli telepathically situates Oskar in the castle room where he was castrated and then the moment when he was transformed into a vampire. In this film-like sequence it is Oskar who undergoes the transition from human to vampire, so that when Oskar returns to the everyday world of Blackeberg he confuses Eli's world with his own, Eli's past with his own history.

The novel ends with Eli and Oskar travelling on the train from Stockholm to Karlstad. Or rather, Oskar sits in the train compartment while Eli is transported in the stout, old-fashioned trunk that occupies the luggage rack. When the conductor, Stefan Larsson, checks Oskar's ticket he notices the trunk and boxes with which the boy travels, and asks him what is in the trunk. Oskar replies, 'A little bit of everything' (581). Larsson registers Oskar's cheerfulness and reflects that if he were travelling with such heavy luggage he 'would hardly have looked so *happy*. But then, it's probably different when you're young' (582). Eli's radical hybridity incorporates apparently irreconcilable differences, inviting readers to imagine a world in which corporeal and temporal boundaries do not circumscribe identities and relationships. The buoyant mood of the novel's conclusion leaves open the questions which hover over the future of the two protagonists: how Eli will access human blood; to what extent Oskar will be implicated in this search; what might become of their relationship as Oskar ages but Eli does not. Nevertheless, the hyperrealism with which the novel's world is constructed works to offset such questions, so that the narrative gestures towards possibilities rather than problems.

'Both my peoples': Being dragon, being human

In his essay 'Radical Fantasy', Fredric Jameson remarks that in fantasy the dragon 'is a living being and the narrative must centrally come to terms with the human relationship to it' (2002: 274).[14] Jameson turns to Ursula Le Guin's Earthsea novels as an example of how fantasy has shifted its orientation towards ethics and history. Tolkien, he argues, epitomises fantasy's 'reactionary nostalgia for Christianity and the medieval world' (279–80), whereas Le Guin 'switches train-tracks from the Church of England to the politics of imperialism and modernisation' (280).

In Tolkien's fantasy the medieval is associated with virtue and modernity with corruption. Andrew Lynch observes that '*The Lord of the Rings* is considerably more romance than epic or novel, because it gives an absolute aesthetic and moral privilege—aesthetics and morality becoming quite indistinguishable—to one side only' (2008: 111). The side of virtue, led by Aragorn, is associated with a 'medieval' style of war waged by 'named volunteers and pledged faith, while the bad side is "modern," with its nameless conscripts, machines, slaves, and creatures of Sauron' (111). In this mode of fantasy dragons are implacable enemies of humans, incorrigibly evil in their origins,[15] attributed with cunning and greed. They are also ancient, majestic and highly intelligent.

Le Guin's treatment of the dragon figure in the Earthsea novels stands in sharp contrast to Tolkien's, most centrally in the novels' depictions of the relationship of dragons to humans. Peter Hollindale summarises the progress of this relationship as follows: 'The dragons move steadily closer to humanity as the Earthsea books progress, but they finally break with it' (2003: 192). The fearsome antagonists of *A Wizard of Earthsea* modulate in the later books into named characters who are the familiars of certain humans such as the dragonlords, Ged and Arren. In *Tehanu*, Le Guin provides a retrospective history of the shared origins of humans and dragons which affords an explanation for the hybrid nature of Tenar's foster-child Therru/Tehanu, who knows dragon language and is in effect a human-dragon. The explanation offered in *Tehanu* is that humans and dragons were once one people, but 'the principle of Change caused their division' (2003: 193). Tehanu has been badly burned; her face is scarred, she has lost an eye, and the fingers of one of her hands have fused, resembling a claw. These 'two sides' of Tehanu come to signify her dual identity, which enables what Mike Cadden calls a 'double vision' (2004: 105) of the human and dragon worlds.

The distinctions between Tolkien's and Le Guin's dragons speak to the contrasting world views which inform their fiction. Tolkien's dragons occupy an invariant position in taxonomies of monsterhood and hierarchies of value: they are always antagonistic to humans and sharply distinguished from them. Le Guin's dragons, on the other hand, occupy much more ambiguous relations to humans, reflecting the collapse of the sturdy binaries (good and evil, human and dragon, light and dark) that inform Tolkien's fiction. The novels I discuss in this section, Rachel Hartman's *Seraphina* (2012) and Janet Lee Carey's *Dragon's Keep* (2007), feature hybrid human–dragon identities, but in these novels the dragon elements uncannily present in the protagonists' bodies refer to interspecies relationships prohibited within the social, political and legal regimes of medievalist settings.

Seraphina's dragon mother Linn, living in disguise as a human, concealed her dragon nature from her human husband, Claude, who discovered that she was a dragon only when Linn died at Seraphina's birth. Since then Claude has destroyed all records of his dead wife and has invented a fictitious mother for Seraphina. Her dragon lineage manifests at the age of 11, when a band of scales appears on her left arm from her wrist to her elbow, another around her midriff. In *Dragon's Keep*, Rosalind was born with a dragon talon in place of the ring finger of her left hand. Her mother, who consulted a witch to enhance her fertility, ingested a dragon egg as part of a spell, and Rosalind's talon is the proof of genetic dragon material in her body.

Both novels are set in societies where the idea of dragon–human hybrids is anathema to lawmakers and citizens. Seraphina and Rosalind must conceal their dragon ancestry to protect their lives, and the action of both novels plays out against a history of violent struggle between humans and dragons. While the imagined world of *Seraphina* is more elaborately drawn than that of *Dragon's Keep*, both novels adhere to Jameson's description of the Earthsea novels: that they engage with 'the politics of imperialism and modernisation' (2002: 280). As in most paranormal romances, their narratives are shaped by stories about romantic attachments between human and non-human characters; the hybrid human-dragons, Seraphina and Rosalind, develop romantic relationships with humans unaware of their hybridity. These romantic trajectories play out against the background of other narrative strands, incorporating political intrigue, social unrest, and struggles over power and control.

When the action of *Seraphina* begins, the nation state of Goredd is in crisis because the Crown Prince, Rupert, has been assassinated. The manner of his death suggests that he has been killed by dragons, an unwelcome turn of events since the nation is about to celebrate the fortieth anniversary of Comonot's Treaty, an agreement forged between Goredd and dragonkind.[16] The treaty allows for dragon-only territory; and when dragons enter Goredd they are obliged to take human forms, as *saarantrai*. The citizens of Goredd are divided as to their view of the treaty. Some, convinced that dragons are by nature antagonistic to humans, resent the fact that dragonkind has been allocated territory, although this territory is pitifully small. A schismatic group of dragons, too, seeks to undermine the treaty and to resume the unremitting enmity which preceded it.

By locating Seraphina in the royal court, where she is the assistant to the court composer, the first-person narration foregrounds her experience as an outsider to the dominant court culture. Witnessing the denigration of dragons by courtiers, she is obliged to remain silent; so absolute is the prohibition against interbreeding that neither dragons nor humans imagine that someone of her kind might exist. In effect she is forced to pass as wholly human, experiencing guilt and shame both because of her hybrid nature and also because she must disguise it. Narratives of passing, according to Monique Rooney, contest 'essentialist categories such as race, gender and sexuality', casting the passer as 'a marked and marking threshold figure' (2001) on whose body is inscribed the instability of these categories. The scales on Seraphina's arm and body comprise a constant reminder that she is just such a 'threshold figure' in Goredd society. When she falls in love with Lucian Kiggs, who is betrothed to Princess Glisselda, second in line to the throne, Seraphina attempts to cut the scales from her arm in an attempt to normalise her appearance. But the pain and bloodshed involved in this drastic manoeuvre are too much to bear, and Seraphina comes to the conclusion that she is and will always be a monster.

The speciesism which so disables relations between humans and dragons in Goredd maps on to forms of discrimination in contemporary societies, notably those in which ethnic majorities exclude or oppress minorities. Like the ruptures of imperialism and civil wars, the history of violent struggle between dragons and humans in Goredd is never over and done with, but lives on in the views and attitudes of its citizens and is the principal cause of discord in the nation. Yet the narrative draws a distinction between the hardened anti-dragon forces, those who oppose Comonot's Treaty, and Goreddis with more progressive views. When Seraphina ventures into the section of the city known as Quighole, defined in the novel's glossary as a 'dragon and quigutl ghetto' (2012: 367),[17] she discovers to her surprise that it is frequented by humans, saarantrai and quigutl. Her uncle Orma, the saarantras brother of her dead mother, meets her in a public house where 'humans and saarantrai sat at the same table ..., students engaged in deep discussions with teachers' (147). Seraphina finds herself overcome with emotion at seeing 'both my ... peoples together' (147).

In line with Foucault's discussion of the human monster, the human-dragon figure in *Seraphina* is situated within a 'juridico-biological domain' (1997: 51) which is incapable of managing the disturbances the monster presents. Seraphina's father, a lawyer, warns her that 'few cases of cohabiting with dragons have ever come all the way to trial; the accused have usually been torn to bits by mobs, been burned alive in their houses, or simply disappeared' (2012: 36). When she asks him what happens to offspring of such alliances, he tells her that there are no records of such children, but that the scriptures of St Ogdo, the founder of dracomachia,[18] prescribe particularly gruesome methods of extermination. This telling silence about actual human-hybrid people is belied by Seraphina's discovery of hybrids (ityasaari) other than herself; she experiences visions of a garden populated by 17 such characters, some of whom appear in human form during the narrative and at its denouement, when the young princess Glisselda assumes command of Goredd and faces down revolt by hard-line humans and dragons.

These dissidents, on both sides, have maintained their opposition to Comonot's Treaty during the 40 years of its operation. Now they reiterate their complaints. The Earl of Apsig complains of the concessions made to the dragons: 'They've won. Nowhere is exclusively human; no side in this conflict is ours alone' (347). For their part, the rebel dragons accuse their leader Comonot of 'seeking to alter our fundamental dragon nature and make us more human-like' (335). The rebels' complaints are based on a conception of dragon and human identities as fixed, permanent and stable; according to this version of history, the 40 years of the treaty have leached away identities by requiring each side (dragon and human) to make concessions to the other in regard to territory and power. But these old arguments, which hinge upon essentialist conceptions of dragon and human, are inconsequential in comparison with the impact of the monstrous *arrivants*, Seraphina and the other hybrids, whose very existence demands a reformulation of what is normal. Ardmagar Comonot points to this conceptual shift: 'Can you not see that it's no longer a question of dragon versus human? The division now is between those who think this peace is worth preserving and those who would keep us at war until one side or the other is destroyed' (339). Comonot observes that 'the young have been raised with peaceful ideals' (339) and they will not acquiesce to war between humans and dragons. Princess Glisselda herself models the new order, refusing to countenance the demands of the rebels, and welcoming the ityasaari as valued citizens of Goredd.

The novel ends, like so much contemporary fantasy fiction, with unfinished business calling for a sequel. The trajectory of Seraphina's romance with Kiggs is poised for development in such a sequel, as are the rumbling threats of conflict. But the primary work of the narrative has been to foreground the redefinition of the monster as citizen; as Derrida suggests, the monstrous *arrivant* ushers in new modes of thought, new practices and relationships. At the same time, the novel tracks the identity formation of a hybrid figure as she progresses from self-hatred and shame to self-acceptance; finally Seraphina reflects: 'We were all monsters ..., and we were all beautiful' (358).

Like *Seraphina*, the narration of Carey's novel *Dragon's Keep* takes the form of a first-person account by its human-dragon protagonist.

Whereas *Seraphina* concerns itself with the enmeshing of state and personal politics, *Dragon's Keep* focuses more on the psychological development of Rosalind, the privileged and beautiful daughter of the king and queen of Wilde Island, and her relationship with her mother, Gweneth. The dominant mode of the novel is that of melodrama, exemplified by the highly coloured events of the plot, an over-worded style of narration, a moral scheme in which individuals are definitively good or evil, and a sense that characters are very much larger than life.[19] As Peter Brooks observes in his seminal work *The Melodramatic Imagination* (1976), in melodrama 'life tends … toward ever more concentrated and totally expressive gestures and statements' (1976: 4), building towards climactic scenes which often incorporate legal or quasi-legal public hearings.

The novel is set in the twelfth century, during the civil war between King Stephen and the Empress Matilda, and is based on the conceit that Rosalind is the descendant of Evaine, the younger sister of King Arthur, and is predestined to be the twenty-first queen of Wilde Island. The island is beset by dragon attacks; and Rosalind is consumed with shame over her dragon talon, for which her mother constantly seeks remedies. In *Unruly Girls, Unrepentant Mothers*, Kathleen Rowe Karlyn observes that 'melodrama has long been the primary popular narrative form available for examining mothers and mother–daughter relationships' (2011: 9). The narrative of *Dragon's Keep* turns upon such a relationship; at its core is the revelation that Queen Gweneth resorted to witchcraft in order to conceive Rosalind, and has murdered all those who know her secret or who have seen Rosalind's talon.

The queen's monstrousness derives from her obsessive determination that Rosalind should marry Prince Henry, son of the Empress Matilda. Mother and daughter are at odds on this matter, which comes to its head after Rosalind is abducted by Lord Faul, the dragon leader. Put to work as a drudge, a servant to Faul's progeny, she realises that her talon is the reason why he has not destroyed her. When her mother encounters Lord Faul and demands her daughter's liberation, Rosalind peels off the golden gloves which conceal her talon and tosses them at her mother's feet as 'a flag of peace' (2007: 199). Her mother 'sobbed and fell on her knees. It seemed to me then it would have been a kinder thing to plunge a knife into her heart. This her eyes told me …' (199). The melodramatic mode externalises inner conflicts through extravagant gestures; here the conflict between mother and daughter centres on Rosalind's talon, which signifies disgrace and shame to Gweneth, a portent of dragon–human peace to Rosalind.

Dragon's Keep ends in a set-piece trial in which Rosalind is accused of being a witch. She is forced to walk on hot coals as a test, and when her feet fail to heal she is sent to the gallows, from which she is saved by her lover, Kye, disguised as a Benedictine monk. This sequence, replete with histrionics, reaches a conclusion similar to that of *Seraphina*. The young protagonists, it is implied, are alive to the liberatory meanings of monstrous hybridity, leading their nation states towards a future characterised by mutual respect between species, and the promise of peace. The novel closes with a tableau in which the dragons bow and the people chant as the new queen raises her dragon claw over them: 'My curse – a blessing' (302). The medievalist allusions, settings and characters of *Dragon's Keep* afford a theatrical and spectacular backdrop distanced from the contemporary world but informed by its anxieties about normality and bodily difference.

Were- today, -wolf tomorrow: werewolves and metamorphosis

The monstrous and hybrid figures I have so far discussed are fixed in their monsterhood: the vampire cannot revert to human, the hybrid-dragon to dragon or human, the once-human fairy back to human. Werewolves, in contrast, are subject to metamorphic changes which generally work both ways: from the *were-* (human) to the *wolf* (animal) and back, over and over again. Jeffrey Cohen observes that in medieval literature werewolves inhabit a 'state of unsettled animality' defined by its 'irreducible hybridity, its ethical complexity, and its dispersive instability, pro-animal yet posthuman' (2012: 353). Markers of ambivalence are common, too, in contemporary werewolf texts for the young, which are inflected by modern debates over ecology, race and ethnicity, and concepts of speciesism.

While such concerns shape the treatment of werewolf figures in YA texts, narratives of metamorphosis are peculiarly pertinent to young readers experiencing the bodily changes of puberty. Shelley Chappell notes that 'the connection between metamorphosis and puberty may allow the metamorphosis motif to signify not merely hybridity but maturation or a process of becoming adult' (2007: 38–9). Narratives of werewolf metamorphosis vary according to the versions of lycanthropy to which they adhere, and which Chappell has defined as follows: 'monstrous and sympathetic werewolves, benevolent and idealised werewolves, non-essentialist werewolves, and incommensurable werewolves' (2009: 22). In this discussion I consider Sue Bursztynski's

Wolfborn (2010), which is loosely based on *Bisclavret*, a twelfth-century *lai* (short story in verse) by Marie de France,[20] and the Canadian teen film *Ginger Snaps* (2000), which features a female werewolf.[21] *Wolfborn* adheres, in the main, to the model of the sympathetic werewolf of its pretext; *Ginger Snaps* deploys the werewolf figure to construct a sharp critique of cultural attitudes towards young women, treating the protagonist's transformation into werewolf as a final and irrevocable event.

Marie de France's *Bisclavret* is a complex and evocative story featuring a nobleman living in Brittany, who acts as a proper and worthy knight for four days of the week, but for three days disappears, returning 'happy and delighted' (de France 1978: 92) to his castle. When his wife asks him about these regular absences Bisclavret admits that he is a werewolf, and that he is in the habit of leaving his clothes in the forest prior to his transformation. Devastated at this revelation, she arranges for her husband's clothes to be stolen by a knight who has 'loved her for a long time' (1978: 94). Thus trapped in wolf form, Bisclavret wanders the forest for a year, during which time his wife marries the knight. Eventually the king, out hunting, discovers Bisclavret in wolf form, and is so charmed by his docility and loyalty that Bisclavret becomes a pet at court. When his former wife visits the court Bisclavret attacks her and bites off her nose. She is tortured into confessing her behaviour and Bisclavret's clothes are restored, resulting in his transformation into a knight. His wife and her husband are banished:

> She had several children
> who were widely known
> for their appearance:
> several women of the family
> were actually born without noses,
> and lived out their lives noseless. (1978: 100)

Cohen remarks that the noselessness of the wife's daughters is 'an infinitely repeating historical sign of the misogyny that has limned this tale, with its closing vision of a thoroughly homosocial world' (2012: 356).

The homosociality to which Cohen refers, like the drastic punishment meted out to Bisclavret's wife, is moderated in Bursztynski's novel *Wolfborn*, which is directed to a young adult audience rather than the adult readers implied by Marie de France's *Bisclavret*. The novel's relationship to its pre-text is one of homage or citation rather than adaptation. Hutcheon argues that for the readers of a text, 'adaptation *as adaptation* is unavoidably a kind of intertextuality *if the receiver is acquainted with the adapted text*' (2012: 21, emphasis in original). Since few if any young readers are likely to have come across Marie de France's *Bisclavret*, they are likely to approach *Wolfborn* through the prism of other more recent werewolf fiction and film. Located in a medieval setting, the novel incorporates elements of Celtic and Germanic folklore as well as allusions to the *Satyricon* of Petronius. This melange of references and narratives is grounded in a rite-of-passage narrative involving Etienne, who leaves home and family as a boy to train with Lord Geraint, who approximates to the Bisclavret of Marie de France's *lai*.

The story of Etienne's identity formation propels him towards his own 'coming out' as werewolf. This eventuality is presaged in the novel's Prologue, in which a young boy afflicted with the 'hairy curse' (2010: 2) is executed at the orders of Etienne's father, and also in the opening chapter, when Etienne's mother takes him aside to tell him a secret which he must not pass on to his father: that her great-grandmother's brother was 'hairy. Very hairy … It happens in the best of families' (5). With this knowledge tucked uneasily in his mind, Etienne is not entirely surprised to find that his master Lord Geraint is a werewolf – or that Geraint's former lover, the wise woman Sylvie, and their daughter Jeanne, are likewise werewolves, forming a hunting pack with Geraint during his pleasurable interludes in the forest.

The werewolves in *Wolfborn*, then, experience their animal lives *en famille*; they form a pack isomorphic with human families, are descendants of werewolf ancestors, and while outsiders to human society in their animal forms, as humans they possess aristocratic lineage and close relationships with their kin. They are familiars to the fairy occupants of the forest, unlike the unnatural and murderous baron Dupré, who makes a pact with the evil force known as 'the Dark One' (65) and who becomes a *loup-garou*, hunting down humans as well as the animals of the forest.[22] It is precisely this appetite for anthropophagy which distinguishes Dupré from Lord Geraint and, by extension, from Etienne, whose loyalty is all for Geraint and not for his vain, affected wife Eglantine. This hierarchy of werewolves pits 'natural' lycanthropes – that is, those genetically programmed to become werewolves at puberty – against those, like Dupré, who elect to become wolves in order to achieve their murderous desires.

For all its emphasis on the naturalness of the werewolf condition, *Wolfborn* privileges human over animal in its depiction of werewolves 'trapped' in their lupine forms. Etienne saves Geraint by restoring his clothes to him; later, seeking to deliver Jeanne from her entrapment, he encounters Kernun, the god of the forest, whose intervention is contingent upon Etienne's acceptance of his own werewolf identity: 'She [Jeanne] will have some of your humanity, you some of her wildness, which I think will not harm you at all. You will be partly mine, then, and I protect my own' (273). The novel ends with the dispensation of justice by King Luiz in conjunction with Kernun: Eglantine is packed off to a women's community, while her lover forfeits some of his land; Geraint's marriage to Eglantine is annulled and the way cleared for him to marry Sylvie; and Jeanne and Etienne are betrothed. Far from functioning as monstrous *arrivants* who usher in new practices and identities, the virtuous werewolves of *Wolfborn* are confirmed in their hybridity; King Luiz promises Geraint that in the unlikely event that his people reject him merely because he 'turn[s] into a wolf now and then' (241), he will endow him with a new estate. The hierarchies of power are affirmed and the happy hybrids look forward to lives in which their animality is contained and regulated by their humanness. Their social status (Sylvie and Jeanne, like Etienne and Geraint, are of aristocratic lineage) shields them from the harsh treatment meted out to werewolves of lower status, such as the young man executed in the novel's first chapter.

Wolfborn claims authority through its allusions to medieval narratives and figures which scaffold its construction of a world in which hybrid beings coexist with human, animal and supernatural populations. While this novel incorporates female werewolves (Sylvie and Jeanne) among its lycanthropes, their femaleness is incidental to their lupine states. In *Ginger Snaps*, in contrast, metamorphosis and menstruation are intimately linked in a narrative which deploys the werewolf figure to reflect on the cultural norms which determine how the female body should look and perform. Set in the Canadian suburbs, this film affords a vivid example of Canadian gothic, which, as Cynthia Sugars explains, adapts the gothic to colonial and postcolonial experience 'expressly because the Gothic was tied to the very elements that settlement Canada seemed to be lacking: cultural mythology and historical antiquity' (2014: 4). Devoid of medievalist ruins, graveyards or churches, the blandness of the suburban setting belies a sense of disquiet, a 'form of constitutive haunting' (Sugars 2014: 4).

Ginger Fitzgerald and her younger sister Brigitte attend a high school in the suburb of Bailey Downs. Here they stand out from the other girls for their gothic style and their resolute misanthropy. They defend themselves from the world through clothing which hides their bodies, in what Ernest Mathijs describes as 'a nineteenth-century North-American interpretation of puritanical feminine dress code: a mix of Quaker,

Mennonite, and Pilgrim styles' (2013: 36). The pre-credit sequence of the film introduces the white-bread suburb in which the girls live, showing orderly, conventional rows of houses, tidy streets and yards, children playing hockey. The camera pans to a small boy playing in a sandpit, shovelling sand and patting it down. His face expresses puzzlement at something he discovers in the sand, and when he touches his face a smear of blood is visible. His mother, noticing the blood, investigates and discovers that the object he has picked up is a dismembered dog's paw. The camera then follows her as she snatches up the boy and runs to check the family's dog. Through her eyes we see a trail of body parts and gore leading to the interior of the dog's kennel. This sequence introduces some of the film's key ideas and images: the sense of a Canadian blandness which conceals an ancient horror; violence haunting suburban streets; childhood innocence cruelly violated; narratives filtered through female eyes.

The female eyes in question are those of Ginger and Brigitte, whose intense relationship is exemplified by the pact the sisters made when they were eight, and to which they constantly return: 'Out by sixteen or dead in the scene, but together forever' (2000). The word 'out' might refer to leaving Bailey Downs, or to coming out as lesbian, an ambiguity which lingers at the end of the film. In brief, the film's action involves a werewolf which prowls the suburb, killing pet dogs, and which attacks Ginger because it is attracted by the blood she sheds at the onset of her first period. Infected by the werewolf, she grows hair and a tail and becomes sexually active, infecting her boyfriend, Jason. Brigitte diligently researches werewolf lore, watching old horror films and consulting herbology, until she discovers that the herb monkshood (*Aconitum*) is suggested as an antidote to lycanthropy. However, this remedy is of no avail to Ginger, who becomes sexually active and murderous before she is fully transformed as a lycanthrope. In the final scenes of the film she is killed, impaled on the knife with which Brigitte defends herself.

The sisters' preoccupation with death is foregrounded in the scenes which play as the opening credits roll, showing the two girls staging vignettes of gruesome and unusual suicides and fatal accidents interspersed with Brigitte's polaroid photographs of the vignettes. These scenes modulate into a sequence in which a selection of the photographs are shown to the girls' class as part of a school project under the innocuous title 'Life in Bailey Downs'. At the end the students are silent for a moment before bursting into applause and cat-calls, while their teacher bumbles and stutters, at a loss as to how to respond, finally asking the sisters to see him (separately) in the guidance office after class.

It is the boys in the class who most openly relish these images; Jason asks 'Can we see the ones of Ginger again?', a request ignored by the teacher but greeted by excited applause from the boys. This sequence dramatises the sisters' difference, the boys' delight in objectified female bodies (a common trope in gothic traditions), and the incomprehension of adults, representational strands which permeate the film. The girls' deployment of symbols, clothing and bodily behaviours is calculated to disrupt the insipid normality of Bailey Downs, the euphemisms which surround the bodily changes of menstruation, and the limitations placed on girls and young women. In this sense they anticipate the advent of the monstrous being which gives shape to their fears.

Ginger's first period is an affront, an insult; she complains to Brigitte: 'I just got the curse ... kill yourself to be different and your own body screws you' (2000). Her body is out of her control, like the werewolf's attack. Moreover, the world of Bailey Downs conspires to deny the facts of menstrual bleeding: the supermarket shelves are stacked with 'feminine products' whose pink and mauve packaging falsifies girls' experience; and her mother makes a cake crowned with strawberry icing to celebrate the fact that 'our little girl's a young woman now' (2000). When the sisters visit the school first aid office, the school nurse explains the bodily processes of menstruation in lurid terms: 'a thick, syrupy, voluminous discharge is not uncommon' (2000). But the nurse's most alarming observation concerns the inexorability of the menstrual cycle: 'expect it every twenty-eight days, give or take, for the next thirty years' (2000). Ginger is now on one side of the menstrual divide, Brigitte on the other, so that they can no longer be 'together forever'.

The final scenes of the film take place in the girls' bedroom, formerly a shrine to their mutuality and their difference from others. The basement room, dark and full of shadows, is replete with ghostly images: photographs of the sisters, their childhood drawings, snatches of writing, cross-shaped picture frames. Ginger rampages through this setting, her werewolf musculature far too powerful for Brigitte, who takes refuge between and beneath the plain metal beds where the sisters have slept, where they have renewed their pacts and planned their suicide vignettes. The film ends with Brigitte cradling the dying Ginger, in a gothic space full of artefacts that resemble, but are not, religious icons. The film's gothic elements of excess, monstrosity and foreboding combine feminist with postcolonial treatments of a Canada haunted by ancient beings and troubled by girls' sexuality.

In the narratives I have discussed, medievalist monsters figure bodily difference and the cultural responses it evokes. The fairy and dragon novels discussed in this chapter, taking up some of the narrative features of paranormal romance, play down the monstrosity of their protagonists, although in *Wicked Lovely* and *Lament* they flatter their readers by treating old age as monstrous. The films *Let the Right One In* and *Ginger Snaps* present the most complex treatments of monstrous identities. These texts disrupt binary thinking, requiring a radical reconfiguration of the distinction between normality and monstrosity. The monstrous *arrivants* they depict point to futures just beyond the horizon of the expected and the normal, offering young readers imaginings of new ways of thinking and being. Their deployment of medievalist elements is dispersed and allusive, drawing attention to the potency of ancient narratives in contemporary settings whose blandness and newness conceal but cannot expunge the irruption of monstrous identities.

6
Medievalist Animals and Their Humans

My heading for this chapter, 'Medievalist Animals and Their Humans', nods to Donna Haraway's discussion of companion species which, she says, include a variety of human and non-human relationships and which involve reciprocity: 'Possession – property – is about reciprocity and rights of access. If I have a dog, my dog has a human; what this means is concretely at stake' (2003: 53–4). As I have argued throughout this book, imaginings of the Middle Ages for the young conjure up a world which reflects, mediates and transforms modernity. This tendency is particularly prominent in texts which address relations between humans and animals in the Middle Ages, many of which incorporate the reciprocal engagement to which Haraway alludes.

Such texts proceed from the supposition that for modern children, especially those living in urban settings, there exists a vast gap between animals and animal products. Modern forms of consumption treat these products as commodities – high-fashion belts; trays of chicken thighs; leather boots; woollen garments – which bear little or no relationship to the actual animals whose bodies have been harvested or used to produce these products. Countering these practices, texts set in the Middle Ages imagine the medieval as a time and place where humans were cognisant of what they owed to animals – even, perhaps, specific animals – for the food and products which enabled their survival.

A further impetus to revisionings of human–animal relations in medievalist texts lies in the assumption that modern children experience minimal contact with animals apart from those they encounter as pets. Texts set in the Middle Ages, in comparison, often represent medieval people and animals living in close proximity as they share living and working spaces. Further, representations of chivalric and military practices, especially in historical fiction, inevitably entail descriptions of the horses, dogs and hawks which enable these practices and participate in them, and of the human–animal relationships which they involve.

Throughout this book I have emphasised that my intention is to examine how the medieval functions in texts for the young. The matter of animal–human relations in such texts comprises a particularly slippery field of signification, since conceptions of animal rights and welfare seem to derive from post-Enlightenment understandings of subjectivity which emphasise what human and non-human animals have in common. The fact that medievalist texts for the young frequently advocate relationships of mutuality and powerful affection between humans and animals is, then, readily explained as another manifestation of *present past* interpretations which treat the Middle Ages as a romanticised pre-industrial past when humans directly experienced the natural world.

But this is too simple an explanation, relying as it does on a clear break between medieval and modern perspectives of relations between humans and animals. Instead, as Susan Crane observes, 'Thought about animals was as complex, diverse, and even contradictory in medieval centuries as it is today' (2013: 126). Discussing the animal trials which took place during the Middle Ages (and continued until the eighteenth century), Bruce Holsinger refers to Luc Ferry's argument that the animal trials are 'indicative of a premodern, which is to say a prehumanistic, relationship to the animal kingdom as well as to nature in general' (1995: xiii). Holsinger concludes that these trials 'represent a provocative (if oblique) prehistory of animal rights that relates in intriguing ways to the more recent past of the subject' (2009: 618).[1]

In reaching for ways of representing interspecies engagements, medievalist texts for the young often embody resistant readings of modernity. I do not argue that these texts knowingly return to or draw upon 'medieval' modes of thought and affect in regard to human–animal relations; rather, imaginings of the medieval in texts for the young seem to chime, on the one hand, with pre-modernity's 'fascination with life on earth' (Fradenburg 2012: 28), and on the other with what Erica Fudge describes as a central tenet of animal studies: 'to acknowledge and engage with animals as active presences in the world' (2012: 87).

Many medievalist texts for the young move away from or resist anthropocentric treatments of animal behaviour which assume that animals derive value only from their utility to humans, as objects and never subjects. Instead, these texts often treat animals as agents, active participants in social networks. Bruno Latour's formulation of actor-network theory (ANT) offers a productive way of thinking about textual animals as 'active presences' which are not necessarily attributed with human subjectivity. A network in Latour's version of ANT is 'a concept, not a thing out there. It is a tool to help describe something, not what is being described' (2005: 131). Humans, animals, inanimate beings, architecture and texts participate in social networks, mediating communication and producing effects such as power and inequality. Latour characterises the text as a 'laboratory', a 'precious little institution to present, or more exactly to re-represent – that is, to present *again* – the social to all its participants, to *perform* it, to give it a form' (139). As Rita Felski observes, Latour's ANT incorporates an understanding of the social world in which 'actors only become actors via their relations with other phenomena, as mediators and translators linked in extended constellations of cause and effect' (2011: 583). In this sense, texts for the young do not merely comment on the times in which they are produced or those in which they are set (for my purposes, imaginings of the medieval), but enable myriad connections between contemporary readers and fictive worlds in which past and present meet. Latour's conceptualisation of the alliances, networks and exchanges which exist between humans and non-humans is taken up by Jane Bennett in *The Enchantment of Modern Life*, to which I referred in Chapter 1. In this chapter I draw upon Bennett's discussion of 'the enchanting effect of interspecies and intraspecies crossings' (2001: 17), including engagements between human and non-human animals.

Intimate relations

When the girl known as Brat is introduced in Karen Cushman's *The Midwife's Apprentice* (1995), she has taken refuge in a smelly, 'rotting and moiling' (1) dung heap which offers her a crucial benefit: warmth. The waste matter of the dung heap originates from animals and plants, comprising a combination of 'animal droppings and garbage and spoiled straw' (1) in which bacteria, microbes and invertebrates break down organic matter, producing the life-sustaining warmth which Brat needs during a cold winter's night. Two forms of abjection meet in this scene: the discarded or eliminated products of humans and animals; and Brat herself, a young girl on the edge of puberty whose life has so far comprised a history of rejection or not-knowing, since she has no memory of home or parents but only of the strategies which have enabled her to survive, one day at a time.

Latour defines an 'actor' as 'an entity that modifies another entity' (2004: 237). In this sense the dung heap might be regarded as one actor and Brat as another, the two modifying each other as Brat burrows into the steaming heap. As I have suggested, both Brat and the dung heap can be read as abject entities; but more importantly for the narrative of *The Midwife's Apprentice*, Brat derives material benefit from the animal and human waste which provide her with warmth. That is, the network produced through Brat's self-insertion in the dung heap consists of human and non-human entities connected because of Brat's drive for survival. Another component of the network comprises implied readers of *The Midwife's Apprentice*, young (probably female) readers whose experience of the world will almost certainly not include dung heaps where young girls might find a warm haven during a cold night. Rather, Brat's deployment of the dung heap is likely to appear to young readers as a sign of a disgusting and filthy Middle Ages defined by a lack of hygiene and of social support for orphaned children. Given the durability and popularity of narratives based on a rags-to-riches script, Brat's abjection at the beginning of the novel sets up expectations of a personal transformation of some kind.

The name 'Brat' derives from the girl's internalisation of her inferiority, deduced from her encounters with other humans. The next name bestowed on her, Beetle (as in dung beetle), is again the product of unequal relations between the girl and others: in this case a group of boys who tease her because they are 'the scrawniest or the ugliest or the dirtiest or the stupidest' (3) and who look for a victim lower in the pecking order. The name is taken up by Jane Sharp, the midwife, who recognises in Brat/Beetle a lackey whom she can use and abuse at will. Yet if we adopt Latour's approach and consider how actors create relationships with fellow actors, it is also the case that Jane provides Beetle with sustenance, shelter and an education, consisting of training in herbs and their uses, household management, and the practices of midwifery.

The actor who most interests me here is the cat, orange with a patch of white, who observes Beetle from his vantage point at the fence post near the river. Beetle leaves food for the cat when she can, but he has his own survival strategies which appear to afford effective protection from the village boys until the day when they stuff him into a sack, together with an eel, and throw the sack into the pond to see which of the two will survive, cat or eel. Beetle, 'more afraid to attract the taunts and torments of the boys than to lose the cat' (8), hides until the boys have gone, when she rescues the cat, barely alive, from the pond, and deposits him in a hollow in the dung heap with some scraps of cheese. When she returns to check on him she finds that the cat has disappeared, to return two days later, at his usual post: 'Finally Beetle came and they sat and ate their cheese together ... And Beetle told him what she could remember of her life before they found each other, and they fell asleep in the sun' (10).

As Bennett observes, Latour 'rejects the categories of "nature" and "culture" in favor of the "collective," which refers to an ecology of human and nonhuman elements' (2010: 103). *The Midwife's Apprentice* can be read as just such an ecology, in which Beetle and the cat are actors who form a connection resulting from the random presence of both, and their movement (physical and emotional) towards each other. It is of course the case, as Philip Armstrong notes, that 'humans can only represent animals' experience through the mediation of cultural encoding, a reshaping according to our own intentions, attitudes and preconceptions' (2008: 2–3). Nevertheless, *The Midwife's Apprentice* treats the cat with a careful detachment, as if seeking to avoid an anthroponormative interpretation of the animal. When Beetle is unfairly blamed because Jane Sharp will not assist women who cannot pay her fees, she complains to the cat, who 'listened and sometimes rubbed his head on her legs in sympathy' (1995: 14). The expression 'in sympathy' departs from the novel's more usual treatment of Beetle's relationship with the cat, since the narrative does not often project human emotions and motives onto his actions. The fact that this moment of attributed sympathy is unusual in the novel suggests a kind of textual struggle over the representation of animals.

The episode when Beetle gives the cat a name incorporates a playful reflexiveness which captures something of this struggle. Beetle attends the fair to purchase spices for the midwife, and when a fair-goer mistakes her for someone called Alyce she decides that Beetle is 'no name for a person' (1995: 31) and resolves to call herself Alyce. This agential self-naming prods her into contemplating a name for the cat, and she experiments with a variety of possibilities, including Purslane, Gypsy Moth, Lentil, Bryony, Millstone, Dartmoor, Holly and Fleecy. When she experiments by addressing the cat by these names, the cat merely stares. Finally Beetle attends to what the cat says:

> The cat wound himself around Beetle's ankle and purred. 'Columbine? Cuttlefish?'
> 'Purr,' the cat responded.
> 'Clotweed? Shrovetide? Wimble?'
> 'Purr,' the cat responded.
> 'Horsera-'
> 'Purr,' the cat demanded.
> 'Purr?' Beetle asked.
> 'Purr,' the cat responded. And that was that. (35)

This exchange does not, of course, imply that Purr is a talking cat but rather that he is an actor in the ecology of the text, that his motivations are unknown to Beetle, and that the appropriate way to behave towards a non-human actor is to attend to the signs he affords, respecting his autonomy.

As Beetle/Alyce gains knowledge and skills she becomes known to the villagers as a midwife rather than merely the midwife's servant. When Emma Blunt calls for her, rather than for Jane Sharp, to deliver her baby, Alyce does not possess the experience required for a protracted and complicated labour, and at length is obliged to call for the midwife, who sees the labour through. After this humiliating experience Alyce runs away from the village to 'she knew not where. And the cat went with her' (71). When Alyce walks on, cold, hungry and homeless, 'the cat stalked behind, stomach empty and feet wet, but unwilling to let Alyce go on without him' (73). The intentionality of the cat is embodied in his actions; he could, after all, return to the village where he survived before associating himself with Alyce. Later, the cat becomes a mediator (Latour 2005: 40) when Alyce is befriended by Magister Richard Reese, a scholar who is a guest at the inn where she has found work, and who is engaged in writing 'an encyclopaedic compendium' called 'The Great Mirror of the Universe' (1995: 78). Alyce is too shy and unconfident to take up Magister Reese's offer of tuition, so that the scholar devises the fiction that he is teaching the cat to read, while Alyce listens: 'The cat listened carefully, although sometimes he lost patience with the tutoring and began to bite at the tantalizingly moving pen' (78). This playful characterisation of the cat as pupil is folded within the larger fact of his presence during Alyce's self-imposed banishment from the village.

When she returns to the midwife's cottage Jane at first refuses to take her back. Alyce turns from the village, intending to run away again, but the cat will not leave: 'Purr laid himself down, tucked his front paws under the white spot on his chest, and looked at her with his gooseberry eyes' (116). The cat is, in Fudge's words, an 'active presence' in the world of the text (2012); his gaze, like that of the cat Derrida discusses in his lecture 'The Animal That Therefore I Am', is direct and 'insistent' (Derrida 2002: 372). Derrida remarks that the question of 'the said animal in its entirety comes down to knowing not whether the animal speaks but whether one can know what *respond* means. And how to distinguish a response from a reaction' (377). Alyce chooses not to leave the village, taking the cat's purr as meaningful: 'Corpus bones, you are right, cat!' (1995: 116). But in fact the gaze of the cat, and his purring, do not allow themselves to be encapsulated into a meaning such as 'You should stay!' Rather, Alyce shows herself to be agential and determined, using the cat's gaze as confirmation of what she has decided: that she will return to the midwife's cottage and tell her that she knows 'how to try and risk and fail and try again and not give up' (1995: 117). As a narrative device Purr comprises an audience for Alyce's words, providing readers with access to her debates with herself over how she should be and what she should do. The cat thus performs narrative functions, but he is not merely a projection of Alyce's emotions and desires, but is an actor within the network of the novel, since 'if an actor makes no difference, it's not an actor' (Latour 2005: 130). Like Derrida's cat, he troubles the boundaries between human and animal.

Arthur de Caldicot, the protagonist and first-person narrator of Kevin Crossley-Holland's Arthur trilogy,[2] occupies a place at the other end of the social spectrum from Alyce, and his interactions with the horse Bonamy are inflected by his duties as a squire. The trilogy combines historical fiction with Arthurian stories, its framing narrative tracing the progress of Arthur de Caldicot from a page to a young knight. In *The Seeing Stone* (2000), Merlin gives Arthur de Caldicot a piece of obsidian in which he first sees himself reflected, and then observes episodes from the Arthuriad, which obliquely relate to his own life. At the end of this novel Arthur learns two things: that he is to go into service as squire to Lord Stephen de Holt, accompanying him on the Fourth Crusade; and that Arthur is not, as he has always believed, the son of Sir John and Lady Helen de Caldicot but of Sir John's older brother, Sir William de Gortanore, by a woman living on William's manor. These events turn the narrative towards what Susan Crane refers to as 'the medieval subculture of chivalry' (2011: 83) in which the horse is central to the two 'defining acts of chivalry, warfare and adventure' (81).

What is very clear at the beginning of *At the Crossing-Places* (2001), the second novel of the trilogy, is that the knight's horse forms part of a chivalric economy. Sir William, Arthur's father, is to pay for his armour and arms, his foster-father Sir John will pay for his horse, and his employer, Lord Stephen, will pay for the horse's upkeep. Inducted into this web of obligations and reciprocities, Arthur is made to understand that the horse is both a thing and a sentient creature. Lord Stephen tells him that the warhorse is 'a piece of equipment, and like all your other equipment he must be well-made and strong and a good fit. But a destrier is also your friend. He'll travel with you, sometimes sleep next to you. If you cherish him, he'll protect you and even lay down his life for you' (2001: 43). A multiplicity of actors, present and absent, contribute to the sequence in which Arthur chooses his horse from the three colts bred by the Welsh horse breeders he visits with Lord

Stephen. These actors include the knights with whom he is enmeshed by familial and chivalric ties and the horse breeders whose Welshness reminds Lord Stephen of past conflicts between English and Welsh in the Marches. Arthur's choice is treated as a moment of ceremony which speaks to chivalric and dynastic networks.

But the trilogy's revisioning of the heroic ideal also incorporates a *present past* reconfiguration of masculinity, in which Arthur is a relatively conventional modern boy[3] who loves writing and solitary thought, enjoys the companionship of the farm-girl Gatty, and is intuitive about the emotions of others. His selection of a destrier discloses both his reverence for tradition and also the emotional lability which characterises him throughout the trilogy: 'His eyes were like ripe damsons, and a silver-white star shone on his forehead; his coat was the colour of a horse-chestnut as it breaks out of its spiky shell, gleaming like silk. I gazed at him, he gazed at me, and that was the moment we made up our minds' (42). Lord Stephen, watching on, compares this meeting to 'love at first sight' (42); like Derrida with his cat, and Alyce with hers, Arthur and the horse gaze at each other, his description of its eyes and colouring conjuring up a moment of enchantment. But this moment soon gives way to a reminder of the economic and material implications of Arthur's choice, as the breeders talk of pedigrees, take the horse's measurements, and negotiate with Lord Stephen over price.

These signals that the horse is 'a piece of equipment' fitted to the requirements of war and adventure shape the novel's treatment of the relationship between boy and horse, creating a dense web of ideas, actors and images. Alyce and Purr are alone in the world and their relationship is shaped by their daily routines and interactions. In comparison, Arthur's life is lived in crowded environments: a large manor house or castle; the throng of crusaders and servants undertaking the Holy War of crusade. He is almost always observed, kindly or not, by a lord, fellow squire or servant; his choice of a horse is, then, a social act as much as a personal decision so that, in Latour's terms, a 'plurality of associations' (2005: 139) complicates human–animal relations. Arthur's choice of a name for his horse, Bonamy, is telling. He explains to the groom Rhys that the name is French for 'good friend …. And that's what he'll be when we're crusading' (2001: 78). The doubleness of the horse's function is here evident: he is to be both Arthur's friend and also a piece of equipment fit for the chivalric self.

As I have noted, Arthur is self-reflective and imaginative. His love of language and poetry manifests in the names by which he addresses Bonamy when Lord Stephen's party is in London before crossing the

English Channel: 'oat-guzzler, London-destrier, channel-crosser' (2001: 328).[4] The enjoyment Arthur derives from gaining Bonamy's trust is, however, vitiated by the realities of war. During the third novel of the trilogy, *King of the Middle March* (2003), the narrative traces Arthur's growing disillusionment with the failures of ethics he observes on both sides of the conflict. When a small boy is brutally and publicly murdered by Lord Stephen's French allies, Arthur is traumatised. His groom Rhys tells him that his 'moping was troubling everyone' (2003: 207) and that 'even if I was no use to other men, I could be of use to my beast, and I should exercise him' (208). Arthur finds solace in Bonamy's presence, reflecting on their friendship: 'My hoof-weaver! My trail-blazer!' (208). But the horse senses Arthur's distress and rears up, throwing Arthur to the ground and then butting him and licking his face. Bonamy's actions are mysterious to Arthur: 'Bonamy, you've never done that before' (208). Yet the palpable differences between boy and horse – on Arthur's side, despondency manifested in 'moping', on Bonamy's, the act of rearing followed by the horse's affectionate nuzzling – expose the strangeness of each to the other, emphasising the limitations of cross-species communication.

When Arthur's father, Sir William, dies in a drunken fight and Lord Stephen is seriously wounded, Arthur carries out his duties to his lord and escorts him back to England. This decision means that Arthur must leave Bonamy with the remaining English forces in the city of Zara. He is desolate at the prospect: 'Poor Bonamy!' I cried. But really, I meant poor me' (282). Arthur's love for Bonamy, he says, 'is so simple. So blessed' (288). But this account of the connection between human and non-human actors conflicts with Arthur's consciousness of the complexity of a world where animals constitute part of the machinery of battle. When he observes warfare in his stone, it seems 'quick and clean, almost painless, not foul and excruciating. Right fights against wrong. But really it's nothing like as simple as that' (315).

Arthur's loss of Bonamy when he returns with Lord Stephen to England is thus the price he pays for restitution to a more comprehensible and simple world where he is reunited with his horse Pip, left behind when Arthur departed Holt for the crusade. Bonamy and Pip resemble the obverse and reverse of a coin: Bonamy the warhorse, Pip the companion; Bonamy the destrier, Pip the palfrey, both animals ascribed signification and purpose by the social worlds of which they are part. If dealings between human and non-human actors are generally informed throughout the trilogy by the principle of human ascendancy over animals, the relationship of Arthur and Bonamy is infused with the ambiguity which derives from the combination of *present past* imaginings of the Middle Ages, and contemporary ideas about relations between human and non-human animals.

The narrating animal

The companion animals I have so far discussed, Purr and Bonamy, are represented through the perspectives of humans; in *The Midwife's Apprentice* that of the narrator and the focalising character of Alyce; in the Arthur trilogy through Arthur's first-person narration. Henrietta Branford's *Fire, Bed & Bone* (1998) takes the less usual approach of narration by an animal, the hunting dog known only as 'the old dog'. Anna Sewell's *Black Beauty* (1877) is the best-known animal autobiography for the young, one of many such texts published during the long nineteenth century (Cosslett 2006: 63–92). These nineteenth-century novels are set in the times and places where they are produced, whereas *Fire, Bed & Bone* locates its characters in the fourteenth century, against the backdrop of the 1381 Uprisings.[5]

Like historical fiction for children more generally, *Fire, Bed & Bone* foregrounds the experience of those marginal to systems of power and government, subaltern populations comprising the poor and especially children. The dog narrator might, then, be expected to be doubly subaltern, except that the novel takes pains to imagine the world from her point of view, including her observations of humans. She lives with Rufus and Comfort, whose home is a meeting place for those agitating against taxes, laws and government. Plotted against seasonal change, the action of the novel begins with the birth of the dog's pups and concludes two years later. During this time the dog observes the imprisonment of Rufus and Comfort; later, the execution of Rufus, who has taught her to hunt and to whom she is powerfully attached. She is captured and forced to hunt for the man who appropriates Comfort's home; after her escape she lives in the forest, returning when Comfort is restored to her cottage.

The dog's perspective is conveyed through its focus on the odoriferous world in which she lives, the bodily experience of hunting and eating her prey, and her intimate knowledge of place. She is amusingly scornful of the cat, Humble, whose allegiances to humans are determined by who feeds her, and she is a close observer of the worlds she inhabits:

> I am a creature of several worlds. I know the house and the village and have my place in both. I know the pastureland beyond the great

field. I know the wildwood. I know the wetlands all along the river, where every green leaf that you step on has a different smell. I know the high, dry heath. (1998: 2)

This outline of the worlds the dog occupies sketches the various and overlapping networks in which she is an actor. It names places (house, village, pastureland, wildwood, wetlands, heath) which traverse human and animal habitations, treating spatiality as the organising principle of her life as a 'creature of several worlds'. Hierarchies of place (Rufus and Comfort's cottage compared to the manor house or the priest's residence) have no meaning for her apart from her associations with animals and humans. Nor are humans privileged over animals (which, however, does not imply that the old dog does not make judgements about particular humans on the basis of their behaviour towards Rufus, Comfort and their three children).

The narrative filters its account of the Uprisings through the old dog's perspective as she relays what she hears, sees and smells, acting as an observer with no personal investment in politics. In an episode during which Rufus, Comfort and their friends discuss John Ball, the old dog reflects, 'For myself, I did not care which side was which, nor what King Richard might do about it. My place was with Rufus' (57–8). Her wariness of humans, learned over a lifetime of experience, locates her at a critical distance from the events of the uprisings. The rebels hear news of a royal pardon promised by the young Richard II, and imagine a transformed society in which the poor will farm their own land, free from the imposition of taxes. Rufus asks Comfort, 'Can it be true, do you think?', to which she replies, 'It must be, Rufus, if the king says so.' The old dog recalls, 'I did not believe it. But I am only a dog' (62–3). This mocking self-deprecation is juxtaposed against a sequence in which Rufus and Comfort return to the village only to experience the same conditions that they previously endured. The old dog turns out to possess a surer sense than Rufus and Comfort of the weight of economic and social practices which maintain power and privilege.

Tess Cosslett observes that nineteenth-century animal autobiographies commonly end with 'a peaceful rural retirement with sympathetic owners' (2006: 89) without whose support these animals could not survive, since they can enjoy no life 'outside human ownership' (91). This style of narrative closure in which docile, dependent animals rely on benevolent humans is entirely absent from *Fire, Bed & Bone*. The old dog returns to her human family towards the end of the novel not because she needs the company of Comfort and her children and a warm place by the fire, but because Comfort needs her. Having lost her holding, Comfort has been fined for grinding corn at home, and has been obliged to pay funeral costs to the priest; her two young sons are exploited by the miller as child labourers. The old dog leads the boys to safety during a violent storm in which the miller falls to his death in the river, and subsequently Comfort regains her house. Throughout the novel the old dog moves between and across the 'several worlds' to which she refers at the beginning of the narrative. In doing so she exemplifies the agentive networks described by Latour, networks which are 'collective because they attach us to one another, because they circulate in our hands and define our social bond by their very circulation' (1993: 89). These networks override distinctions between culture and nature, human and non-human, since they incorporate 'bodies and souls, property and law, gods and ancestors, powers and beliefs, beasts and fictional beings' (107).

The old dog is attuned, as the humans in the novel are not, to echoes and memories of the archaic human and non-human inhabitants of the round stone tower where Rufus and Comfort take refuge following the execution of John Ball. More accurately, she smells the traces of their ancient presence 'but faintly, like an old scent left long ago' (1998: 71); and she hears vestiges of their voices. The dog observes these 'shadow people' (71) at twilight, and witnesses their demise when they are attacked by 'the newcomers' (72), who kill adults and children, 'them and their dogs. Even the small boy on his sister's lap. Even the sister. The old bitch and her puppies' (72–3). The dog's access to these stories of resistance and displacement are swiftly transmuted to an anticipatory vision of Rufus, 'my Rufus, standing in air, his feet high above the ground' (73), which prefigures his execution. Her vision of Rufus's death, triggered by the scents and sounds of the shadow people, positions young readers to attend to the continuities and discontinuities of local and national histories.

The novel begins when the dog selects the place where she will give birth to the litter of pups born just before the Uprisings; it ends with a roll-call of litters, recalling the pups she has lost to wildcats, those who have died, those she has raised to adulthood. The narrative is punctuated by the old dog's engagement with human children as well: her protection and care of Comfort and Rufus's two boys and their daughter Alice, and of the red-headed baby born following Rufus's death. As she lies in the yard, listening to Comfort, the dog hears 'messages from the past', those of the 'small, plump wrigglers and scrawny squabblers, wet-nosed nuzzlers, blind-eyed, wet-furred, helpless scraps' (116) she has nurtured. Her principal human allegiance has been to Rufus, through an investment in time and mutuality: 'It takes time for a dog and a man to fit together and it takes time for them to part' (93). The vision of human–animal relations proposed in this novel does not involve polarities, since 'the human is not a constitutional pole to be opposed to that of the nonhuman' (Latour 1993: 137). Rather, the old dog's story is one of intricately connected networks in which identities and affective relations are interwoven.

Magical and metaphorical creatures

In the texts I have so far discussed, cultural formations are inflected by the material presence of animals as they interact with and influence humans. The enchanting possibilities of what Bennett refers to as *crossings* are also at play in various modes of medievalist fantasy in which animal bodies take on shapes and properties which exceed or transform what is taken to be normal. Metaphorical treatments of animals evoke a more problematic set of ideas, since as Susan McHugh notes, the 'aesthetic structures of metaphor, though precariously supporting the human subject, seem unable to bear animal agency' (2009: 488). We might, for instance, wonder what to make of Tamora Pierce's deployment of canine metaphors in her Beka Cooper series, whose eponymous protagonist progresses from Puppy to Dog as she trains to become a member of the Provost Guard in the kingdom of Tortall.[6] In this series the world of trainees and fully-fledged guards who patrol the streets of Corus is replete with dog metaphors, from their guard stations (kennels) to street names (Mutt Piddle Lane) and woven through their conversations. Not only are canine metaphors integral to Beka's identity as a trainee Guard, but real animals are everywhere in Corus, including the four-legged dogs who accompany two-legged Dogs on their round. In the Lower City, where Beka carries out her duties, pigs, dogs and cats, horses and mules frequent the streets and pigeons hunt out food. Then there are animals which possess magical abilities, notably Pounce, Beka's purple-eyed cat,[7] and the pigeons which serve the Black God of death and which carry the spirits of the dead who have not yet entered the 'Peaceful Realms' (2006: 76). As well, dust spinners, eddies of air which gather dust, debris and leaves, accumulate snatches of talk by humans and pass these on to Beka, whose access to the language of animals and dust spinners is inherited from her father.

This assortment of hybrid beings – humans who compare themselves to animals, magical animals and particles of matter – is drawn together under the sign of the medieval, residing in the novel's evocation of a hierarchical and ordered political structure, its emphasis on heroics, swordplay and hand-to-hand combat, and its references to paranormal and magical events, especially those involving Beka. As Beka embarks on the trajectory of her emotional and psychological development she attracts beings (cat, pigeons, dust spinners) which transit from one state to another. She is herself at odds with the hierarchical social world of Tortall, which is structured by ranks and orders: royalty, knights, provost guards, and citizen populations whose class status is defined by the districts they inhabit, from the aristocratic precincts of Highfields and Prettybone to the crime-ridden Lower City. In *Terrier* (2006), the first novel of Pierce's trilogy, animal metaphors distinguish the Dogs of the Provost Guard from the Rats (criminals) they pursue. But the figure of Beka transgresses this distinction, since she grew up as a child in the Lower City and possesses associations and habits at odds with the culture of the Dogs of the Provost Guard.

Beka's partners and mentors, Clara Goodwin and Matthias Tunstall, are charged with training her as a Dog, including rules of deportment and language. When Beka uses the language of the Lower City to chase away children who swarm around her begging for money, Clara Goodwin reprimands her: 'Don't talk Cesspool cant anymore. You're a Dog, not a Rat' (2006: 93). Goodwin's disapproval is symptomatic of her adherence to hierarchical distinctions between groups. However, the narrative disrupts these social hierarchies by foregrounding Beka's attachment to the Lower City, and the strategic advantages which accrue from her familiarity with the people and practices of this stigmatised precinct of Corus. As Goodwin's reprimand 'You're a Dog, not a Rat' indicates, animal metaphors in *Terrier* divide between positive and negative conceptions of animality. Whereas canine metaphors draw on assumptions about the dog's status as man's best friend, rat metaphors evoke notions of rats as vermin and as definitively other to humans. Whether positive or negative, the animal metaphors of *Terrier* occlude reference to actual animals, since they always use the animal to produce ideas about humans.[8]

The novel's treatment of magical animals and beings takes a more complex approach to animality. Beka's cat Pounce moves across social hierarchies, ingratiating himself with Goodwin and Cooper, and accompanying Beka's team on their rounds. He is at once cat and mage, charming Beka against her will, advising her in language which only she can understand, warning her of danger. The enchanting effects of the novel's treatment of Pounce derive in large part from the double-edged games he plays. To Beka's friends Aniki and Kora he masquerades as a conventional cat, purring when they stroke him. At the same time he complains to Beka: 'Pounce muttered in cat. At least, Aniki and Kora heard it so. Aniki petted and admired him for being "such a talky little pippin". I heard, *Humans. Always getting ideas and interrupting important business with them at the stupidest times*' (182). Pounce's capacity to communicate with Beka is matched by her ability to comprehend his language, constructing a relationship built partly on their shared history, partly on the magical abilities they both possess. As in *The Midwife's Apprentice*, the cat functions as a narrative device. In the novel's final scene, Beka is obliged to report to the Magistrate's Court on her identification of the Shadow Snake, the person responsible for terrorising the Lower City by abducting and killing children. Pounce leaps on her shoulder as she approaches the court, scolding her: *'Calm down, will you? It will be over soon and then you can find a rock to hide under'* (557). The narrative uses the cat's reassurance to disclose Beka's anxieties, anticipating her successful court appearance and the approbation of the Dogs and citizens of Corus. Crossing between material cat and magical being, Pounce performs cat-ness, offering humans the qualities they desire in a cat: aloofness or affection, amusing antics or a dignified stillness.

The pigeons that serve the Black God carry the fears and sorrows of humans who occupy a liminal space between life and the 'Peaceful Realms' of death; in particular, those who have died violently and suddenly. The white pigeon which carries the spirit of Rolond, a small boy kidnapped and killed by the Shadow Snake, has undergone a kind of crossing between bird and human which is evident to Beka but not to other humans; Beka proves to be remarkably attuned to the unresolved grief of humans enmeshed in traumatic events, including her friend Tansy, Rolond's mother. In a scene where the white pigeon visits Beka and Tansy, they hear Rolond's voice as he details the events of his kidnapping and death. What is absent from this episode is a sense of the pigeon's being as pigeon; rather, the bird is prey to the ghost who rides him, and so to Tansy's anger and confusion as she blames the bird for her son's entrapment in the liminal space between life and the Peaceful Realms. It falls to Beka to persuade Rolond's ghost and Tansy to assent to their separation from each other.

The animals in *Terrier* circulate, then, within an anthropocentric framework in which their capacities and functions enhance Beka's self-determination. Pounce is, in effect, Beka's more assured alter ego, articulating the selfhood to which she aspires; and the pigeon ghost-carriers endow her with a significance which derives from her access to the spirit world, an access mediated by these birds. Pounce and the pigeons thus serve the cause of Beka's emergence as a hero. The dust spinners Aveefa, Hasfush and Shiaa are the most agential of Beka's non-human companions, conjuring up what Latour calls 'flip-flop', the capacity of objects to be 'at once compatible with social skills ... and then totally foreign to any human repertoire of action' (2005: 194). They gather up matter (dust, leaves, debris) and the utterances of humans, 'songs, fights, whingeing, laughter, baby wails and giggles, whispers' (2006: 335), which they pass on to Beka. The names Aveefa, Hasfush and Shiaa are sharply differentiated from the Western-associated names of Beka and her family and companions – for instance, Matthias, Clara, Verene, Diona, Lorine. This suggestion of a foreignness identified as 'oriental' alludes to the strangeness of the spinners, whose lineage stretches back over their long presence in Corus, and their previous associations with generations of Beka's family. The mediating presence of the spinners, intriguing and mysterious, seems to enable a sense of the 'masses of entities [which] circulate' (Latour 2005: 196) in places inhabited by humans. In contrast, the animals of *Terrier* are represented in line with discourses of animality which play to human/non-human binaries.

The medievalism of *Terrier* resides in its treatment of the government of Tortall, the quest structure of its narrative, and its magical and paranormal figures. In Rosemary Sutcliff and Emma Chichester Clark's picture book *The Minstrel and the Dragon Pup* (1993), Clark's illustrations, drawing upon Italian art of the fifteenth century, evoke a medievalist world offset by Sutcliff's ironic and playful text. The prologue establishes a matter-of-fact and authoritative narrative perspective which both foregrounds romance traditions and gently mocks them. The narrative tells of a she-dragon which lays three eggs near a cliff-top and sits on them in order to hatch them. A knight on a white horse comes by, certain in the knowledge that 'it was the duty of all good knights to kill any dragons they met with' (6). The she-dragon, however, is loathe to fight, having eggs on her mind, and she runs away from the dragon, accidentally tipping one of the eggs over the cliff and onto a beach where it is discovered by a passing minstrel. Having shaken off the knight and his horse, the she-dragon returns to her eggs, oblivious to the fact that only two remain: 'dragons cannot count very well, so she never noticed the loss' (7).

The minstrel notices that the egg is hatching and invents a melody to help the process. In brief, he befriends the dragon pup, whom he calls Lucky, taking him on the road until the young dragon is abducted by a travelling showman who exploits Lucky as an attraction. The minstrel searches for him, arriving at a great city whose king owns a kind of zoo of monstrous creatures such as wyverns and griffins. Here the minstrel discovers Lucky, languishing miserably in the cage which he has occupied since the king's beast-master purchased him from the showman. The king's son is ill, trapped in a coma-like condition; the minstrel saves him by playing the melody he invented to invite the dragon from its shell, and the king frees Lucky, issuing a royal proclamation which places the minstrel and the dragon under royal protection.

Throughout this sequence of events the text treats the dragon's relationship with the minstrel as entirely unremarkable. Readers are disabused of the idea that dragons are 'as big as houses ... and fire-breathing fierce by nature'. Rather, the text explains that they 'only stand about as high as a Shetland pony' (11) when fully grown, and that their vaunted fierceness is simply a matter of training. These tongue-in-cheek observations are coupled with close descriptions of the dragon's appearance: 'It had green goose-pimply skin and a long tail, and two little flapping things rather like small damp kid gloves that were the promise of wings on its back, and a round pink stomach' (11). Clark's illustrations adopt a larger perspective, locating the minstrel and the dragon in natural and social spaces. In one illustration the two lie together in a clearing fringed by palm trees, on the shore of a river. The dragon lies on his back while the minstrel rubs his belly, the faces of minstrel and dragon suggesting a moment of enchanted accord in a utopian space which seems to welcome the interspecies relationship of minstrel and dragon.

The cultural and economic imperatives which threaten this relationship are visible in an illustration depicting the interior of a village inn, where the dragon sits under a table, his bowl in front of him, while the minstrel eats his supper at the table. The scene is shown from the perspective of an observer (the showman) whose vision takes in the minstrel and the dragon, marked out by the play of light on the floor where the dragon sits. As well, we see the bystanders who watch the dragon, including a mother and child who lean forward to catch a view of him. The posture of the bystanders suggests curiosity, constructing the dragon as an exotic spectacle which attracts the attention of villagers and, in a more sinister sense, that of the showman who registers their interest and imagines the possibility of gaining income from his abduction of the dragon. The enchantment evoked by the interspecies accord of dragon and minstrel is undermined both by the villagers' suspicion of the dragon's otherness, and by the mercantile ambitions of the showman.

Clark's illustrations present as a series of pictures, each framed to stand out from the black ground of the page. This strategy creates the impression of a moment suspended in time, directing the attention of the audience to the embedded narratives visible within each illustration, and inviting a meditative and exploratory style of viewing. The affective focus in each illustration is the relationship between dragon and minstrel, both in pictures where the two are present and also in those where

Figure 6.1 Illustration from *The Minstrel and the Dragon Pup* by Rosemary Sutcliff and Emma Chichester Clark

the minstrel is searching for the absent Lucky. The depicted relationship of minstrel and dragon is, of course, isomorphic with more conventional depictions of relationships between humans and animals, and in most respects Lucky is represented in dog-like poses: sitting before his bowl, walking along next to the minstrel. But there is no ignoring his dragon body and the incongruity of his appearance. Clark's deployment of framed moments invites audiences to linger on an interspecies relationship which is not unlike that of romance lovers: separated from the dragon, the minstrel sings sad songs, and both minstrel and dragon pine away in their grief. The narrative treatment of their relationship is pertinent to 'the ethical demands of a sociality that is increasingly multicultural, multispecied, and multitechnical' (Bennett 2001: 32).

The book's penultimate illustration depicts the moment when Lucky and the minstrel are reunited (Figure 6.1). Like the illustrations more generally, this picture refers to the paintings of Piero della Francesca in its geometric design, its play of colour and light and the emblematic import of its human figures. The light which illuminates the dragon's wings draws attention to its body and head as the minstrel embraces Lucky and gazes on him. Writing on Piero's True Cross cycle of frescoes, Christopher Wood comments on the typological schemas of these paintings, which enable Piero to 'invest bodies with emblematic status' (2006: 257). Clark's figures suggest such typological significances, displaying varieties of strangeness: the dragon which is like but also unlike a dog; the minstrel's unorthodox attachment; the ethnic difference visible in the clothing and appearance of the royal beast-master; the exotic creatures glimpsed through the bars behind the beast-master. The relationship between the dragon and the minstrel is both an instance of interspecies engagement, and also an emblem of the enchanting capacity of such engagement.

Barely animals

In a significant proportion of children's texts, especially those for younger children, anthropomorphic animals substitute for humans. Cary Wolfe argues that the discourse of animality enables a framework within which 'the law of culture arranges its species significations on a kind of grid' marked by the categories of 'animalized animals', 'humanized animals' 'animalized humans' and 'humanized humans' (2003: 101). The first and fourth of these categories exist, Wolfe says, as 'pure (and hence immensely powerful) ideological fictions' (101–2) which inform constructions of relations between species. Wolfe names pets as the primary example of 'humanized animals', noting that humans exempt such animals 'from the sacrificial regime by endowing them with ostensibly human features' (101). Anthropomorphic narratives comprise another subcategory of 'humanized animals', conventionally deployed in children's literature to distance audiences from human behaviour. Such distancing allows for encodings of narrative details and ideologies which would be less palatable or less engaging in texts incorporating human protagonists.

Brian Jacques's Redwall series locates its action in a medievalist world whose central focus is Redwall Abbey in Mossflower country. The first book of the series, *Redwall* (1986), traces the progress of the mouse protagonist, Matthias, from an unregarded orphan to the hero of Redwall. His development is plotted against a struggle between the inhabitants of Redwall and an invading army led by the rat Cluny the Scourge.[9] The sandstone abbey, with its cloisters, bell tower, Great Hall and infirmary, houses a utopian community whose members vow to 'heal the sick, care for the injured, and give aid to the wretched and impoverished' (1986: 15). Monastic terminology is frequently invoked; thus, the inhabitants of Redwall refer to themselves as an Order, are led by Abbot Mortimer, and occupy hierarchies from Brothers to Friars. However, the ethos of the Order is staunchly secular, privileging humanist ideas concerning an essential human nature which transcends social and cultural formations. These ideas are promoted through distinctions between animal species aligned with Redwall Abbey, and those which seek to destroy the abbey.

The animals of the abbey are intensely anthropomorphic: they wear clothes (in Matthias's case, a habit and sandals), they eat vegetarian food at long tables, sleep in beds, and maintain records of the abbey's history. In contrast, depictions of their principal antagonist, Cluny, linger on his animality: 'He was big and tough; an evil rat with ragged fur and curved, jagged teeth. He wore a black eyepatch; his eye had been torn out in battle with a pike' (17). His clothes embody trophies of his violence upon other animals: 'His long ragged black cloak was made of batwings, fastened at the throat with a mole skull. The immense war helmet he wore had the plumes of a blackbird and the horns of a stag beetle adorning it' (49). The more anthropomorphic animals are, the more closely they are aligned to the virtuous heterotopia of Redwall Abbey. Matthias, his love-interest Cornflower Fieldmouse, and the other inhabitants of the abbey are, however, read as animals by their enemies; thus, when Cluny the Scourge visits the abbey to challenge the Abbot, he refers to the inhabitants of Redwall as 'a load of mice in funny robes' (50).

Cluny himself comes from somewhere beyond the abbey and the country in which it is located: 'Some said that Cluny was a Portuguese rat. Others said he came from the jungles far across the wide oceans. Nobody knew for sure' (17). He is, then, a dangerous outsider implacably opposed to Redwall Abbey and what it signifies – that is, a medieval British culture defined by values such as honour, chivalry, and principles of justice. Maria Cecire argues that British fantasy for children, including J. K. Rowling's Harry Potter series, calls on the nationalistic agendas of C. S. Lewis and J. R. R. Tolkien, who inaugurated what Cecire refers to as 'the Oxford School of Children's Literature' (2009: 398). Hogwarts, Cecire says, is a 'medieval-castle-turned-British-boarding-school' which functions as a 'loaded nationalistic symbol' (403), incorporating in its student population ethnically marked minor characters, such as Cho Chang and the twins Parvati and Padma Patil, whose difference is subsumed into a culture defined by Britishness and whiteness. Like the fantasies to which Cecire refers, *Redwall* demonstrates the potency of nationalistic medievalism, which deploys the past to make meaning in the present.

In *Redwall* this meaning hinges upon practices of inclusion and exclusion which maintain the cultural norms of Redwall by drawing a line between virtuous and evil species. Virtuous animals, who include various species of mice as well as badgers, beavers, hares, red squirrels, otters and hedgehogs, are set against the evil horde of rats, weasels, stoats and ferrets who follow Cluny. It is enough for animals to align themselves with either Redwall or Cluny to establish their standing in the world of the novel; thereafter the contrasts between members of the two armies are folded into descriptions of their relations with allies and foes and the military strategies they deploy. Cluny's lack of chivalry is evident in his exploitation of the weak and vulnerable, notably the unfortunate family of dormice who are taken prisoner by his troops. The dormouse leader, Plumpen, threatened with the violent death of his family, is blackmailed into opening the abbey door to Cluny and the invaders. Expecting to be released once he has carried out his part of the bargain, he is betrayed, clubbed to the ground at Cluny's orders. Positioned to sympathise with the helpless dormouse, readers are prompted to assent to an ideological scheme which assumes that outsiders are to be feared and resisted.

The conservative politics of *Redwall* are manifested in the novel's celebration of hierarchies and heroes. At the end of the narrative, following the defeat of the invaders, the old Abbot dies, poisoned by Cluny's barbed tail, but not before naming Brother Alf as his successor.

In another sign of continuity and lineage, Abbot Mortimer designates Matthias as Warrior Mouse of Redwall, successor to the first such champion, Martin, whose likeness is depicted on the ancient tapestry in the Great Hall of the abbey. Releasing Matthias from his intention of becoming a Brother, the Abbot calls on Cornflower Fieldmouse to marry Matthias, since 'a warrior needs a good wife' (348). Just as Matthias represents a link with the tradition of Warrior Mice inaugurated by Martin, so the abbey itself stands for Britishness and nationhood. Published in the year before Margaret Thatcher's third election victory for the Conservative Party, *Redwall* depicts a community comprising orders and classes of animals who know their place in society. The aristocratic figures of Basil Stag Hare and the marmalade cat Squire Julian Gingivere are at once revered for their noble lineage and treated as remnants of an outmoded system; Squire Julian laments the degradation of his property and his lack of 'trusty servants' (276), while the foppish Basil is a Bertie Wooster figure whose voice carries 'a slightly affected quaver' (86). Redwall is governed by a bourgeois ruling class of industrious mice, backed by a warrior caste exemplified by Matthias. Even the trade union movement is incorporated into the imagined community of the abbey: the shrews, once estranged from Redwall because of their propensity for taking industrial action at the slightest provocation, are welcomed back following the heroic death of their leader, Guosim, whose name is an acronym for 'Guerilla Union of Shrews in Mossflower' (254).

As old enmities are healed and the utopian community settles back into its routines, its lands and buildings are secured against the encroachment of outsiders. The novel ends with an extract from the annals of Redwall, written by John Churchmouse, detailing the calm routine of an ordinary day a year after the defeat of Cluny the Scourge. Cornflower and Matthias's son plays with his father's sword, the Guerilla Shrews collect honey, Cornflower gathers flowers in the meadow, and the abbey farm is burgeoning with produce. This evocation of a green and pleasant land governed by a benevolent but firm leadership proposes a highly conservative model of Britishness and nationhood. Its animal inhabitants are, of course, barely animals at all. Rather, the forces of animality associated with Cluny have been expunged, routed by humanised animals in a clear display of the ascendancy of humans.

This chapter demonstrates the wide range of significations surrounding representations of animals in medievalist texts for the young. While the anthropomorphic fantasy of *Redwall* and the sword-and-sorcery medievalism of Pierce's *Terrier* tend towards depictions of animal figures subordinated to the needs and agendas of humans, the example of

Sutcliff and Clark's *The Minstrel and the Dragon Pup* suggests that genre alone does not determine representations of relations between humans and non-humans. Medievalisms are readily captured by conservative agendas that privilege hierarchies such as those which structure the grid of 'species significations' (Wolfe 2003: 101) which Wolfe describes. Yet medieval settings in children's literature also enable imaginings of networks in which human and non-human actors influence and shape each other. In Crossley-Holland's Arthur trilogy, Cushman's *The Midwife's Apprentice*, and particularly in Branford's *Fire, Bed & Bone*, humans and animals share lives which are experienced differentially, represented in ways which tend towards a revisioning of humanist assumptions about the subordinate place of animals.

7
The Laughable Middle Ages

Of the many pleasures offered by medievalist texts, laughing at the Middle Ages is foremost among them. This is especially the case in regard to texts for the younger readers who constitute the main audience of picture books and animated films. Older children and YA audiences are less likely to come across comic representations of the Middle Ages in medievalist fantasy and historical fiction, although authors such as Terry Pratchett, Philip Reeve, Eoin Colfer and Catherine Jinks deploy comic and ironic modes in novels for older readers; and comic medievalisms abound in non-fiction for young audiences. Henri Bergson's celebrated essay *Laughter* (*Le rire*) (1911) observes that 'to understand laughter, we must put it back into its natural environment, which is society, and above all we must determine the utility of its function, which is a social one' (1911: 13). This chapter follows Bergson's lead by focusing on the social functions of children's texts that make fun of the Middle Ages.

Contemporary cultural production for children is keenly conscious of the ethical considerations which attend representations of cultural Others; for instance, members of ethnic minorities. Making fun of the past is, it seems, immune from such concerns because past figures and cultures are safely out of reach, incapable of outrage or indignation, devoid of defenders and apologists. It is clear, however, that some pasts are more risible than others. Children's texts, especially those for younger audiences, are far more likely to make fun of the Middle Ages than of classical antiquity, the early modern period or the Victorian age. Simon Critchley, borrowing from John Morreall, summarises theories of humour as follows: 'the superiority theory, the relief theory and the incongruity theory' (2002: 2).[1] In practice, medievalist humour for children blends and combines modes and practices, so that it is rarely possible to confine discussion of texts to one or other of the theories of humour to which Critchley refers.

Fiction for children seeks to engage readers with ideas and values by offering them reading positions where they align with young protagonists, typically through narrative strategies such as focalisation. Whereas these strategies seek to narrow the gap between implied readers and protagonists, comic medievalism distances audiences by inviting them to observe the Middle Ages from the safe vantage point of modernity. Medieval protagonists may be represented either as exemplifications of what is comical about the Middle Ages, or as exceptions to the rule, characters who stand out from their medieval settings as somewhat 'like us' and hence capable of reading their own time as comical. Both these forms of comic medievalism imagine the Middle Ages as the *present past* (see Chapter 1), projecting the past in the light of present-day mores and values.

Making fun of the Middle Ages

Babette Cole's *Princess Smartypants* (1986), for instance, treats the Middle Ages as a comic exemplar of outdated gender relations. The text establishes its parodic orientation in the coat of arms which appears on the book's opening page (Figure 7.1). Here a fat green frog prince replaces the crest, helm and coronet which traditionally signify status and lineage; the shield is adorned with pink ribbons and three pairs of pink, lace-trimmed knickers; the supporters stationed on either side of the shield are two of Smartypants' pet dragons; and the motto reads 'Smartypantus Rulus O.K.us'. In heraldic tradition the coat of arms, with its conventions of shape, colours and significations, is a formal and rule-bound assemblage. In *Princess Smartypants* this sense of order and tradition is disrupted by the insertion of fantasy elements (the frog prince and the dragons), a mildly naughty reference (pink knickers), and a motto which is a variant of the slang phrase 'rules, ok'.

The coat of arms introduces a narrative which pits modernity against medieval practices, and feminism against social orders which privilege patriarchy. What defines comic medievalism in this text, as in many others, is that the Middle Ages is attributed with what Bergson refers to as '*inelasticity* of character' (1911: 23, emphasis in original). Bergson observes that sociability relies on movement, action and adaptability, and that comedy is to be found in 'anything rigid, ready-made, mechanical in gesture, attitude and even facial expression' (103). In *Princess Smartypants* such comic rigidity is evident in the behaviour

Figure 7.1 Illustration from *Princess Smartypants* by Babette Cole

of Smartypants' suitors, who insist on seeking her hand in marriage because she is 'pretty and rich', even though it is clear that she has no interest in marriage and is determined to thwart the suitors by allocating them unpleasant or impossible tasks. The contrasts between the suitors and Smartypants are sustained through their appearance and bodily actions. Whereas the suitors adopt stereotypical poses (smiling hopefully, clutching flowers) as they approach Smartypants, she does not adhere to norms of princess-like behaviour but sits on her throne nonchalantly painting her fingernails and regarding the suitors with distaste. The suitors wear spit-and-polish uniforms; Smartypants sports casual wear: a colourful T-shirt, denim overalls, and red espadrilles, her royal status signified by an attenuated crown perched on her spiky, blond hair.

This contrast between the suitors' rigid adherence to traditional modes of behaviour and Smartypants' mobility and dissidence enforces a wider contrast between medieval and modern, in which medieval settings and references provide a shorthand for unreformed and outdated versions of gender. The narrative modulates into comic excess as Smartypants' suitors fail the tasks she sets them: Prince Vertigo collapses in panic at the thought of climbing her tower; Prince Bashthumb, sent to chop firewood, is pursued by Rackhamesque monster trees; Prince Grovel is utterly humiliated when he takes Smartypants' mother shopping and is trapped in the lingerie section of Harrolds department store. The ineptitude of the suitors is associated precisely with their rigidity, which manifests in their fixation on outdated narratives of heroic achievement, quests and chivalry. Smartypants rejects these in favour of a narrative of female agency which replaces rigidity with energetic movement, mechanical behaviour with spontaneity, medieval with modern.

A similar style of comic medievalism is apparent in Munsch and Martchenko's *The Paper Bag Princess* (1980). In the closing pages of the narrative, Elizabeth, like Smartypants, rejects a script in which princesses are treated as marriage trophies. The final image of the book depicts her dancing off, free and alone, into a bright future. In contrast, Prince Ronald adheres to outmoded ideas about what 'a real princess' (1980, unpaged) is like: pretty, well dressed, subservient. In Bergson's terms, Ronald manifests a comical determination to 'keep strictly to one path, to follow it straight along, to shut their ears and refuse to listen' (Bergson 1911: 165), even when it is clear to readers that the old order has changed in the face of 1980s feminisms.

In *Princess Smartypants* and *The Paper Bag Princess*, then, the Middle Ages constitutes a comic foil in narratives which mock patriarchal versions of gender relations. Another version of medievalist humour appears in the many picture books featuring knights, kings or monsters who are comically inept at performing tasks associated with chivalric or heroic narratives. Princess Smartypants' suitors and Prince Ronald in *The Paper Bag Princess* adhere to this pattern, although they are minor figures in comparison with the female action heroes on whom these texts are built. Medievalist texts with male protagonists often take up notions of masculinity, sometimes in relation to wider concepts of sociality. In Colin McNaughton's *King Nonn the Wiser* (1980), a bookish king who 'liked nothing better than to be alone with his books' is forced into adventures because his people 'want a king who can fight dragons and slay giants' (1980, unpaged). Oblivious to the dangerous spaces and antagonists he encounters, King Nonn inadvertently behaves like the hero his people expect, and is astonished to receive their accolades on his return.

A comparable pattern is evident in Barbara Shook Hazen and Tony Ross's *The Knight Who Was Afraid of the Dark* (1989), which features Sir Fred, a 'bold and much loved knight' (Figure 7.2) whose fearless

Once long ago in a time known as the Dark Ages, there lived a bold and much loved knight. He was called Sir Fred.

Figure 7.2 Illustration from *The Knight Who Was Afraid of the Dark* by Barbara Shook Hazen and Tony Ross

encounters with monsters, dragons and dishonest merchants are belied by the 'one crack in Sir Fred's armour. Sir Fred was afraid – knee-bumping, heart-thumping afraid – of the dark' (1989, unpaged). He is even more afraid of the possibility that his fatal flaw will be discovered, and the narrative revolves around the risk of exposure at the hand of Sir Fred's rival, Melvin the Miffed, who 'couldn't stand Sir Fred because he was better loved, especially by Lady Wendylyn' (1989, unpaged). Sir Fred's dilemma is resolved when he discovers that Lady Wendylyn is just as afraid of his fireflies and electric eel as he is of the dark. The final image of the book shows Sir Fred and Lady Wendylyn riding together through the dark, their fears overcome by their romantic attachment to each other: 'Meanwhile Sir Fred was clutching his True Love and telling her, "Hmmm, the dark's not so scary .... *With* someone"' (1989, unpaged).

When adult protagonists in picture books are shown to experience doubts and fears, young audiences are positioned to enjoy the pleasure of observing adults evincing vulnerability. However, King Nonn and Sir Fred are comic figures not merely because they are vulnerable adults, but because they are medieval. Their paraphernalia of shields, swords, steeds and armour, which should make them impregnable and powerful, do not afford them immunity from everyday insecurities, but rather render these insecurities ludicrous. Tony Ross's illustrations in *The King Who Was Afraid of the Dark* depict Sir Fred as a statuesque figure with enormous shoulders and a hawk-like profile, so that his fear of the dark is comically inappropriate to his appearance. In these picture books, the Middle Ages is inherently comical because the knights, kings and warriors who feature in their narratives are prone to doubts and fears that undermine the heroic narratives associated with the medieval.

How to Train Your Dragon (2010), which I have discussed in Chapter 4 in relation to the disabled bodies it incorporates, affords an example of how medievalist humour blends with conventional story scripts to cater to a global audience. Like other medievalist films for children, *How to Train Your Dragon* builds on what Arjun Appadurai refers to as mediascapes, repertoires of images and narratives which circulate globally to produce 'images of the world' (1990: 9). As Michael Mulkay observes, the mass production of humour relies on 'a restricted range of techniques, themes and semantic scripts' (1988: 179), and the film's treatment of Viking culture draws on just such a 'restricted range' of representations, familiar to global audiences from cartoons, other films, and visual images. In summary, Berk is represented as a harsh and violent place and Viking culture as endemically masculinist and hierarchical, with physical strength valued above intellectual pursuits. The iconic popular visual image of the Viking warrior – bearded, broad-shouldered, unkempt, dentally challenged, wearing a horned helmet – recirculates in the film's depiction of Stoick and his warriors. Although some few female warriors are members of Stoick's army, they are incorporated into its masculinist ethos and do not figure as leaders or even as identified characters.

The film's stock picture of Viking identity is, however, undermined by Hiccup's ironic narration. The film commences with his voice-over description of the village of Berk: 'Twelve days north of Hopeless, and a few degrees south of Freezing to Death. It's located solidly on the Meridian of Misery .... We have fishing, hunting, and a charming view of the sunsets. The only problems are the pests. You see, most places have mice or mosquitoes. We have dragons' (2010). Hiccup explains that the village is old but all its buildings new because they are constantly destroyed by dragons, and rebuilt: 'Most people would leave. Not us. We're Vikings. We have stubbornness issues' (2010). Claire Colebrook notes that irony 'challenges any ready-made consensus or community' while also 'claiming a point of view beyond the social whole and above ordinary speech and assumptions' (2004: 150). Even as Hiccup's narration undercuts the idea that Viking life is built on heroic ideals, it constructs Hiccup as sceptical and critical of the received values of the community of Berk so that he is seen to claim 'a point of view beyond the social whole'. In particular Hiccup's perspective punctures heroic rhetoric; for example, the stoical determination prized by Stoick and his warriors is reduced to 'stubbornness issues'.

The humour of *How to Train Your Dragon* relies on the comical juxtaposition of modern and medieval, since Hiccup is, like so many other protagonists in medievalist texts (including Smartypants and Princess Elizabeth in *The Paper Bag Princess*), an exceptional figure in his culture, one with whom contemporary audiences are positioned to align themselves. Hiccup befriends a young dragon whose tail has been injured and who is thus unable to return to his den. The progress of Hiccup's relationship with the dragon Toothless (so called because of his retractable teeth) is similar to the many story scripts in which antagonists become friends, and it intersects with another common script involving father–son conflict. In *How to Train Your Dragon*, this generational conflict centres on Stoick's and Hiccup's respective attitudes to dragons: Stoick adheres to the belief that the only good dragon is a dead dragon, while Hiccup, who understands that the dragons who attack Berk are themselves enslaved by the monstrous Red Death dragon, advocates a strategy of peaceful coexistence.

Hiccup is selected for the dragon-training classes run by Gobber, the blacksmith, in a training ring which doubles as an arena for public performances. The training session in *How to Train Your Dragon* evokes myriad scenes in films involving martial and sporting contests, in which training itself constitutes an extreme test of initiates and sometimes results in injury or death. The setting of the training ring in the film echoes action films, such as *Demetrius and the Gladiators* or *Spartacus*, in which novice fighters are placed in settings isomorphic with the Roman Colosseum[2] where they are expected to demonstrate their skills and showmanship. In the opening moments of the scene Hiccup's five classmates enter the training ring, their faces and bodies alive with nervous exhilaration. The directions in which they look guide viewers' eyes towards stone walls, a vast expanse of floor, a domed ceiling, secure doors behind which lurk the dragons the trainees will fight as part of their training. That the young dragon-fighters are accountable to their community is signified by glimpses of the stadium walls, where villagers will later stand to observe the trainees in combat.

The trainees are differentiated as to their attitudes, articulated in the dialogue which opens the scene:

Gobber: Welcome to Dragon Training!
Astrid: No turning back.
Tuffnut: I hope I get some serious burns!
Ruffnut: I'm hoping for some mauling, like on my shoulder or lower back.
Astrid: Yeah, it's only fun if you get a scar out of it. (2010)

The comic impact of the scene derives in part from the disjunction between signifiers of antiquity (Roman and Viking), and the twenty-first-century demotic of the dialogue. The twins Tuffnut and Ruffnut disclose their try-hard posturing, while Astrid's 'No turning back' and her wry 'it's only fun if you get a scar out of it' points both to her ambition and also to her hard-headed disdain for empty rhetoric. It is at this point that Hiccup enters, saying 'Yeah, no kidding, right? Pain, love it.' A skinny, awkward youth, Hiccup possesses none of the swagger of the recruits Snotlout, Tuffnut and Ruffnut, who model their demeanour on senior warriors such as Stoick and Gobber. Voiced by the Canadian actor Jay Baruchel, Hiccup is presented as a nerdy outsider to the dominant culture, his nasal tones suggesting urban cool rather than the belligerence espoused by his companions.

While the comedy of this scene revolves around its portrayal of Hiccup as a figure at odds with the dragon-training culture, the dragon Toothless represents a far more radical form of difference. In the opening moments of the film, Hiccup hits Toothless with a missile so that the dragon plunges to the ground, but is unable to convince his father of his success. Subsequently he discovers the stranded dragon in a glade near the village[3] and fashions a prosthetic tail fin so that Toothless can fly. A pivotal moment occurs when Hiccup presents Toothless with a fish to eat. Toothless devours the fish with gusto, then corners Hiccup so that he is trapped against a rock. A close-up of Hiccup's face, inches away from Toothless, discloses his fear, followed by a mixture of relief and disgust when Toothless regurgitates half of the fish (fittingly, the lower half including the tail) and lays it on Hiccup's lap. This moment of cultural incommensurability is rendered comical through alternating images of the two characters' faces as Toothless waits expectantly for Hiccup to enjoy the treat he has offered him. The moment when Hiccup bites into the fish plays to the film's emphasis on Hiccup's bookish and fastidious nature, which distinguishes him from other Vikings.

In comparison with the inelasticity and rigidness attributed to the Middle Ages in the picture books I discussed earlier, *How to Train Your Dragon* relies for its comic effects on the dynamics between its broadly drawn depictions of Viking culture and the ironic playfulness encapsulated in the character of Hiccup. The film ends with a scene in which Vikings and dragons frolic together, with Hiccup and his friends riding dragons through the village of Berk, swooping around the harbour and soaring into the sky. Hiccup's voice-over echoes the words of the film's opening: 'The only upsides are the pets. While other places have ponies or parrots, we have dragons' (2010). The film's narrative is based on Hiccup's transformation from an outsider to a valued member of the community of Berk, but the village is also transformed as it embraces interspecies cooperation. The film contrives to nod to the medieval past even as it parodies popular-culture depictions of Viking culture. Hiccup functions both as an ironic commentator and as a boy engaged in the work of identity formation, simultaneously drawing in young audiences and inviting them to laugh at the Middle Ages.

Facticity, humour and the Middle Ages

So far my discussion of medievalist humour has focused on fiction and film for younger audiences. Humorous non-fiction dealing with the Middle Ages and other pasts has proliferated over the last few decades in the form of books of fun facts, and series such as the 'You wouldn't want to be' books, which outline why readers 'wouldn't want to be' a slave in Ancient Greece, a medieval knight, a pyramid builder, and dozens of other undesirable occupations. Such texts typically seek to engage young children with history through narratives that emphasise the alterity of past times by focusing on gory, scatological and unhygienic elements. But humorous non-fiction has a much longer pedigree, including W. C. Sellar and R. J. Yeatman's *1066 and All That* (1930), which purports to comprise 'A Memorable History of England, comprising all the parts you can remember including 103 Good Things, 5 Bad Kings, and 2 Genuine Dates' (1930, title page). *1066 and All That* implies an educated audience familiar with the history textbooks of the time, and satirises these through outrageous puns, mangled facts and running jokes. Its account of Joan of Arc, for instance, reads as follows:

> ... the Hundred Years War was brought to an end by *Joan of Ark*, a French Descendant of Noah who after hearing Angel voices singing *Do Re Mi* became inspired, thus unfairly defeating the English in several battles. Indeed, she might even have made France top nation if the Church had not decided that she would make an exceptionally memorable martyr. Thus Joan of Ark was a Good Thing in the end and is now the only memorable French saint. (46)

As this description demonstrates, *1066 and All That* pillories nationalism and unthinking binarisms ('top nation'; 'Good Thing') while evoking the untroubled dogmatism of British textbooks. Like most texts in the genre it turns to the Middle Ages for ready examples of outrageous historical 'facts'.

Terry Deary's Horrible Histories books seem at first glance to follow in the lineage of *1066 and All That*, since they too incorporate amusing pen-and-ink drawings, quizzes and lists of facts; but the purposes of the two publications are very different. The Horrible Histories books imply a less knowing readership than *1066 and All That*, and are far less dissident; rather, they buy into a reflex suspicion of teachers and educational institutions, while proclaiming a narrow vision of Britishness centred on Anglo-Saxon society.[4] Lesley Milne notes that whereas *1066 and All That* satirises school history books, the Horrible Histories are, in fact, 'cunningly disguised children's textbooks' (2005: 738). Their didactic and pedagogical agendas butt up against their frequent and explicit assaults upon teachers, the discipline of history, and educational institutions.

The book series, written by Terry Deary and illustrated by Martin Brown, numbers more than 60 titles. The first of these, *Terrible Tudors* and *Awesome Egyptians*, were published in 1993. During the two decades since, the books in the series and their repackaged editions have sold over 25 million copies and have been widely translated. The highly popular live-action series, which incorporates some animation, was launched on the BBC in 2009, followed by five further series. The Horrible Histories franchise incorporates multiple spin-offs including stage productions, a television game show and a series of magazines, some of which were released as audiobooks in conjunction with a promotion for breakfast cereal. Other products include video games, activity books, toys and much, much more. While the book series and its spin-offs address a wide range of historical periods, the Middle Ages comprises its core content, with titles such as *Cut Throat Celts*, *Measly Middle Ages*, *Smashing Saxons*, *Stormin' Normans* and *Vicious Vikings* reissued and repackaged multiple times.

The cover of the 2013 edition of *The Measly Middle Ages* is symptomatic of how the series promotes itself, promising 'Splats, hats and lots of rats!' (2013). That is, the book focuses on violence (splats), nobles (steeple hats) and disease and filth (rats). Bergson remarks that laughter is 'a kind of social "ragging"' (1911: 122) which is incompatible with sympathy. The Horrible Histories books avoid dealing with history after the Second World War, and the TV series have generally followed suit, although Series Five has profiled twentieth-century figures such as Jesse Owens and Rosa Parks. Deary has compared writing on the Tudors with his writing of *The Woeful Second World War*: 'With a book like *Even More Terrible Tudors* you can talk about someone having their head chopped off after ten hacks and it's almost comical because you're so removed from it. But there's very little humour to be had from the Second World War' (2000: 169). The telling phrase in Deary's account of writing about history is 'because you're so removed from it'. Medieval bodies are, it is implied, more readily treated as 'mere machines' (Bergson 1911: 32) than modern bodies precisely because they are 'so removed' from modernity.

Throughout the Horrible Histories books readers are positioned as amused observers of medieval bodies which emit wastes and gases, suffer diseases, endure punishments, are tortured, dismembered and die. The book *The Smashing Saxons* (2000), for instance, includes a sequence on Saxon punishments in which readers are asked to consider which penalty they would select if caught in criminal activities: stoning, beheading, hanging, drowning, burning, or having their necks broken. Alternatively, they are offered options of mutilation involving various body parts: hand, nose, upper lip, scalp, tongue, eye, ear or foot. The bodies represented in the text and illustrations are already dismembered on the page, offered up as components of Bergson's 'mere machine'. Objectified as options in a quiz ('Which of these Saxon punishments would you choose to suffer?'), they are both ancient and also machinic. The indignities visited on bodies during the Second World War were, of course, equally gross, but these bodies cannot so readily be consigned to a past discontinuous with our own. As Louise D'Arcens notes, the unstable logic of the Horrible Histories' depiction of the Middle Ages acknowledges historical alterity 'under the star of pre-modern weirdness' (2014: 160).

To draw readers into their brand of historical comedy, the Horrible Histories books create what Peter Berger calls a 'comic culture' (1997: 68), which creates boundaries between insiders and outsiders. Like all books in the series, *The Measly Middle Ages* opens by articulating its position on what constitutes history:

> History is horrible. **Horribly confusing** at times. People can't even agree what happened yesterday. When events happened last year, last century or hundreds of years ago we have no chance of knowing the whole truth ....
>
> You see the problem? Queen Isabeau was described as a tall, short, dark, fair woman, while French peasants were starving, well-fed, smelly people who had regular baths. Historians and teachers have usually said what they thought and that's not the same as giving the facts. **Who can you believe?** No one! Your schoolbooks will probably give you one side of the story .... Look at the facts and make up your own mind! (Deary 2013: 5–7, emphasis in original)

The generalised *they*, 'people [who] can't even agree what happened yesterday', modulates to the pronoun 'we' in 'we have no chance of knowing the whole truth' and then to 'you' in 'You see the problem?', thus gradually reducing the distance between narrator and implied readers. The accompanying cartoon distinguishes 'you' from 'them', showing two pupils arguing over medieval populations. The intervention of their teacher aligns him with historians who have 'argued both ways', inviting the girl's sceptical response: 'Huh! They can't both be right!'.

The 'you' in 'Who can you believe?' interpellates readers as anti-historian, anti-schoolbooks and anti-teacher, offering the Horrible Histories as the alternative source of reliable information: 'Look at the facts and make up your own mind!' The cartoon illustrations go further: in the first, a schoolboy reads *Pleasant History for the Young*, which tells him that 'Knights were brave and noble warriors! They were called Sir' (2013: 7). In the second illustration the same boy reads *Horrible Histories*: 'Knights were ignorant, vicious bullies! Is that why *teachers* are called "Sir"?' (2013: 7). The lexical chain produced through this sequence proceeds as follows: knights ... sir ... bullies ... teachers ... sir. Between *Pleasant History for the Young* and *Horrible Histories*, then, the comic culture of the series is defined: schools, historians and teachers are excluded, while child readers are insiders, encouraged to 'make up their own minds' by attending to the facts provided by the narrator.

The approach used here draws audiences in by constructing them as the narrator's allies in opposition to school versions of history. This illusion of solidarity is sustained by a combination of strategies, including the books' frequent use of colloquial language, such as:

1066
Nutty Norman Knights aren't satisfied with living in France. The fighting fellers want Britain too. They invade, and hack English King Harald to bits. Their boss, William the Conqueror, pinches his throne. (Deary 2013: 8)

Second, the Horrible Histories rely on readers' familiarity with sporting terms and popular culture references:

1099
European armies set off to capture Jerusalem for the Christian Church. These religious expeditions to the Holy Land are known as **Crusades**. Away win for Crusaders! (Deary 2013: 9)

A third strategy is the deployment of graphic devices such as cartoons, handwritten letters, diary entries, newspaper mock-ups, recipes and lists.

These informal and irreverent styles of address readily fold into Deary's projection of his persona as a character and media personality, the development of which accompanied the formation of the Horrible Histories franchise. His public and online pronouncements, suggesting a blend of libertarian and contrarian perspectives, commonly express his disdain for institutions, particularly education, and his project of reattributing power to the powerless and oppressed by mocking the failings of the mighty and providing readers with knowledge. But even as Deary inveighs against education and the discipline of history, the Horrible Histories position readers as docile subjects subjected by the dogmatism of the books' narratives.

The Horrible Histories are in many ways at odds with the disciplinary shifts which have reshaped history over the last few decades, and which are visible in the approach and content of history teaching, so that in effect they set up an Aunt Sally version of school history which they then knock down. School history has moved away from a focus on 'the view from above' concentrating on the 'great deeds of great men' (Burke 2001: 4), and now tends to treat history 'from below' (Sharpe 2001: 26), with particular reference to the lives of children and young people in the past. In addition, pedagogies of history have to a large extent de-emphasised the acquisition of knowledge in the form of dates and lists of rulers in favour of 'a more interpretative, source-based approach' (Scanlon and Buckingham 2002: 143) which invites children to consider the ideological frameworks and cultural assumptions on which accounts of history are based. Occasionally the Horrible Histories books gesture towards this latter approach by citing sources, but they are typically dogmatic in their treatment of how such sources are to be interpreted.

In *Vicious Vikings* (1994), for instance, a chapter entitled 'Vicious Viking historians' quotes the words of the monk Alcuin and the Arab trader Al-Tartushi:

What they said about the Vikings ...
... Never before has such a terror appeared in Britain as we have now suffered from this pagan race.
Alcuin 735–804 AD – a monk and a very bad loser
(Deary 1994: 87)

The town of Hedeby (in Denmark) is poor in goods and wealth .... If a child is born there it is thrown into the sea to save bringing it up. I have never heard anything more horrible than their singing.
Al-Tartushi – an Arab trader and a bit of a snob
(Deary 1994: 87)

The words of Alcuin (a monk and a very bad loser) and Al-Tartushi (a bit of a snob), selectively quoted here,[5] play to a generalised suspicion of religion and wealth. The next page refers to a phrase commonly attributed to the British during the Viking raids of the ninth century:

... And what they didn't say! *A furore Normannorum, libera nos Domine.* (From the fury of the Northmen, deliver us, O Lord.)

This is what the poor English were *supposed* to have chanted as they trembled in their tiny churches. Nearly every book on the Vikings quotes this prayer of terrified people. The truth is there is no evidence that anyone ever actually said these words! It's simply something that scholars and teachers think they should have said. (Deary 1994: 88)

Monks and traders, scholars and teachers are, then, unreliable sources: not only do they present 'facts' through the prism of their skewed view of the world, but they invent history. The implication is that the Horrible Histories offer a truthful and plain-speaking version of the past and reliable readings of sources.

The humour of the Horrible Histories books bifurcates along two lines. The first of these pokes fun at teachers and historians, as well as ancient commentators whose views of the Middle Ages are at variance with the narratives of the Horrible Histories. This style of humour relies on what Andrew Stott describes as 'a discrepancy between the way a character presents him- or herself and the substance of their actions' (2005: 9); that is, teachers and historians are shown to assume the status of authorities, while the Horrible Histories books purport to demonstrate their ignorance, timidity or bias. Thus, *Vicious Vikings* commences with a promise to tell 'the *truth* about the Vikings. The things that teacher never tells you because teacher's too chicken-livered. Now you can watch Miss faint in fright as you describe some vicious Viking inventions ... for torture!' (1994: 6). Here the discrepancy is between the authority of 'Miss' and her 'chicken-livered' refusal to tell 'the truth'.[6] The narratives of the Horrible Histories position readers as allies and confidants of an omniscient narrator identified closely with the implied author, implying an anti-authoritarian ethos calculated to appeal to schoolchildren. This approach clothes itself in claims to facticity in comparison with the unreliability of 'authorities'.

Second, the book series makes fun of medieval people and cultures. While Deary has made much of his resolve to alert his audiences to the injustices of history and the plight of the poor and oppressed, the Horrible Histories' focus on horror, cruelty and gore does not give a voice to the powerless but depicts them, in the manner of the sequence on Saxon punishments discussed above, as objects of cultural and institutional brutality. As D'Arcens notes, Deary's claims to subversion are limited by his propensity for reproducing 'caricatures of pre-modern barbarism, bizarre superstitions, tolerance of filth, absurd customs and laws, thereby confirming the greater civility, rationality, and hygiene of modernity' (2014: 158).

The television series *Horrible Histories*, launched in 2009, markets itself in relation to Deary's book series, but caters to a wider audience of adults and children. It fits within the category of 'edutainment', defined by David Buckingham and Margaret Scanlon as 'a hybrid mix of education and entertainment that relies heavily on visual material, on narrative or game-like formats, and on more informal, less didactic styles of address' (2005: 46). These styles of edutainment incorporate what D'Arcens refers to as *jocumentary*, televisual forms which 'use comic technique while simultaneously appealing to the cultural weight accorded to their historical content and ... the pedagogic authority vested in television documentary as a genre' (2014: 141).

The cultural weight to which D'Arcens refers is exemplified by high-profile history academics such as Simon Schama, David Starkey and Niall Ferguson, who have headed up television history documentaries including *A History of Britain* (Schama), *Monarchy* (Starkey) and *Empire* (Ferguson), which occupy the 'serious history' end of the TV spectrum. At the 'entertain' end of 'edutainment', British television history shows such as Terry Jones's *Medieval Lives*, Tony Robinson's *The Worst Jobs in History*, and *The Supersizers* series deploy a combination of comedic and historical content, with a focus on gross and disgusting aspects of the past. The *Horrible Histories* TV series is similarly concerned with entertainment; however, its 'made for children' orientation plays out in its claim to historical accuracy, materialised through the figure of Rattus Rattus, the rat glove puppet which addresses audiences, pointing to the truth of depictions of the past. Although publicity for the TV series always emphasises its allegiance to the books, in fact content from the books accounts for only a small proportion of the material in the series. To feed what is a hungry medium, the producers recruited researchers and writers to develop additional sketches, commentaries, quizzes and songs.

Like British jocumentaries for adults, the *Horrible Histories* TV series is powerfully influenced by traditions of satirical and absurdist comedy in British television and film, including *Blackadder*, the Monty Python films, and *Do Not Adjust Your Set*.[7] In addition, many of the sketches parody television genres such as news and weather broadcasts, documentaries, cooking shows, hospital dramas and various forms of reality TV in sequences such as *Historical Wife Swap*, *Ready Steady Feast*, *Historical Shopping Channel* and *This Is Your Reign*. The six principal actors of the Horrible Histories series are individuated personalities; they appear in TV interviews, live performances such as Horrible Histories at the Prom, comedy festivals, and social media. For viewers, part of the pleasure of the Horrible Histories series is recognising the actor behind period costumes and makeup.

In Series Two of the TV series, a sketch in the 'Measly Middle Ages' segment depicts a scene in which a young knight approaches a lord's castle and demands that land and castle be handed over to him. When the lord refuses, the knight cuts off a leg here, an arm there, of the peasants who are working in the vegetable garden outside the castle battlements. The lord protests on the grounds that these workers are his property, but the knight continues to cut limbs off. The lord and knight turn out to be father and son, and the scene ends with the knight promising to return the next day and the next until his father hands over his lands and castle, and the lord performing a Gallic shrug as he exclaims, 'Children, I don't know what to do with them …'[8] The principal marker of Frenchness in this sketch is accent – or rather, Pythonesque performances which evoke the castle siege in *Monty Python and the Holy Grail*. During the *Monty Python* siege scene one of the 'French' knights in the castle responds to the question 'Well what are you then?' with 'I'm French. Why do you think I have this outrageous accent?' In the 'father and son' episode of *Horrible Histories* the comedy of the sketch format, with its reliance on exaggeration, over-the-top acting and intertextual references, is not so much about the French Middle Ages as about how the English like to make jokes about the French, so that this sketch embodies what Critchley refers to as 'a joke about a joke' (2002: 70). When the puppet Rattus Rattus appears at the end of the segment to proclaim that 'A fight like that really did take place in France in the 1100s between a father and his son' (2010), this truth claim thus struggles against the comic impact of the dialogue: 'By the way, give my love to mama.' 'Of course. Au revoir' (2010).

Whereas the comic impact of the Horrible Histories books relies on jokes presented by an omniscient narrator with a very particular view of the Middle Ages, the TV series presents the more pluralistic range of points of view typical of a multi-track medium and conveyed through 'camera angle, focal length, music, *mise-en-scene*, performance, [and] costume' (Hutcheon 2012: 55). The books and the TV series are somewhat at odds, then, in their treatment of the medieval past: whereas the books insist on the truth of their depiction of a gross and gory Middle Ages, the TV series, in line with its allusions to absurdist and counter-cultural comic traditions, undermines historicism and its attendant notions of truth and authority.

'There's no harm in an occasional cackle …'

The medievalist worlds of Tolkienesque epic fantasy rarely incorporate humour or comedy, but trade off the moral seriousness which attaches to narratives based on oppositions between good and evil. Diana

Wynne Jones's *The Tough Guide to Fairyland* (1996) conducts a parodic tour of Fairyland in which she offers tongue-in-cheek accounts of fantasy tropes, artefacts, places and figures for the benefit of tourists set loose in medievalist fantasy worlds. Terry Pratchett's Discworld series prosecutes a similar agenda through comic fantasy, and here I focus on Pratchett's *The Wee Free Men* (2003), the first of the four Discworld novels featuring Tiffany Aching as she progresses from neophyte witch to established practitioner.[9]

In *The Wee Free Men* Tiffany seeks advice from the senior witches, Mistress Weatherwax and Mrs Ogg, as to the training regime she is required to undertake. A serious-minded girl of nine, Tiffany has heard rumours which lead her to fear that she may be obliged to 'dance around with no clothes on' (Pratchett 2003: 297). Mrs Ogg evinces a guarded approval of such practices: 'Well, that procedure does have something to recommend it' (2003: 297). Mistress Weatherwax, on the other hand, assures Tiffany: 'No, you don't have to! ... No cottage made of sweets, no cackling and no dancing!' (297). These opposing stances point to wider debates, in the Tiffany Aching novels and Pratchett's Discworld oeuvre, about the nature and functions of magic. They also exemplify the dialogical interplay which characterises Pratchett's approach to comic medievalisms.

Mistress Weatherwax's dogmatic rejection of cottages made of sweets, cackling and naked dancing is in essence a rejection of medievalist narratives which, in her view, detract from an appreciation of the role and functions of witches in the world of the Tiffany Aching novels.[10] More than this, her deployment of the story of Hansel and Gretel ('cottages made of sweets') to refer to a debate over the everyday practices of witches is symptomatic of the style of ontological humour which pervades the Tiffany Aching novels. Medievalist elements in Pratchett's novels, jostling with a variety of other intertextualities, are always liable to shift from one plane of existence to another. At the beginning of *The Wee Free Men*, for instance, Tiffany encounters a monster in the river, a monster with 'a thin face with long sharp teeth, *huge* round eyes and dripping green hair like waterweed' (5). She snatches up her little brother, Wentworth, just in time to save him from this monster, and returns to her home, where she consults one of the few books in the house, *The Goode Childe's Booke of Faerie Tales*, which is 'so old that it belonged to an age when there were far more 'e's around' (11). Having found the page she is looking for, she takes a soup plate from the crockery cupboard and measures it: 'Hmmm,' she said. 'Eight inches. Why didn't they just *say*?' (12).

Armed with the largest frying pan in the kitchen, a piece of string and a paper bag full of sweets, she drags the unwilling Wentworth back to the river, where she ties the bag to a piece of wood near the edge of the river. Wentworth is partial to sweets, and is lured to the paper bag. The monster is, in turn, lured to Wentworth, and leaps out of the water to snatch him, only to be dispatched by the force of the frying pan wielded by Tiffany. The monster, later identified by the witch Miss Tick as Jenny Green-Teeth, appears both in the material world of the countryside near Tiffany's house and in *The Goode Childe's Booke of Faerie Tales*. Tiffany crosses the boundary between materiality and fairy tale when she consults the *Goode Booke* as a reference, measuring a soup plate to establish Jenny's identity. Readers are positioned to follow the logic of Tiffany's investigation, and to accede to the ontological shifts involved. When, later in the novel, Tiffany asserts that she is 'careful and logical and I look up things I don't understand' (256), the narrative signals that readers who align themselves with Tiffany may well assent to this description of their own reading practices.

The comic doubleness which pervades the Tiffany Aching novels derives from what Stott describes as 'incompatible orders, such as the displacement of people or discourses, to produce ambiguity and the feeling that normality has been momentarily decentred for pleasurable ends' (2005: 10). Specifically, the discourses of the witches destabilise normality for comical effect by playing with the gap between conventional representations of witches as practitioners of the dark arts of magic, and the pragmatic and everyday lives of the witches of Discworld. Mistress Weatherwax assures Tiffany that magic 'doesn't take much intelligence, otherwise wizards wouldn't be able to do it' (2003: 295), and Mrs Ogg advises her that she needs a paying job since 'there's no money in witchcraft' (295). Being a witch in Discworld is, according to Mistress Weatherwax, 'a bit like life' (298) in that one learns, at it were, on the job, which in the main revolves around mundane and repeated tasks and activities.

A prominent comic mode in the Tiffany Aching novels is that of the carnivalesque, most evident in the novels' depictions of the species of fairy known as the Nac Mac Feegles, who are six inches tall, with red hair, blue skin (from tattoos and paint), kilts and a preoccupation with fighting, drinking and stealing. Although Mikhail Bakhtin's *Rabelais and His World* (1968) has been highly influential in studies of comedy and humour, its treatment of medieval folk culture is commonly regarded as somewhat utopian and historically improbable (Critchley 2002: 51; Gurevich 1988: 178–9; Stott 2005: 34; Strohm 1992: 45). Nevertheless,

Bakhtin's theorisation of the carnivalesque suggests some useful strategies for considering the narrative and comedic functions of the Feegles in *The Wee Free Men*. The first of these revolves around the notion of the grotesque carnivalesque body, which according to Bakhtin does not comprise the individuated and private subject, but takes on a kind of collectivity as 'the collective ancestral body' (1968: 19). This grotesque body is, Bakhtin says, based on the materiality of bodily experience, with an emphasis on 'food, drink, defecation, and sexual life' (18); and its ambivalence derives from the fact that it combines the principles of death and life, rather than consigning death to a separate realm.

Indeed, death and life coalesce in the Nac Mac Feegles, who believe that they have died and now live in the heaven that is the Discworld, which offers them ample sunshine, animals to hunt and alcohol to drink. In deference to the young readers implied by the Tiffany Aching books, the carnivalesque qualities of the Feegles play out in their frenetic fighting tactics and the exuberance with which they steal, eat and drink, rather than in 'acts of defecation and copulation' (Bakhtin 1968: 21). This textual reticence is itself cleverly parodied in an episode following Tiffany's accession to the status of kelda, a role which requires that she should marry Rob Anybody, the Big Man of the Chalk Hill clan of Feegles.[11] Neither Tiffany nor Rob Anybody regards such a marriage as feasible or desirable, and Tiffany overhears part of the Feegles' debate on the topic:

'*Ach, she's a bit on the big side, no offence to her.*'
'*Aye, but a kelda has to be big, ye ken, to have lots of wee babbies.*'
'*Aye, fair enough, big wimmin is a' very well, but if a laddie was to try tae cuddle this one he'd had tae leave a chalk mark to show where he left off yesterday.*' (2003: 155)

This exchange exposes the Feegles' uncertain comprehension of reproduction and invites readers to speculate about Tiffany's reaction to what she has heard. The omniscient narration of the next paragraph points out that Tiffany, raised on a farm, is relatively well informed: 'It's amazing what a child who is quiet and observant can learn, and this includes things people don't think she is old enough to know' (2003: 155). The amusing prudishness of the Feegles, set alongside Tiffany's matter-of-factness, involves a comical disjunction accessible to young readers, while offering an oblique reference to interspecies copulation which might or might not be apparent to this audience.

Whereas Tiffany is in essence a modern girl inhabiting a world in which witches are a normal part of society,[12] the Nac Mac Feegles are conspicuously folkloric, referring to themselves as Pictsies and speaking in a style which evokes Lowland Scots language of an archaic kind. Thus, when Tiffany discovers that the Feegles have stolen one of her father's sheep, Rob Anybody explains, 'We wuz hungering', mistress .... But when we kenned it was thine, we did put the beastie back in the fold' (2003: 82). The archaic forms 'kenned' and 'thine', and the verb form 'did put' combine to convey the impression that the Feegles come from an earlier era. They ascribe, too, to beliefs associated with folkloric traditions, such as their conviction that names embody power, and that what is written down is particularly potent and dangerous. Their fear of lawyers stems from this belief, since they know from experience that documents such as summonses, 'wanted' posters and writs of distrainment always lead to unpleasant consequences.[13] The carnivalesque aspects of the Feegles – in particular their energetic pursuit of opportunities to steal, drink alcohol and fight – are thus folded into their collective identity as inhabitants of an earlier (medieval) time. Like other texts for children, *The Wee Free Men* modifies its depiction of carnivalesque identities to minimise their potential for anarchy: the Feegles are Tiffany's allies and protectors in her quest to save her brother Wentworth from the queen of Fairyland, so that their wildness is harnessed to support Tiffany's identity formation. Their resistance to authority and their delight in the bodily pleasures of eating and drinking remind readers that rules and prohibitions are culturally constructed, produced by 'an official culture that consolidates its power through seriousness' (Stott 2005: 131).

Playing with history

Chapter 1 alluded to the historiographical shifts which inform *Here Lies Arthur* and *Catherine, Called Birdy*, both of which incorporate metafictional devices drawing attention to how narratives shape versions of the past. Here I discuss some of the comedic effects which stem from Catherine Jinks's postmodern treatment of the Middle Ages in the Pagan Chronicles. *Pagan's Crusade* (1992) follows the progress of Pagan Kidrouk, a 16-year-old boy who joins the Knights Templar in Jerusalem as the squire of the French knight Lord Roland.[14] In this novel Pagan's first-person narration is in the present tense, a strategy which restricts readers to what Pagan himself knows, sees and feels from moment to moment, so conveying the impression that his knowledge is contingent and partial. The *present past* of the novel is foregrounded through the language of Pagan's narration which, like that of Hiccup in *How to Train*

Your Dragon, is wry, sceptical and above all modern. Hutcheon observes that postmodern fiction suggests that 'to re-write or re-present the past in fiction and in history is, in both cases, to open it up to the present' (1988: 110). In its metafictive commentary and its close attention to historiography, *Pagan's Crusade* both rejects the possibility of historical authenticity and also flaunts its inauthenticity, treading a line between fiction and history.

The novel introduces Pagan as he approaches the Standard-Bearer of the Knights Templar:

'Name?' he says.
'Pagan.'
'Pagan what?'
'Pagan Kidrouk.'
'Pagan Kidrouk, *sir.*'
(Christ in a cream cheese sauce.)
'Pagan Kidrouk, sir.'
Scratch, scratch. He writes very slowly.
'Age?'
'Sixteen. Sir.'
'Born in?'
'Bethlehem.'
Rockhead looks up. The brain peeps out from behind the brawn.
'Don't worry, sir. It didn't happen in a stable.'
Clunk. Another jest falls flat on the ground.
'Rule number one, Kidrouk. In the Order of the Temple you speak only when you're spoken to.'
'Yes, sir.' (Jinks 1992: 1)

This exchange, redolent of many fictive encounters between authority figures and recalcitrant young people, parodies the language of authority and its reliance on nothing more than its own claims to such authority. Pagan's 'Christ in a cream cheese sauce', a leitmotif throughout the narrative, enforces the novel's anachronistic stance at the same time that its mild suggestion of blasphemy evokes a frisson of surprise. It is Pagan's joke about being born in a stable in Bethlehem that most clearly functions as an ideological tool, for it positions young readers to enjoy a witticism lost on Rockhead. The rueful comment 'Another jest falls flat on the ground' further invites readers to align with Pagan in opposition to an intimidating adult devoid of a sense of humour. Like the language of the novel more generally, jokes in *Pagan's Crusade* self-consciously point to the enunciative situations in which they occur. In the 'born in Bethlehem' joke Pagan's narration sets up the context and receiver ('Rockhead looks up. The brain peeps out from behind the brawn'), delivers the punchline ('Don't worry, sir. It didn't happen in a stable'), reflects on Rockhead's lack of reaction ('Clunk. Another jest falls flat on the ground'), and finally uses a conversational exchange to provide a wider context for the joke's lack of success, expressed in Rockhead's invocation of a rule-governed social order in which squires speak only when spoken to.

Discussing the history of humour, Critchley argues against a periodised approach in which 'the transition from a medieval-Renaissance world-view to that of modernity is defined in terms of the gradual disappearance of the ludic, playful element in culture' (2002: 83). Rather, Critchley says, humour constitutes a form of *sensus communis*, a term which he defines as 'sociableness' (80). Seen in this light, jokes appeal to members of social worlds united by common languages, assumptions and practices, and either reinforce a community's sense of distinctiveness or challenge it by making fun of what is regarded as normal and understood. Pagan's 'born in Bethlehem' joke sketches an analogy between Pagan and Jesus Christ, both born in Bethlehem. The irreverence of this analogy, and the slickness of Pagan's delivery, imply a modern audience quite distinct from that of the social world to which Pagan seeks entry, that of the Knights Templar. Rockhead's refusal even to entertain the possibility of interaction with Pagan halts the joke in its tracks, both directing it towards its contemporary audience and also pointing to the narrative's negotiations between history and fiction.

Pagan's identity formation in *Pagan's Crusade* is plotted in relation to his developing friendship with Roland, an odd-couple pairing complicated by differences of ethnicity, personal history, religious belief, and world view. These differences afford rich opportunities for humour, many of which call on the signifying practices which have shaped post-medieval representations of the medieval. When Pagan first views Roland he reads the knight's body in the light of just such practices: 'Lord Roland, son of Saint George. He looks like something off a stained-glass window. Tall as a tree, golden hair, wide shoulders, long nose, eyes as blue as the Virgin's mantle. He's wearing a white robe (spotless, of course) and a knife at his belt. If he's as good as he looks, I'm in big trouble' (1992: 6–7). Pagan's comparison between Roland and Saint George accords with Western iconographic and hagiographical traditions which represent the saint as an English knight dressed in armour,[15] a model of chivalry and of military prowess. Pagan, on the other hand, is an example of the many 'ex-centrics, the marginalized, the peripheral figures' (Hutcheon 1988: 114) who feature as protagonists in historiographic metafiction. Viewing Roland from the marginal position of an orphaned Palestinian boy living off his wits, Pagan initially misrecognises Roland as the stained-glass figure of his imaginings, 'piously raised as a living dedication to God. Weaned on the sacred host and holy water. His only playmate, a statue of Saint Sebastian' (Jinks 1992: 37). The very extravagance of Pagan's references to hagiographical traditions parodically undermines these traditions by drawing attention to their fictionality and their excess.

More broadly, the novel incorporates parodic representations of the multiple contradictions which characterise religious beliefs and practices, especially those associated with medieval pilgrimages to the Holy Land. The Templars are charged with the protection of pilgrims undertaking the dangerous return trip from Jerusalem to the River Jordan, during which Pagan observes the petty criminal Joscelin playing on the credulity of Sister Agnes, one of the nuns in the party. To Sister Agnes every detail of the desert landscape carries meaning; seeing a rock cloven in three parts she demands to know its significance, whereupon Joscelin provides an explanation: 'That's where they buried the man who ate one of the swine that had devils in them, from the Gospel of Matthew chapter eight. He wouldn't lie down when he was dead, you see, so they had to roll that big rock on top of him. And God smote the rock to kill the devil. And that's why it's now in three parts' (1992: 24). Fluent and specious, Joscelin misses no opportunity to exploit the pilgrims; Pagan, listening to his account of the rock's spiritual meaning, is caught between his dislike of Joscelin and his uneasy history of collusion with him. But there is also something compelling about Joscelin's inventiveness and imagination, so that the narration points to the appeal of such stories not only for pilgrim audiences but also for modern readers who will recognise in them analogies with the sensationalist modes of tabloid journalism.

After the pilgrims return safely to Jerusalem, clutching the eight bottles of water they have been permitted to draw from the River Jordan, the narrative incorporates a snippet of their conversation:

'So what do *you* have left? Or are you finished?'
'No, we're not finished. We've still got Mount Sion, and Our Lady of Josophat, and the Pool of Bethesda. And the shrine of the Ascension.'
'Oh, haven't you seen the shrine yet? Oh, you must. They've got the autograph text of the Lord's prayer.' (1992: 41)

The intertexts at play here are those of contemporary 'pilgrimages' to tourist destinations. What unites Christian pilgrims and modern tourists, the narration suggests, is a compulsive (and competitive) quest for authenticity, comprehensiveness and high-status destinations. The religious motivations of the pilgrims are swept up into an ironic comment on the shallowness of such touristic impulses and their emphasis on trophy sites and sights. Hutcheon argues that postmodern parody is 'fundamentally ironic and critical, not nostalgic or antiquarian in its relation to the past' (1989: 98). Indeed, there is nothing nostalgic about the irony of *Pagan's Crusade*, which plays with past and contemporary practices and representations by denaturalising both.

This chapter has touched on various modes and styles of comic medievalism, considering how humorous fiction, non-fiction and films for children and young people treat the relationship of the present to the past. In these texts the Middle Ages is the object of humour which serves to illuminate questions such as what constitutes masculinity, what the past means in the present, and the ethical implications of laughing at the Middle Ages. In all the texts I have discussed, what is at issue is not simply or exclusively the Middle Ages, but the multifarious, contradictory discourses which have shaped comic medievalism in the post-medieval world.

Conclusion

In Philip Reeve's novel *No Such Thing as Dragons* (2009), a young boy, Ansel, is sold by his father to Brock, a charlatan who passes himself off as a dragon-slayer. Ansel, shrewd and observant, strongly suspects that there is no such thing as a dragon and that the dragon-slayer holds the same conviction. Both turn out to be wrong: a dragon turns up in the mountains near the village of Knochen in Saxony, and hunts Brock, Ansel and Else, the girl designated by the villagers as a sacrifice to appease the dragon. At the end of the novel, after the wounded dragon has escaped from its cage in the village and has flown back to its mountain lair, Ansel too flees his life of servitude. Having departed Knochen, he finds a hollow under some birch trees and lies down to sleep. But 'the dragon got into his dreams again, as he knew it always would. It was as if it had not flown away at all, just made itself small and crept inside his head' (2009: 182).

Ansel's dragon, always getting into his dreams, is something like the medieval, always claiming a space in the dreams of modern people. To some degree the dragon of *No Such Thing* is represented in accord with tropes of medievalist melancholy; alone in its mountain fastness it is the sole survivor of its kind, so that Ansel, observing it, comes to the realisation that: '*It is waiting for another dragon to come. It wants to build a nest, and raise a brood of little dragonlets.* And for a moment, just for a moment, he was not scared of the creature any more. He felt sorry for it' (136). The sense of sadness prompted by the dragon's lonely existence is replicated in instances of regret or mourning for medieval pasts which feature in many of the texts I have considered in this book. But the narrative of *No Such Thing* also underscores the lability of Ansel's emotions: 'for a moment, just for a moment'. Rather than a pure or singular emotional reaction, he is attributed with a complex mingling of sentiments as he contemplates the dragon: sympathy for the dragon, fascination with its physicality, curiosity about its intentions, fear of its teeth, 'icicle white and sharp as nails' (78). In a similar vein, many medievalist texts for the young treat the medieval as a site where multiple forms of engagement and affect meet.

Not all medievalist texts for the young manifest this degree of affective and narrative complexity. Rather, some treat the Middle Ages as a homogeneous and static period and/or culture insulated from modern times. Yet even such shallow versions of the medieval can tell us much about the desires which prompt them, and about the forms of socialisation which they intend. In the hazy realms of fairy narratives for very young readers, for instance, can be detected a powerful anxiety about girls' sexuality, channelled into an imagined world where girl protagonists are fixed in a state of innocence. Directed to the adults who purchase them, these books offer a version of the Middle Ages which offers immunity from the unstable ground of puberty and female sexuality.

Over the time I have been researching and writing this book, I have frequently been asked to explain the ascendancy of the medieval in the popular imagination. What, I am asked, is the appeal of the Middle Ages and what might explain why medievalist texts proliferate in comparison with texts grounded in other times and cultures – for instance, in classical antiquity. Umberto Eco suggests that the explanation for this phenomenon is to be found in what he refers to as the 'utilitarian bricolage' (1986: 67) of medievalism:

> In the case of the remains of classical antiquity we reconstruct them but, once we have rebuilt them, we don't dwell in them, we only contemplate them as an ideal model and a masterpiece of faithful restoration. On the contrary, the Middle Ages have never been reconstructed from scratch: We have always mended or patched them up, as something in which we still live. (67–8)

We might argue that classical antiquity, just as much as the Middle Ages, is recursively 'rebuilt' as successive generations make sense of classical texts and artefacts in the light of their own times and cultures, while drawing upon previous interpretations and imaginings of the classical heritage. It is the case, however, that in 2014 'people like the Middle Ages' (Eco 1986: 61) just as much as they did in 1986, when Eco published his essay 'Dreaming of the Middle Ages'. To me, the most telling aspect of Eco's argument is his assertion that the Middle Ages comprises a time or place 'in which we still live'.

The 'we' of Eco's 'in which we still live' refers to adults who purchase, read and view the popular and filmic texts to which he refers. In this book I have focused, rather, on a body of texts distinguished by the fact that their producers and their audiences occupy quite different cultural locations; that is, texts for the young are always shaped by the views and interests of adults engaged in the production and mediation of such texts. Medievalism in texts for the young is, then, necessarily implicated in socialising agendas, some overt and others embedded in cultural assumptions. It follows that the Middle Ages in children's literature carries a wide range of significations, from the social conservatism of Brian Jacques's Redwall series to the sceptical posthumanism of Reeve's *No Such Thing as Dragons*.

As Louise D'Arcens and Andrew Lynch observe, modern medievalism is 'increasingly intelligible as a cultural lingua franca, produced in transnational and international contexts with a view to reaching international audiences, some of mass scope' (2014: xii). We learn this lingua franca as children, carrying it through into our adult lives as consumers or scholars of medievalism, or both. Given the global expansion of medievalism for the young, it is inevitable that tomorrow's authors, illustrators and film-makers will sustain the engagement with the medieval which is such a prominent feature of today's texts.

In this book I have frequently observed that contemporary medievalisms for the young are not 'about' the Middle Ages so much as 'about' our own times and cultures, and the future worlds they project and advocate. If young audiences live in the Middle Ages (to return to Eco's assertion), the Middle Ages also lives in the everyday experience of children and young people who encounter the medieval as a multi-temporal and geographically dispersed world of narratives, images, tropes and registers. Recursively mobilising previous versions of the medieval, texts for the young offer a rich repertoire of stories and symbols which reveal the potency of the medieval and its enduring capacity to enchant.

Notes

Introduction

1. See also David Matthews, in 'What the Trumpet Solo Tells Us' (2008), which reaffirms his conviction that there is 'no hard distinction between medievalism studies and medieval studies' (2008: 124); and Clare A. Simmons' argument, in her introduction to *Medievalism and the Quest for the "Real" Middle Ages*, that 'medievalism and medieval studies need no longer represent an opposition' (2001: 12).
2. Fradenburg notes that animals have to 'stand in for peasants' (1997: 205) in *Babe*.
3. Here I draw upon John Frow's distinction between genres and modes, treating *modes* as 'qualifications or modifications of particular genres' (2005: 106).

1 Thinking about the Middle Ages

1. Michael Alexander argues that the beginnings of the Medieval Revival occurred in 1835, following a fire which destroyed the Houses of Parliament. A Select Committee of the House of Commons resolved that the new Houses of Parliament were to be built in 'the national style', defined as 'Gothic or Elizabethan' (2007: xviii). Alexander contrasts this choice of a medievalist style with the rebuilding of St Paul's Cathedral, designed by Christopher Wren following the Great Fire of London 'in a modern style deriving from classical antiquity' (2007: xviii).
2. Michael Saler points out that Tolkien's treatment of Middle-earth changed 'as broader cultural representations of English national identity changed' (2012: 168). His early writing reflected 'a heroic, Anglo-Saxon or "Northern" understanding of English identity' (2012: 179), shifting to a 'less heroic, and more bourgeois and domestic, understanding of Englishness' (2012: 168) in the 1920s and 1930s, when the notion of 'little England' dominated formulations of national identity.
3. This section owes much to research I conducted in conjunction with the 'International Medievalism and Popular Culture' symposium, University of Western Australia, December 2011, convened by Louise D'Arcens and Andrew Lynch. I draw here on sections of the paper I presented at this symposium. See 'Here Be Dragons' (Bradford: 2014).
4. The bulk of dragon picture books adhere to Category 2. The following titles are representative. **Category 1 (dragons in everyday settings)**: Astrid Lindgren and Ilon Wikland, *The Dragon with Red Eyes* (1986); Margaret Mahy and Helen Oxenbury, *The Dragon of an Ordinary Family* (1969); Anna Walker, *I Don't Believe in Dragons* (2010); **Category 2 (dragons in medieval settings)**: David McKee, *The Magician and the Dragon* (1986); Mercer Mayer and Diane Dawson Hearn, *Whinnie the Lovesick Dragon* (1986); Martin Baynton, *Jane

184 Notes

    and the Dragon (1988); Bill Peet, *How Droofus the Dragon Lost his Head* (1972); **Category 3 (the postmodern dragon)**: David Wiesner, *The Three Pigs* (2001); Spike Milligan and Carol Barker, *Sir Nobonk and the Terrible, Awful, Dreadful, Naughty, Nasty Dragon* (1982); Allan Baillie and Wayne Harris, *DragonQuest* (1996).
5. Picture books incorporating similar narrative patterns include Tomie de Paola's *The Knight and the Dragon* (1980), David McKee's *The Magician and the Dragon* (1986), James Cressey and Tamasin Cole's *The Dragon and George* (1977), and Bill Peet's *How Droofus the Dragon Lost his Head* (1972).
6. As Catherine Butler and Callie O'Donovan note, the novel's title alludes to the epitaph on Arthur's tomb as described by Malory: '*Hic Iacet Arthurus, Rex Quondam Rexque Futurus*' ('Here lies Arthur, the once and future king'). The word 'lies' in the novel's title refers to the trickery wrought by Merlin and Arthur, but it also evokes the unreliability of 'historical' accounts of Arthur (see Butler and O'Donovan 2012: 58).
7. The Welsh name 'Myrddin' was attributed to the earliest appearances of Merlin in medieval Welsh poems. The name 'Merlin' was popularised by Geoffrey of Monmouth, whose *Historia Regum Britanniae* ('History of the Kings of Britain') incorporated Merlin's 'Prophecies'. The most authoritative account of the history of the Merlin myth is Stephen Knight's *Merlin: Knowledge and Power Through the Ages* (2009).
8. See Cherie Allan, *Playing with Picturebooks: Postmodernism and the Postmodernesque* (2012), which examines the influence of postmodernism on picture books, and the emergence in recent years of the postmodernesque.
9. The term 'script' refers to 'how a sequence of events or actions is expected to unfold' (Stephens 2011:14). See Stephens' essay 'Schemas and Scripts' for a discussion of how schemas and scripts produce ideas about and attitudes to cultural diversity and multiculturalisms.

2 Temporality and the Medieval

1. See, for instance, Kathleen Biddick, *The Shock of Medievalism* (1998); Paul Strohm, *Theory and the Premodern Text* (2000); Bruce Holsinger, *The Premodern Condition: Medievalism and the Making of Theory* (2005); Kathleen Davis and Nadia Altschul (eds), *Medievalism in the Postcolonial World: The Idea of 'The Middle Ages' Outside Europe* (2009); Elizabeth Scala and Sylvia Federico (eds), *The Post-Historical Middle Ages* (2009); Carolyn Dinshaw, *How Soon Is Now? Medieval Texts, Amateur Readers, and the Queerness of Time* (2012).
2. See Jeffrey Jerome Cohen, 'Introduction: Midcolonial', in *The Postcolonial Middle Ages*, pp. 4, 16, for an account of the history of this phrase in scholarly writing.
3. Examples include Charlie Carter's Battle Boy series, Jan Lister's Time-Tripper series, Linda Bailey's Good Times Travel Agency series, Mary Pope Osborne's Magic Tree House series, Damian Dibben's History Keepers series, and Linda Buckley-Archer's Gideon trilogy, among many others.
4. China Mieville's Young Adult fantasy novel *Un Lun Dun* (2007) employs a similar conceit to refer to a mirror version of the real London inhabited by creatures and discarded objects which have found their way into the fantasy realm.

Notes 185

5. The exception to this rule is the cat-faced gargoyle from St Pancras Railway Station whom George names 'Spout' because his function is to channel water from the station's roof. Spout saves George from death; in return George mends Spout's broken wing. Spout functions as a comical sidekick to George in *Ironhand* and *Silvertongue*.
6. The London Stone is a remnant of a larger limestone stone, now located in Cannon Street in the City of London. See John Clark, 'London Stone: Stone of Brutus or Fetish Stone – Making the Myth' (2010).
7. Although opinions are divided on the origins and nature of the Cnihtengild of London, it is likely that this body comprised men involved in the administration of the developing city during the reign of King Edgar (957–75) and charged with the defence of part of the city wall (see S. E. Kelly, ed., *Charters of St Paul's London*, 2004). The Cnihtengild statue against which George conducts his duels is Denys Mitchell's *The Cnihtengild*, Cutlers Garden Estate, dedicated in 1990.
8. Whereas the Temple Bar dragon was created by C. B. Birch in 1880, most of the City Dragons are 1960s replicas of Victorian dragon sculptures.
9. The statue of Ernest Shackleton in Exhibition Road was created by Charles Sargeant Jagger, whose First World War soldier statues also feature prominently in the trilogy.
10. There has been a noticeable increase in the popularity of First World War settings and protagonists in narratives for young readers over the last three decades, evident in many high-profile works including Michael Mopurgo's *War Horse* (1982), Theresa Breslin's *Remembrance* (2002), Michael Bedard's *Redwork* (1990) and David Metzenthen's *Boys of Blood and Bone* (2003).
11. See Louise d'Arcens, 'Laughing in the Face of the Past' (2011), for a cogent discussion of the role of 'medieval' odours in the production of the Middle Ages for modern consumers.
12. See the archived National Curriculum website for a list of topics to be taught to primary school children at Key Stage 2, including 'the Romans, Anglo-Saxons and Vikings', and the suggestion that children learn through 'visits to museums, galleries and sites': http://webarchive.nationalarchives.gov.uk/20130802151143/https://www.education.gov.uk/schools/teachingandlearning/curriculum/primary/b00199012/history/ks2 (accessed 22 April 2014).
13. See the Jorvik Viking Centre website for a vivid example of such use of faces from the past: http://jorvik-viking-centre.co.uk/ (accessed 22 April 2014).
14. The Old Norse term *skald* means 'poet'. In *Dream Master Nightmare* the word is used to refer more broadly to storytelling and to Cy's role as narrator of the play performed by his classmates.
15. The journal *Studies in Medievalism* 16 (2008) includes a section of essays on video games, and individual essays appear in other medieval(ism) journals, including *The Year's Work in Medievalism* 27 (2012) and *Medium Aevum* 77.2 (2008). See also these edited collections: Daniel T. Kline, *Digital Gaming Re-imagines the Middle Ages* (2013), and Carol L. Robinson and Pamela Clements, *Neomedievalism in the Media: Essays on Film, Television and Electronic Games* (2012). Tison Pugh and Angela Jane Weisl's *Medievalisms: Making the Past in the Present* (2013) includes a chapter on video games, 'Experiential Medievalisms: Reliving the Always Modern'. Numerous essays

186 *Notes*

on medievalist games and tropes also appear in the large and lively field of game studies.

16. See, for instance, Jesper Juul, *Half-Real: Video Games between Real Rules and Fictional Worlds* (2005), Espen Aarseth, 'Aporia and Epiphany in Doom and "The Speaking Clock": The Temporality of Ergodic Art' (1999), and Mark J. P. Wolf, *The Medium of the Video Game* (2001).
17. A first-person shooter game involves an avatar engaged in combat using various weapons. The player sees the action through the perspective of the avatar.
18. For a discussion of the various forms post-disaster fiction has taken in children's literature, see Bradford et al., *New World Orders Orders in Contemporary Children's Literature*, pp. 13–16.
19. The term 'Dark Ages' as used of Britain generally refers to the period following the withdrawal of Roman rule in the fifth century, and up to the 'High Middle Ages' of the eleventh to the thirteenth century. The term is no longer used in modern scholarship because it conjures up concepts of barbarity and political chaos unsustainable in the light of more recent research by archaeologists and historians of the early Middle Ages. See Guy Halsall, *Worlds of Arthur: Facts and Fictions of the Dark Ages* (2013) for a thorough historical account of the figure of Arthur and the times in which he is believed to have lived.
20. The 'Ray Dio' plays a version of the patriotic anthem based on William Blake's poem 'Jerusalem' and set to music by Hubert Parry.

3 Spatiality and the Medieval

1. In this chapter I distinguish between the terms *space* and *place*. 'Space' refers to large, abstract concepts of spatiality, while 'place' refers to local and bounded locations.
2. Edith Nesbit's Bastable novels comprise *The Story of the Treasure Seekers* (1899), *The Wouldbegoods* (1901) and *The New Treasure Seekers* (1904). Lucy M. Boston's Green Knowe series comprises *The Children of Green Knowe* (1954), *The Chimneys of Green Knowe* (1958), *The River at Green Knowe* (1959), *A Stranger at Green Knowe* (1961), *An Enemy at Green Knowe* (1964) and *The Stones of Green Knowe* (1976). Other examples of manor houses in canonical British literature include Frances Hodgson Burnett's *The Secret Garden* (1911) and Philippa Pearce's *Tom's Midnight Garden* (1958). Although Susan Cooper had migrated to the United States by the time she wrote her series The Dark Is Rising, she set the novels in Wales and England, incorporating Huntercombe Manor and its mistress, Miss Greythorne.
3. These soldiers are probably preparing to fight in the second Boer War (1899–1902), following failed negotiations between the British government and the South African republic.
4. See Clare Bradford, Kerry Mallan, John Stephens and Robyn McCallum, *New World Orders in Contemporary Children's Literature* (2008), on utopian and dystopian tropes in children's literature. In *Retelling Stories, Framing Culture* (1998), John Stephens and Robyn McCallum identify Peter Dickinson's *The Weathermonger* (1968) as the first example of post-disaster fiction in which societies that survive cataclysmic disasters are modelled on medieval modes of organisation.

5. For a history of the English manor house, land tenure and regional variations, see Mark Bailey, *The English Manor c. 1200–c. 1500* (2002).
6. The exception is *The River at Green Knowe* (1959), in which the manor house is rented by two elderly women, Maud Biggin and Sybilla Bun, who invite three children, Ida (Maud Biggins's great-niece), and two refugee children, Oskar and Ping, to stay at Green Knowe for the summer.
7. Like the 1939 film *Hunchback of Notre Dame*, in which Charles Laughton plays Quasimodo, the Disney version steps away from the anti-clericalism of Victor Hugo's novel by avoiding the depiction of Frollo as an evil churchman. In the 1939 film Frollo is a virtuous archdeacon and his young brother Jenan, a judge, is the villain. The Disney *Hunchback* makes Frollo the villain but changes him from an archdeacon to a judge, the minister for justice.
8. Harvey is at pains to emphasise, however, that such experiences of rootlessness are not confined to postmodernity but manifest at times of political and social turmoil such as the turn of the twentieth century.
9. Rose is of mixed race, human and vampire, and is thus of lower caste than Lissa, a *moroi* (vampire) and a member of the vampire aristocracy. The *strigoi* (undead) prey on the *moroi* because they derive strength from *moroi* blood. In the world of *Vampire Academy*, humans occupy the lower end of the spectrum of beings. At the Academy they supply blood to the *moroi*.
10. *Marked* is the first of a series of 12 novels by the mother-and-daughter team P. C. and Kristin Cast, published between 2007 and 2014.
11. That is, Zoey's forehead has been imprinted with the sign of the crescent moon which marks her as a vampyre.
12. The Cherokee princess effect is remarkably common in American texts for children and young people and appears in narratives where protagonists who are effectively white claim Native American ancestry while maintaining a careful distance from Native Americans. See Clare Bradford, *Unsettling Narratives* (2007: 89–93).
13. In *The Fairy Mythology: Illustrative of the Romance and Superstition of Various Countries* (1892), the historian and folklorist Thomas Keightley describes boggarts as mischievous spirits which occupy houses and tease their inhabitants, particularly children, by snatching their food, shaking their beds at night, and overturning jugs and pitchers. Cooper's boggart is of this kind, but has developed strong friendships with two humans: Duncan MacDevon, a clan chief who held Castle Keep a thousand years before the events of *The Boggart*, and the most recent clan chief, Devon MacDevon.

4 Disabilities in Medievalist Fiction

1. See, for instance, Marguerite de Angeli's *The Door in the Wall* (1949), Rosemary Sutcliff's *Blood Feud* (1976), Elizabeth Alder's *The King's Shadow* (1997), Sheryl Jordan's *The Raging Quiet* (1999), Karleen Bradford's *Lionheart's Scribe* (1999), Merrie Haskell's *Handbook for Dragon Slayers* (2013), as well as numerous other titles.
2. Eyler's edited collection, *Disability in the Middle Ages*, comprises essays which draw on theories from disability studies to reflect on medieval texts and institutions. See also Irina Metzler's *Disability in Medieval Europe* (2006) and the same scholar's *A Social History of Disability in the Middle Ages* (2013); Tory Vandeventer

188 Notes

   Pearman's *Women and Disability in Medieval Literature* (2010); Kristina L. Richardson's *Difference and Disability in the Medieval Islamic World* (2012).
3. See Rosemarie Garland-Thomson, *Extraordinary Bodies: Figuring Physical Disability in American Culture and Identity* (1997: 8).
4. The film *How to Train Your Dragon* is loosely based on Cressida Cowell's series of junior novels, from *How to Train Your Dragon* (2003) to the ninth book in the series, *How to Betray a Dragon's Hero* (2013). These adventure novels follow the exploits of Hiccup the son of Stoick, and his companions.
5. Stith Thompson's compendium *The Folktale* (1946), for instance, refers to variants of a story (Type 503) about a hunchback who befriends fairies, and is rewarded when they remove his hump. However, his friend, another hunchback, seeks to gain the same boon, whereupon the fairies give him his friend's hump as well as his own.
6. Sutcliff herself contracted Still's disease, a form of juvenile arthritis, at the age of two, and used a wheelchair for most of her adult life. It is clear that her lived experience provided Sutcliff with particular insight into the identity formation of children and young people with disabilities, who feature in much of her historical fiction. While I do not subscribe to the view that only writers with disabilities can write effectively about disabled figures, it is not necessarily the case that writers without such insight are in a position to identify stereotypes and naturalised assumptions in their own work.
7. See Keir Waddington, *Charity and the London Hospitals, 1850–1898*: 'The first authentic hospital in Britain was established at York in 947, but it was not until Rahere's foundation of St Bartholomew's Hospital and Priory in 1123 that an institution was created specifically as a hospital and not as a hostel for travellers and pilgrims' (2000: 6). Many stories have gathered around the figure of Rahere, who is said to have been employed by Henry I as his jongleur and courtier before Rahere took orders.
8. The beginning of the novel precedes the Siege of Acre (1189–91), held by Saladin from 1187. Muslim and Christian forces fought over this port city until its inhabitants were starving and the water supply was contaminated. After Saladin's forces were defeated, Richard the Lionheart ordered the massacre of almost 3000 Muslim prisoners, including women and children; in retaliation, Saladin ordered that all the Christian prisoners were to be killed.

5 Monstrous Bodies, Medievalist Inflexions

1. That fairy art and literature was largely the province of men during the Victorian era is explained by Nicola Bown as follows: 'Fairies, one tends to think, are mostly female, tiny and beautiful; the word "fairy-like" seems a perfect epithet for that ideal of Victorian femininity which required that women be diminutive in relation to men, magical in their unavailability, of delicate constitution, playful rather than earnest. Why should women be interested in a figure which offered them only an image of a femininity from which so many were struggling to escape?' (2001: 14).
2. See Carole Silver, *Strange and Secret Peoples: Fairies and Victorian Consciousness* (1999) and Nicola Bown, *Fairies in Nineteenth-Century Art and Literature* (2001) for accounts of the Victorian preoccupation with fairies. James Wade's

Fairies in Medieval Romance (2011) and Helen Cooper's *The English Romance in Time* (2004) analyse the narrative and ideational functions of fairies in romance texts.
3. I distinguish between fairy narratives for the young, and what are now referred to as urban fairy/faerie romance. Fairy narratives for younger children form part of the global movement of fairy-themed merchandising which since the 1980s has incorporated products, clothing, accessories and services, marketed through fairy shops and specialist areas in toyshops, bookshops and department stores and identifiable by the lavish use of pink and glitter. The narratives which inform this body of texts and products are socially conservative, promoting versions of female identity focused on appearance, and on caring for babies and small children. See Bradford, 'The Return of the Fairy' (2011).
4. The word 'glamour' is a corruption of 'grammar'. Its first literary use occurs in the novels of Walter Scott, where it refers to a charm or spell which deceives the eye. In Melissa Marr's *Wicked Lovely* and other fairy narratives the term is used of the disguises (human, animal, hybrid) magically assumed by fairies.
5. In *Lament*, Luke is a former human stolen by the Fairy Queen hundreds of years prior to the events of the novel. When he refused to court her she ripped his soul from his body and imprisoned it, forcing him thereafter to act as her assassin. The term 'gallowglass' refers to mercenaries, mainly from the Hebrides, who fought with Gaelic armies between the thirteenth and sixteenth centuries.
6. The figure of Beira is loosely based on the Cailleach, a Gaelic female deity who appears in Irish and Scottish traditions as a divine hag, world-maker, ancestress and monarch.
7. The other novels in the series are *Ink Exchange* (2008), *Fragile Eternity* (2009), *Radiant Shadows* (2010) and *Darkest Mercy* (2011). All are located in the same imagined world as *Wicked Lovely*, but only *Fragile Eternity* and *Darkest Mercy* feature narratives involving Aislinn, Keenan and Seth.
8. *Lament*, the first novel in Stiefvater's Books of Faerie series, is followed by *Ballad* (2009) and *Requiem* (2013).
9. See, for instance, Richelle Mead's Vampire Academy series (2007–10), Rachel Caine's Morganville Vampires series (2006–13), Heather Brewer's Chronicles of Vladimir Tod series (2007–2010), Lynsay Sands's Orgeneau and Rogue Hunter series (2003–13), Kresley Cole's Immortals After Dark series (2006–14), and Kerrelyn Sparks's Love at Stake series (2005–14), among many others.
10. This novel, published as *Låt den rätte komma in* (2004), appeared in English translation in 2007. As is the case with much vampire fiction, television and film, the readership of *Let the Right One In* crosses between YA and adult readerships. The novel's protagonists are a 12-year-old boy and a vampire, Eli, who appears to be around the same age. Its themes of bullying and friendship and its settings of home and school fit within YA fiction; its treatment of paedophilia is, however, more explicit than is common in this fiction. The novel has been reviewed in YA review journals including *Viewpoint: Books for Young Adults*, as well as in general review sites such as *Kirkus*. Lindqvist wrote the screenplay for the film *Let the Right One In* (2008), directed by Tomas

Alfredson; subsequently an American English-language film version was developed, entitled *Let Me In* (2010), directed by Matt Reeves.
11. That is, the Judarn forest, in the borough of Bromma in the west of Stockholm. Blackeberg is one of the districts of Bromma.
12. Norma Montesino (2001) points out that a similar reaction has dominated official representations and policies in regard to Gypsy children in Sweden since early in the twentieth century, when 'experts' on Gypsies began to enunciate the 'Gypsy Question' as a problem which 'lies in the existence of a people that is different' (20).
13. See Bruce Holsinger, 'Empire, Apocalypse, and the 9/11 Premodern' (2008) for a compelling account of the rhetoric of neo-medievalism.
14. As I demonstrate in Chapter 1, narratives involving relations between humans and dragons in picture books for the very young embody diverse ideologies and narrative strategies. These picture books, along with cartoons and animated films featuring dragons, induct young audiences into medievalist imaginings in which dragons comprise a particularly malleable figure.
15. Dragons in Tolkien were created in the First Age by Morgoth, the main agent of evil in *The Silmarion*, and appear also in *The Hobbit*. They are based on classical and medieval figures, notably Fafnir in the *Volsunga Saga*, and the unnamed dragon fought by Beowulf.
16. Comonot's Treaty is named for Ardmagar Comonot, leader of the dragons, who led negotiations with Queen Lavonda of Goredd, both of whom remain in power at the fortieth anniversary of the treaty's signing.
17. Quigutl in *Seraphina* are 'a subspecies of dragon, which can't transform. They are flightless; they have an extra set of arms and terrible breath. Often shortened to "QUIG"' (2012: 367). Since the Treaty, many quigs have migrated to the city of Lavondaville where they survive on the garbage of the city and participate in an economy in which they create and sell metal jewellery, and panhandle citizens. They live in the ghetto of Quighole, which is locked at sunset by the Queen's Guard. However, there exist multiple entries by which humans, quigs and saarantrai enter and leave the ghetto during the night.
18. Dracomachia is a 'martial art developed specifically for fighting dragons' (366) and its invention is attributed to St Ogdo.
19. Most of the monster narratives I discuss in this chapter incorporate elements of melodrama. However, *Dragon's Keep* consistently adheres to the melodramatic mode in its plotting, characterisation and language.
20. Marie de France's collection of 12 *Lais* is thought to date from around 1170. Her *lais*, short stories in verse, were written in Anglo-Norman, the language used by the English aristocracy, and take the conventional form of the octosyllabic couplet, comprising eight-syllable lines in rhyming pairs. According to Marie de France, 'Bisclavret' is the Breton term for 'werewolf'.
21. *Ginger Snaps* (2000) was directed by John Fawcett and quickly gained cult status. The sequel *Ginger Snaps II: Unleashed* was released in 2004, together with a prequel, *Ginger Snaps Back: The Beginning*.
22. The term *loup-garou* originates from Old French and means 'werewolf'. In *Wolfborn*, *loup-garou* is used to distinguish evil werewolves, in league with the forces of darkness, from 'natural' werewolves like Geraint and Etienne, who are genetically programmed to undergo metamorphosis.

6 Medievalist Animals and Their Humans

1. Holsinger's essay, 'Of Pigs and Parchment: Medieval Studies and the Coming of the Animal', appears in a section entitled 'Animal Studies' in the March 2009 issue of *PMLA*. Other journals have also published themed issues or sections drawing together animal studies and medieval literary studies: *New Medieval Studies* (2010), *postmedieval* (Spring 2011) and *Studies in the Age of Chaucer* (2012). See also scholarly works including Dorothy Yamamoto's *The Boundaries of the Human in Medieval English Literature* (2000), Jill Mann's *From Aesop to Reynard: Beast Literature in Medieval Britain* (2009), Karl Steel's *How to Make a Human: Animals and Violence in the Middle Ages* (2011), and Susan Crane's *Animal Encounters: Contacts and Concepts in Medieval Britain* (2012); and edited collections including Barbara A. Hanawalt and Lisa J. Kiser's *Engaging with Nature: Essays on the Natural World in Medieval and Early Modern Europe* (2008), and Carolynn Van Dyke's *Rethinking Chaucerian Beasts* (2012).
2. The Arthur trilogy comprises *Arthur: The Seeing Stone* (2000), *Arthur: At the Crossing-Places* (2001) and *Arthur: King of the Middle March* (2003).
3. See, for instance, John Stephens's discussion of the New Age Boy in junior fiction as 'the boy who reads for pleasure and may aspire to become a writer himself', and whose 'relationships with peers are other-regarding' (2002: 44). Unlike many contemporary New Age Boys in children's fiction, Arthur is adept at and dedicated to improving the physical skills he requires to become a squire and a knight.
4. The poetic language attributed to Arthur alludes to kennings, metaphorical compound words common in Old English and Old Norse poetry; for instance, 'whale road' for 'sea', or 'ring-giver' for 'lord'.
5. Helen Barr argues that contemporary accounts of the 1381 uprisings routinely depicted the rebels as peasants, giving rise to the phrase 'The Peasants' Revolt'. Barr observes that 'far from being exclusively peasants and bondmen, the social composition of the rebels comprised significant numbers of artisans and tradesmen, as well as a smattering of lesser gentry and clerics in minor orders' (2001: 107).
6. Tamora Pierce's Provost's Dog trilogy is a YA fantasy series, a prequel to Pierce's first quartet, *The Song of the Lioness* (1983–88). The trilogy comprises *Terrier* (2006), *Bloodhound* (2009) and *Mastiff* (2011). Its protagonist and narrator, Rebekah (Beka) Cooper, is the ancestor of George Cooper, the king of thieves in *The Song of the Lioness*; the events of the Provost's Dog trilogy are set two hundred years prior to those of the *Lioness* quartet.
7. Pounce is a constellation (the Cat) which appears in the sky above Tortall. He takes corporeal form occasionally and comes to the assistance of Alanna in the *Lioness* quartet (as Faithful) as well as Beka Cooper.
8. See Steve Baker's seminal discussion of animal metaphors in *Picturing the Beast* (2001: 77–119).
9. Following the success of *Redwall* (1986), Jacques went on to publish 20 further novels in the series, some of which are prequels to the action of *Redwall*. The final novel, *The Rogue Crew* (2011), was published posthumously. The book series gave rise to a television series (1999–2002) and a two-act musical for children (2002).

7 The Laughable Middle Ages

1. According to Critchley, the superiority theory, which posits that we laugh from a sense of superiority over others, 'dominates the philosophical tradition until the eighteenth century' (2002: 3). The relief theory explains laughter as a means of conserving energy that 'would ordinarily be used to contain or repress psychic activity' (2002: 3), while the incongruity theory explains humour in relation to 'a felt incongruity between what we know or expect to be the case, and what actually takes place in the joke, gag, jest or blague' (2002: 3).
2. The essential features of these settings are an amphitheatre in the middle of a town or city, within which an arena provides space for games, contests and training schools, surrounded by seating or standing room for audiences, and with access to stables where animals are caged before they are set loose in the arena.
3. The forest glade setting of *How to Train Your Dragon* evokes other medievalist films, notably Disney's versions of fairy tales, suggesting a peaceful pre-industrial world. The film pays homage to Disney films through its close-up depictions of appealing birds fluttering about their nests.
4. The Horrible Histories books turn repeatedly to 1066, which is treated as a watershed separating Anglo-Saxon society from modernity. D'Arcens observes that the Horrible Histories franchise 'reanimates for [Deary's] young audience the romantic nationalistic notion of the "Norman Yoke", which argued that the brutal totalitarian nature of Norman rule ... led to the demise of Anglo-Saxon society' (2014: 154).
5. Alcuin laments the sacking of the church of St Cuthbert, not merely the invasion of the Normans. Al-Tartushi comments on the freedom of women in Hedeby, and the availability of eye makeup, as well as practices of infanticide and his negative reactions to the singing of the people of the city:

> Alcuin:
> Lo, it is nearly 350 years that we and our fathers have inhabited this most lovely land, and never before has such terror appeared in Britain as we have now suffered from a pagan race, nor was it thought that such an inroad from the sea could be made. Behold the church of St. Cuthbert spattered with the blood of the priests of God, despoiled of all its ornaments; a place more venerable than all in Britain is given as a prey to pagan peoples. (Loyn 1977: 55–6)
>
> Al-Tartushi:
> The town is poorly off for goods and wealth. The people's chief food is fish, for there is so much of it. If a child is born there it is thrown into the sea to save bringing it up. Moreover he relates that women have the right to declare themselves divorced: they part with their husbands whenever they like. They also have there an artificial make-up for the eyes; when they use it their beauty never fades, but increases in both man and woman. He said too: I have never heard more horrible singing than the Slesvigers' – it is like a growl coming out of their throats, like the barking of dogs, only much more beastly. (Jones 1984: 177)

6. This reference to 'Miss' and her 'chicken-livered' dislike of harsh truths implies a male reader, like the Horrible Histories books more generally.
7. See Richard Preston's 'Horrible Histories: 20 years of entertaining children', in the *Telegraph*, 21 February 2013: http://www.telegraph.co.uk/culture/tvandradio/9857326/Horrible-Histories-20-years-of-entertaining-children.html (accessed 22 April 2014)
8. The Gallic shrug is a gesture (raised shoulders, outstretched hands with palms up) which is common in conversational French and which functions, especially in English-speaking cultures, as a stereotype representing French nonchalance or insouciance.
9. Pratchett's Tiffany Aching novels, in which Tiffany's progress as a witch is traced from the ages of 9 to almost 16, are *The Wee Free Men* (2003), *A Hat Full of Sky* (2004), *Wintersmith* (2006) and *I Shall Wear Midnight* (2010).
10. The setting of these four novels is that of Pratchett's Discworld but it bears a strong resemblance to the English countryside; Tiffany comes from the Chalk, a hilly region not unlike Wiltshire. During the novels she journeys to Lancre and Ankh-Morpork to continue her training, to the realm of Fairyland and to the ice palace of the Wintersmith.
11. The Feegles live in a society whose structure is somewhat similar to that of bees and ants. They are predominantly male except for a kelda, a queen who gives birth to hundreds of Feegles, including (very rarely) a female Feegle. Such a female becomes the kelda of a clan other than her own, marrying the Big Man of such a clan and shifting to the new clan's settlement where she gives birth to new generations. Upon the death of the kelda of the Chalk Hill clan Tiffany briefly becomes kelda, but contrives to avoid the marriage which normally ensues as a result of accession to this role.
12. The witches of Discworld often serve local steadings where they exercise considerable power, as is the case with Tiffany's late grandmother, Granny Aching. They perform tasks that include midwifery, the application of herbal remedies, and mediation in disputes, for which they often receive payment in kind from the communities they serve (although they are not supposed to explicitly seek financial or other reward).
13. So intense is the Feegles' fear of lawyers and legal processes that in the presence of lawyers their swords glow blue.
14. Jinks's Pagan Chronicles comprise *Pagan's Crusade* (1992), *Pagan in Exile* (1994), *Pagan's Vows* (1995) and *Pagan's Scribe* (1995), followed by the sequel *Pagan's Daughter* (2006). The four Pagan novels stretch between 1187, when Pagan is employed as squire to Lord Roland Roucy de Bram, and 1209, when the Albigensian Crusade began.
15. Saint George is believed to have been born in Cappadocia in Asia Minor, and to have been a Christian soldier and officer who was martyred in the late third or early fourth century. The cult of Saint George developed first in the East, and later, especially during the Crusades, in Europe and specifically England where he became 'the patron saint of chivalry' (Good 2009: 48) By the fourteenth century he was established as the national patron of the English nation.

Bibliography

Primary sources

Avi. 2006. *Crispin: At the Edge of the World*. New York: Hyperion.
Baynton, Martin. 1988. *Jane and the Dragon*. Auckland: Ashton Scholastic.
Boston, Lucy M. 1976/2005. *The Stones of Green Knowe*. Orlando, FL: Houghton Mifflin Harcourt.
Branford, Henrietta. 1998. *Fire, Bed & Bone*. Somerville, VA: Candlewick Press.
Breslin, Theresa. 2000. *Dream Master Nightmare*. London: Doubleday.
Bursztynski, Sue. 2010. *Wolfborn*. North Sydney: Random House.
Carey, Janet Lee. 2007. *Dragon's Keep*. Orlando, FL: Harcourt.
Carter, Charlie. 2011. *Battle Boy: Black Prince*. Sydney: Pan Macmillan.
Cast, P. C., and Kristin Cast. 2007. *Marked*. London: Little, Brown.
Cole, Babette. 1986. *Princess Smartypants*. London: Collins.
Cooper, Susan. 1993. *The Boggart*. New York: Aladdin.
Crossley-Holland, Kevin. 2000. *The Seeing Stone*. London: Orion.
Crossley-Holland, Kevin. 2001. *At the Crossing-Places*. London: Orion.
Crossley-Holland, Kevin. 2003. *King of the Middle March*. London: Orion.
Crossley-Holland, Kevin. 2006. *Gatty's Tale*. London: Orion.
Cushman, Karen. 1995. *The Midwife's Apprentice*. New York: Houghton Mifflin.
Cushman, Karen. 1994. *Catherine, Called Birdy*. New York: HarperCollins.
Deary, Terry. 1994. *Vicious Vikings*, illus. Martin Brown. London: Scholastic.
Deary, Terry. 2000. *The Smashing Saxons*, illus. Martin Brown. London: Scholastic.
Deary, Terry. 2013. *The Measly Middle Ages*, illus. Martin Brown. London: Scholastic.
Elliott, Janice. 1988. *The Empty Throne*. London: Walker.
Fletcher, Charlie. 2006. *Stoneheart*. London: Hodder.
Fletcher, Charlie. 2007. *Ironhand*. London: Hodder.
Fletcher, Charlie. 2008. *Silvertongue*. London: Hodder.
de France, Marie. 1978. *The Lais of Marie de France*, trans. Robert Hanning and Joan Ferrante. Grand Rapids, MI: Baker Academic.
Gaiman, Neil. 2008. *The Graveyard Book*. New York: HarperCollins.
Ginger Snaps. 2000. Dir. John Fawcett.
Hartman, Rachel. 2012. *Seraphina*. London: Random House.
Hazen, Barbara Shook, and Tony Ross. 1989. *The Knight Who Was Afraid of the Dark*. London: Andersen.
Horrible Histories, Series Two. 2010. Dir. Dominic Brigstocke. Lion TV and Citrus Television.
How to Train Your Dragon. 2010. Dir. Chris Sanders and Dean DeBlois. DreamWorks Animation.
The Hunchback of Notre Dame. 1996. Dir. Gary Trousdale and Kirk Wise. Walt Disney Pictures.
Jacques, Brian. 1986. *Redwall*. London: Hutchinson.
Jinks, Catherine. 1992. *Pagan's Crusade*. Rydalmere, NSW: Hodder.

Jinks, Catherine. 2014. *Saving Thanehaven*. Crows Nest, NSW: Allen & Unwin.
Jordan, Sherryl. 1991. *The Wednesday Wizard*. London: Scholastic.
Laird, Elizabeth. 2008. *Crusade*. London: Macmillan.
Lindqvist, John Ajvide. 2007. *Let the Right One In*, trans. Ebba Segerberg. Melbourne: Text.
Marr, Melissa. 2007. *Wicked Lovely*. New York: HarperCollins.
McNaughton, Colin. 1980. *King Nonn the Wiser*. London: Heinemann.
Mead, Richelle. 2007. *Vampire Academy*. New York: Penguin.
Montgomery, L. M. 1908/1987. *Anne of Green Gables*. North Ryde, NSW: Angus & Robertson.
Munsch, Robert, and Michael Martchenko. 1980. *The Paper Bag Princess*. Lindfield, NSW: Scholastic.
Nesbit, E. 1901. *The Wouldbegoods*. New York: Harper & Brothers.
Pierce, Tamora. 2006. *Beka Cooper: Terrier*. New York: Scholastic.
Pratchett, Terry. 2003. *The Wee Free Men*. London: Random House.
Price, Susan. 1994. *Foiling the Dragon*. New York: Scholastic.
Quindlen, Anna. 1997. *Happily Ever After*, illus. James Stevenson. New York: Penguin.
Reeve, Philip. 2007. *Here Lies Arthur*. London: Scholastic.
Reeve, Philip. 2009. *No Such Thing as Dragons*. London: Scholastic.
Rosoff, Meg. 2004. *How I Live Now*. London: Penguin.
Schlitz, Laura Amy. 2007. *Good Masters! Sweet Ladies! Voices from a Medieval Village*, illus. Robert Byrd. Cambridge, MA: Candlewick Press.
Sellar, Walter Carruthers, and Robert Julian Yeatman. 1930. *1066 and All That*. London: Methuen.
Stiefvater, Maggie. 2008. *Lament: The Faerie Queen's Deception*. Woodbury, MN: Flux.
Sutcliff, Rosemary. 1970. *The Witch's Brat*. London: Oxford University Press.
Sutcliff, Rosemary. 1993. *The Minstrel and the Dragon Pup*, illus. Emma Chichester Clark. Cambridge, MA: Candlewick Press.
Westall, Robert. 1988. *Ghost Abbey*. London: Random House.
Westall, Robert. 1991. *The Stones of Muncaster Cathedral*. London: Mammoth.
Whatley, Bruce. 2010. *Hunting for Dragons*. Gosford, NSW: Scholastic.
Wiesner, David. 2001. *The Three Pigs*. New York: Clarion Books.
Winthrop, Elizabeth. 1985. *The Castle in the Attic*. New York: Holiday House.

Secondary sources

Alexander, Michael. 2007. *Medievalism: The Middle Ages in Modern England*. New Haven, CT: Yale University Press.
Allan, Cherie. 2012. *Playing with Picturebooks: Postmodernism and the Postmodernesque*. Basingstoke: Palgrave Macmillan.
Appadurai, Arjun. 1990. 'Disjuncture and Difference in the Global Cultural Economy'. *Public Culture* 2: 1–23.
Appadurai, Arjun. 1996. *Modernity at Large: Cultural Dimensions of Globalization*. Minneapolis: University of Minnesota Press.
Armstrong, Philip. 2008. *What Animals Mean in the Fiction of Modernity*. London: Routledge.

Bailey, Mark. 2002. *The English Manor c. 1200–c. 1500*. Manchester: Manchester University Press.
Baker, Steve. 2001. *Picturing the Beast: Animals, Identity, and Representation*. Champaign, IL: University of Illinois Press.
Bakhtin, Mikhail. 1968. *Rabelais and His World*. Cambridge, MA: MIT Press.
Barker, Clare. 2011. *Postcolonial Fiction and Disability: Exceptional Children, Metaphor and Materiality*. Basingstoke: Palgrave Macmillan.
Barnhouse, Rebecca. 1998. 'Books and Reading in Young Adult Literature Set in the Middle Ages'. *The Lion and the Unicorn* 22 (3): 364–75.
Barnhouse, Rebecca. 2000. *Recasting the Past: The Middle Ages in Young Adult Literature*. Portsmouth, NH: Boynton/Cook.
Barnhouse, Rebecca. 2004. *The Middle Ages in Literature for Youth: A Guide and Resource Book*. Lanham, MD: Scarecrow Press.
Barr, Helen. 2001. *Socioliterary Practice in Late Medieval England*. Oxford: Oxford University Press.
Bayless, Martha. 2012. 'Disney's Castles and the Work of the Medieval in the Magic Kingdom'. In Tison Pugh and Susan Aronstein (eds), *The Disney Middle Ages: A Fairy-Tale and Fantasy Past*. New York: Routledge, pp. 39–56.
Beck, Ulrich. 1992. *Risk Society: Towards a New Modernity*. London: Sage.
Bennett, Jane. 2001. *The Enchantment of Modern Life: Attachments, Crossings, and Ethics*. Princeton, NJ: Princeton University Press.
Bennett, Jane. 2010. *Vibrant Matter: A Political Ecology of Things*. London: Duke University Press.
Berger, Peter L. 1997. *Redeeming Laughter: The Comic Dimension of Human Experience*. New York: Walter de Gruyter.
Bergson, Henri. 1911. *Laughter: An Essay on the Meaning of the Comic*, trans. Cloudesley Brereton and Fred Rothwell. Copenhagen: Green Integer.
Bérubé, Michael. 2005. 'Disability and Narrative'. *PMLA* 120 (2): 568–76.
Biddick, Kathleen. 1998. *The Shock of Medievalism*. Durham, NC: Duke University Press.
Bloom, Clive. 2012. 'Horror Fiction: In Search of a Definition'. In David Punter (ed.), *A New Companion to the Gothic*. Chichester: Blackwell, pp. 211–23.
Bogost, Ian. 2008. 'The Rhetoric of Video Games'. In Katie Salen (ed.), *The Ecology of Games: Connecting Youth, Games, and Learning*. Cambridge, MA: MIT Press, pp. 117–40.
Botting, Fred. 2014. *Gothic*. London: Routledge.
Bourdieu, Pierre. 1977. *Outline of a Theory of Practice*. Cambridge: Cambridge University Press.
Bown, Nicola. 2001. *Fairies in Nineteenth-Century Art and Literature*. Cambridge: Cambridge University Press.
Bradford, Clare. 2007. *Unsettling Narratives: Postcolonial Readings of Children's Literature*. Waterloo, ON: Wilfrid Laurier University Press.
Bradford, Clare. 2009. 'Muslim–Christian Relations and the Third Crusade: Medievalist Imaginings'. *International Research in Children's Literature* 2 (2): 177–91.
Bradford, Clare. 2011. 'The Return of the Fairy: Australian Medievalist Fantasy for the Young'. *Australian Literary Studies* 26 (3–4): 115–35.
Bradford, Clare. 2014. 'Here Be Dragons'. In Louise D'Arcens and Andrew Lynch (eds), *International Medievalism and Popular Culture*. Amherst, NY: Cambria Press, pp. 207–26.

Bradford, Clare, Kerry Mallan, John Stephens and Robyn McCallum. 2008. *New World Orders in Contemporary Children's Literature: Utopian Transformations*. Basingstoke: Palgrave Macmillan.
Brooks, Peter. 1976/1995. *The Melodramatic Imagination: Balzac, Henry James, Melodrama and the Mode of Excess*. New Haven, CT: Yale University Press.
Buckingham, David, and Margaret Scanlon. 2005. 'Selling Learning: Towards a Political Economy of Edutainment Media'. *Media, Culture & Society* 27 (1): 41–58.
Burke, Peter. 2001. 'Overture. The New History: Its Past and Its Future'. In Peter Burke (ed.), *New Perspectives on Historical Writing*. University Park: Pennsylvania State University Press, pp. 1–24.
Butler, Catherine, and Hallie O'Donovan. 2012. *Reading History in Children's Books*. Basingstoke: Palgrave Macmillan.
Cadden, Mike. 2004. *Ursula K. Le Guin Beyond Genre: Fiction for Children and Adults*. New York: Taylor and Francis.
Cecire, Maria Sachiko. 2009. 'Medievalism, Popular Culture and National Identity in Children's Fantasy Literature'. *Studies in Ethnicity and Nationalism* 9 (3): 395–409.
Chakrabarty, Dipesh. 2000. *Provincializing Europe: Postcolonial Thought and Historical Difference*. Princeton, NJ: Princeton University Press.
Chappell, Shelley. 2009. 'Contemporary Werewolf Schemata: Shifting Representations of Racial and Ethnic Difference'. *International Research in Children's Literature* 2 (1): 21–35.
Chappell, Shelley. 2007. 'Werewolves, Wings, and Other Weird Transformations: Fantastic Metamorphosis in Children's and Young Adult Fantasy Literature'. Thesis, Macquarie University, Sydney.
Clark, John. 2010. 'London Stone: Stone of Brutus or Fetish Stone – Making the Myth'. *Folklore* 121 (1): 38–60.
Cohen, Jeffrey Jerome. 1996. 'Monster Culture (Seven Theses)'. In Jeffrey Jerome Cohen (ed.), *Monster Theory: Reading Culture*. Minneapolis: University of Minnesota Press, pp. 3–25.
Cohen, Jeffrey Jerome. 2000. 'Introduction: Midcolonial'. In Jeffrey Jerome Cohen (ed.), *The Postcolonial Middle Ages*. New York: Palgrave, pp. 1–17.
Cohen, Jeffrey Jerome. 2012. 'The Werewolf's Indifference'. *Studies in the Age of Chaucer* 34: 351–6.
Colebrook, Claire. 2004. *Irony*. London: Routledge.
Collins, Fiona M., and Judith Graham. 2001. *Historical Fiction for Children: Capturing the Past*. London: David Fulton.
Cooper, Helen. 2004. *The English Romance in Time: Transforming Motifs from Geoffrey of Monmouth to the Death of Shakespeare*. Oxford: Oxford University Press.
Cosslett, Tess. 2006. *Talking Animals in British Children's Fiction, 1786–1914*. Farnham: Ashgate.
Crane, Susan. 2011. 'Chivalry and the Pre/Postmodern'. *Postmedieval: A Journal of Medieval Cultural Studies* 2 (1): 69–87.
Crane, Susan. 2013. 'Animality'. In Marion Turner (ed.), *A Handbook of Middle English Studies*. Chichester: Wiley, pp. 123–34.
Craven, Allison. 2012. 'Esmeralda of Notre-Dame: The Gypsy in Medieval View from Hugo to Disney'. In Tison Pugh and Susan Aronstein (eds), *The Disney Middle Ages: A Fairy-Tale and Fantasy Past*. New York: Routledge, pp. 225–42.

Critchley, Simon. 2002. *On Humour*. London: Routledge.
D'Arcens, Louise. 2008. 'Deconstruction and the Medieval Indefinite Article: The Undecidable Medievalism of Brian Helgeland's *A Knight's Tale*'. *Parergon* 25 (2): 80–98.
D'Arcens, Louise. 2011. 'Laughing in the Face of the Past: Satire and Nostalgia in Medieval Heritage Tourism'. *Postmedieval: A Journal of Medieval Cultural Studies* 2 (2): 155–70.
D'Arcens, Louise. 2014. *Comic Medievalism: Laughing at the Middle Ages*. Woodbridge: Boydell & Brewer.
D'Arcens, Louise, and Andrew Lynch. 2014. 'Introduction'. In Louise D'Arcens and Andrew Lynch (eds), *International Medievalism and Popular Culture*. Amherst, NY: Cambria Press, pp. xi–xxvi.
Davis, Kathleen, and Nadia Altschul (eds). 2009. *Medievalism in the Postcolonial World: The Idea of 'The Middle Ages' Outside Europe*. Baltimore, MD: Johns Hopkins University Press.
Deary, Terry. 2000. 'The Woeful Second World War and the Horrible Histories Series'. In David Carter (ed.), *Creating Writers: A Creative Writing Manual for Schools*. Abingdon: Routledge, pp. 166–70.
Derrida, Jacques. 1995. *Points ... Interviews, 1975–1994*, ed. Elisabeth Weber, trans. Peggy Kamuf and others. Stanford, CA: Stanford University Press.
Derrida, Jacques. 2002. 'The Animal that Therefore I Am (More to Follow)', trans. David Wills. *Critical Inquiry* 28: 369–417.
Dinshaw, Carolyn. 2011. 'Nostalgia on My Mind'. *Postmedieval: A Journal of Medieval Cultural Studies* 2 (2): 225–38.
Dinshaw, Carolyn. 2012. *How Soon Is Now? Medieval Texts, Amateur Readers, and the Queerness of Time*. Durham, NC: Duke University Press.
Eco, Umberto. 1986. *Travels in Hyper Reality: Essays*. San Diego, CA: Harcourt Brace Jovanovich.
Elias, Amy J. 2001. *Sublime Desire: History and Post-1960s Fiction*. Baltimore, MD: Johns Hopkins University Press.
Eyler, Joshua (ed.). 2010. *Disability in the Middle Ages: Rehabilitations, Reconsiderations, Reverberations*. Burlington, VT: Ashgate.
Felski, Rita. 2011. 'Context Stinks!'. *New Literary History* 42 (4): 573–91.
Ferry, Luc. 1995. *The New Ecological Order*, trans. Carol Volk. Chicago: University of Chicago Press.
Foucault, Michel. 1980. *Power/Knowledge: Selected Interviews and Other Writings 1972–1977*. Brighton: Harvester Press.
Foucault, Michel. 1997. *Ethics: Subjectivity and Truth*. London: Allen Lane.
Fradenburg, Aranye. 2009. '(Dis)Continuity: A History of Dreaming'. In Elizabeth Scala and Sylvia Federico (eds), *The Post-Historical Middle Ages*. New York: Palgrave Macmillan, pp. 87–116.
Fradenburg, Aranye. 2012. 'Among all Beasts: Affective Naturalism in Late Medieval England'. In Carolynn Van Dyke (ed.), *Rethinking Chaucerian Beasts*. New York: Palgrave Macmillan, pp. 13–31.
Fradenburg, Louise. 1997. '"So That We May Speak of Them": Enjoying the Middle Ages'. *New Literary History* 28 (2): 205–30.
Frow, John. 2005. *Genre*. London: Routledge.
Fudge, Erica. 2012. 'Renaissance Animal Things'. *New Formations* 76: 86–100.

Galloway, Alexander R. 2006. *Gaming: Essays on Algorithmic Culture*. Minneapolis: University of Minnesota Press.
Garland-Thomson, Rosemarie. 1997. *Extraordinary Bodies: Figuring Physical Disability in American Culture and Literature*. New York: Columbia University Press.
Garland-Thomson, Rosemarie. 2005. 'Disability and Representation'. *PMLA* 120 (2): 522–7.
Garland-Thomson, Rosemarie. 2009. *Staring: How We Look*. Oxford: Oxford University Press.
Good, Jonathan. 2009. *The Cult of St George in Medieval England*. Woodbridge: Boydell & Brewer.
Grosz, Elizabeth. 2004. *The Nick of Time: Politics, Evolution and the Untimely*. Crows Nest, NSW: Allen & Unwin.
Gurevich, Aron. 1988. *Medieval Popular Culture: Problems of Belief and Perception*, trans. János M. Bak and Paul A. Hollingsworth. Cambridge: Cambridge University Press.
Haraway, Donna. 2003. *Companion Species Manifesto*. Chicago, IL: Prickly Paradigm Press.
Harvey, David. 1990. *The Condition of Postmodernity: An Enquiry into the Origins of Cultural Change*. Oxford: Blackwell.
Hollindale, Peter. 2003. 'The Last Dragon of Earthsea'. *Children's Literature in Education* 34 (3): 183–93.
Holsinger, Bruce. 2005. *The Premodern Condition: Medievalism and the Making of Theory*. Chicago: University of Chicago Press.
Holsinger, Bruce. 2008. 'Empire, Apocalypse, and the 9/11 Premodern'. *Critical Inquiry* 34: 468–90.
Holsinger, Bruce. 2009. 'Of Pigs and Parchment: Medieval Studies and the Coming of the Animal'. *PMLA* 124 (2): 616–23.
Hutcheon, Linda. 1988. *A Poetics of Postmodernism: History, Theory, Fiction*. New York: Routledge.
Hutcheon, Linda. 1989. *The Politics of Postmodernism*. London: Routledge.
Hutcheon, Linda, with Siobhan O'Flynn. 2012. *A Theory of Adaptation*. New York: Routledge.
Jameson, Fredric. 2002. 'Radical Fantasy'. *Historical Materialism* 10 (4): 273–80.
Jones, Gwyn. 1984. *A History of the Vikings*. Oxford: Oxford University Press.
Karlyn, Kathleen Rowe. 2011. *Unruly Girls, Unrepentant Mothers: Redefining Feminism on Screen*. Austin: University of Texas Press.
Keightley, Thomas. 1892. *The Fairy Mythology: Illustrative of the Romance and Superstitions of Various Countries*. London: George Bell & Sons.
Kelly, S. E. (ed.). 2004. *Anglo-Saxon Charters 10: Charters of St Paul's, London*. Oxford: Oxford University Press.
Knight, Stephen. 2009. *Merlin: Knowledge and Power Through the Ages*. Ithaca, NY: Cornell University Press.
Kutzer, M. Daphne. 2000. *Empire's Children: Empire and Imperialism in Classic British Children's Books*. London: Routledge.
Langton, Jane. 1994. 'Children's Books: *The Ramsay Scallop*, and *Catherine, Called Birdy*'. *New York Times*, 20 August.
Latour, Bruno. 1993. *We Have Never Been Modern*, trans. Catherine Porter. Cambridge, MA: Harvard University Press.

Latour, Bruno. 2004. *Politics of Nature: How to Bring the Sciences into Democracy*. Cambridge, MA: Harvard University Press.
Latour, Bruno. 2005. *Reassembling the Social: An Introduction to Actor-Network Theory*. Oxford: Oxford University Press.
Le Goff, Jacques. 1988. *Medieval Civilization 400–1400*, trans. J. Barrow. Oxford: Blackwell.
Lerer, Seth. 2008. *Children's Literature: A Reader's History, from Aesop to Harry Potter*. Chicago: University of Chicago Press.
Levina, Marina, and Diem-My T. Bui. 2013. 'Introduction: Toward a Comprehensive Monster Theory in the 21st Century'. In Marina Levina and Diem-My T. Bui (eds), *Monster Culture in the 21st Century: A Reader*. New York: Bloomsbury, pp. 1–13.
Linton, Simi. 1998. *Claiming Disability: Knowledge and Identity*. New York: New York University Press.
Lowenthal, David. 1985. *The Past Is a Foreign Country*. Cambridge: Cambridge University Press.
Lowenthal, David. 1996. *Possessed by the Past: The Heritage Crusade and the Spoils of History*. New York: The Free Press.
Loyn, H. R. 1977. *The Vikings in Britain*. London: B. T. Batsford.
Lukács, Georg. 1962. *The Historical Novel*. London: Merlin Press.
Lupack, Barbara Tepa. 2004. 'Introduction'. In Barbara Tepa Lupack (ed.), *Adapting the Arthurian Legends for Children: Essays on Arthurian Juvenilia*. New York: Palgrave Macmillan, pp. xiii–xxi.
Lynch, Andrew. 2008. 'Archaism, Nostalgia and Tennysonian War in *The Lord of the Rings*'. In Harold Bloom (ed.), *J. R. R. Tolkien's The Lord of the Rings*. New York: Infobase, pp. 101–16.
Lynch, Andrew. 2014. 'Swords in Stones / Ladies in Lakes'. In Louise D'Arcens and Andrew Lynch (eds), *International Medievalism and Popular Culture*. Amherst, NY: Cambria Press, pp. 227–44.
Macleod, Anne Scott. 1998. 'Writing Backwards: Modern Models in Historical Fiction'. *Horn Book Magazine* 74 (1): 26–33.
Mallan, Kerry. 2009. *Gender Dilemmas in Children's Fiction*. Basingstoke: Palgrave Macmillan.
Mathijs, Ernest. 2013. *John Fawcett's Ginger Snaps*. Toronto: University of Toronto Press.
Matthews, David. 2006. 'What was Medievalism? Medieval Studies, Medievalism, and Cultural Studies'. In Ruth Evans, Helen Fulton and David Matthews (eds), *Medieval Cultural Studies*. Cardiff: University of Wales Press, pp. 9–22.
Matthews, David. 2008. 'What the Trumpet Solo Tells Us: A Response'. *Parergon* 25 (2): 119–27.
McHugh, Susan. 2009. 'Literary Animal Agents'. *PMLA* 124 (2): 487–95.
Metzler, Irina. 2013. *A Social History of Disability in the Middle Ages: Cultural Considerations of Physical Impairment*. New York: Routledge.
Mickenberg, Julia L., and Philip Nel. 2011. 'Radical Children's Literature Now!' *Children's Literature Association Quarterly* 36 (4): 445–73.
Miller, Miriam Youngerman. 1995. '"Thy Speech is Strange and Uncouth": Language in the Children's Historical Novel of the Middle Ages'. *Children's Literature* 23: 71–90.
Milne, Lesley. 2005. 'Universal History as Reworked by *Satirikon* and *1066 and All That* as Parody History Textbooks: A Suggestion of a Literary Genre'. *The Modern Language Review* 100 (3): 723–9.

Mitchell, David T., and Sharon L. Snyder. 2000. *Narrative Prosthesis: Disability and the Dependencies of Discourse*. Ann Arbor: University of Michigan Press.
Montesino, Norma. 2001. 'The "Gypsy Question" and the Gypsy Expert in Sweden'. *Romani Studies* 11 (1): 1–24.
Mulkay, Michael. 1988. *On Humour: Its Nature and Its Place in Modern Society*. Cambridge: Polity Press.
Munslow, Alun. 1997. *Deconstructing History*. London: Routledge.
Munslow, Alun. 2010. *The Future of History*. Basingstoke: Palgrave Macmillan.
Norden, Martin F. 2013. '"You're a Surprise from Every Angle": Disability, Identity and Otherness in *The Hunchback of Notre Dame*'. In Johnson Cheu (ed.), *Diversity in Disney Films: Critical Essays on Race, Ethnicity, Gender, Sexuality and Disability*. Jefferson, NC: McFarland, pp. 163–78.
Orme, Nicholas. 2001. *Medieval Children*. New Haven, CT: Yale University Press.
Owen, Alex. 2004. *The Place of Enchantment: British Occultism and the Culture of the Modern*. Chicago: University of Chicago Press.
Prendergast, Thomas, and Stephanie Trigg. 2009. 'The Negative Erotics of Medievalism'. In Elizabeth Scala and Sylvia Federico (eds), *The Post-Historical Middle Ages*. New York: Palgrave Macmillan, pp. 117–38.
Preston, Richard. 2013. 'Horrible Histories: 20 Years of Entertaining Children'. *The Telegraph*, 21 February. http://www.telegraph.co.uk/culture/tvandradio/9857326/Horrible-Histories-20years-of-entertaining-children.html (accessed 22 April 2014)
Pugh, Tison, and Angela Jane Weisl. 2013. *Medievalisms: Making the Past in the Present*. New York: Routledge.
Punter, David. 2000. '"A Foot is What Fits the Shoe": Disability, the Gothic and Prosthesis'. *Gothic Studies* 2 (1): 39–49.
Quayson, Ato. 2007. *Aesthetic Nervousness: Disability and the Crisis of Representation*. New York: Columbia University Press.
Ricoeur, Paul. 1984. *Time and Narrative*, trans. Kathleen McLaughlin and David Pellauer. Chicago: University of Chicago Press.
Robinson, Alan. 2011. *Narrating the Past: Historiography, Memory and the Contemporary Novel*. New York: Palgrave Macmillan.
Rooney, Monique. 2001. 'Grave Endings: The Representation of Passing'. *Australian Humanities Review*. http://www.australianhumanitiesreview.org/archive/Issue-September-2001/rooney2.html (accessed 15 August 2014).
Rosaldo, Renato. 1993. *Culture & Truth: The Remaking of Social Analysis*. Boston, MA: Beacon Press.
Rostankowski, Cynthia. C. 2003. 'The Monastic Life and the Warrior's Quest: The Middle Ages from the Viewpoint of Animals in Brian Jacques's Redwall Novels'. *The Lion and the Unicorn* 27 (1): 83–97.
Royle, Nicholas. 2003. *Jacques Derrida*. London: Routledge.
Saler, Michael. 2003. '"Clap if You Believe in Sherlock Holmes": Mass Culture and the Re-enchantment of Modernity, c. 1890–c. 1940'. *The Historical Journal* 40 (3): 599–622.
Saler, Michael. 2006. 'Modernity and Enchantment: A Historiographic Review'. *The American Historical Review* 111 (3): 692–716.
Saler, Michael. 2012. *As If: Modern Enchantment and the Literary Prehistory of Virtual Reality*. New York: Oxford University Press.
Scala, Elizabeth, and Sylvia Federico (eds). 2009. *The Post-Historical Middle Ages*. New York: Palgrave Macmillan.

Scanlon, Margaret, and David Buckingham. 2002. 'Popular Histories: "Education" and "Entertainment" in Information Books for Children'. *The Curriculum Journal* 13 (2): 141–61.
Scott, Robert A. 2011. *Gothic Enterprise: A Guide to Understanding the Medieval Cathedral*. Berkeley: University of California Press.
Sharpe, Jim. 2001. 'History from Below'. In Peter Burke (ed.), *New Perspectives on Historical Writing*. University Park: Pennsylvania State University Press, pp. 25–42.
Simmons, Clare. A 2001. 'Introduction'. In Clare A. Simmons (ed.), *Medievalism and the Quest for the "Real" Middle Ages*. Abingdon: Frank Cass, pp. 1–28.
Stagg, Kevin. 2006. 'Representing Physical Difference: The Materiality of the Monstrous'. In David M. Turner and Kevin Stagg (eds), *Social Histories of Disability and Deformity*. Abingdon: Routledge, pp. 19–38.
Stephens, John. 1992. *Language and Ideology in Children's Fiction*. London: Longman.
Stephens, John. 2002. "A Page Just Waiting to be Written on": Masculinity Schemata and the Dynamics of Subjective Agency in Junior Fiction'. In John Stephens (ed.), *Ways of Being Male: Representing Masculinities in Children's Literature and Film*. New York: Routledge, pp. 38–54.
Stephens, John. 2011. 'Schemas and Scripts: Cognitive Instruments and the Representation of Cultural Diversity in Children's Literature'. In Kerry Mallan and Clare Bradford (eds), *Contemporary Children's Literature and Film*. Basingstoke: Palgrave Macmillan, pp. 12–35.
Stephens, John, and McCallum, Robyn. 1998. *Retelling Stories, Framing Cultures: Traditional Story and Metanarratives in Children's Literature*. New York: Garland, 1998.
Stephens, John, and McGillis, Roderick. 2006. 'Critical Approaches to Children's Literature'. In Jack Zipes (ed.), *The Oxford Encyclopedia of Children's Literature*, Vol. 1. Oxford: Oxford University Press, pp. 364–7.
Stott, Andrew. 2005. *Comedy*. New York: Routledge.
Strohm, Paul. 1992. *Hochon's Arrow: The Social Imagination of Fourteenth-Century Texts*. Princeton, NJ: Princeton University Press.
Strohm, Paul. 2000. *Theory and the Premodern Text*. Minneapolis: University of Minnesota Press.
Sugars, Cynthia. 2014. *Canadian Gothic: Literature, History, and the Spectre of Self-Invention*. Cardiff: University of Wales Press.
Tally, Robert T. 2012. *Spatiality*. New York: Routledge.
Turner, Victor. 1982. *From Ritual to Theatre: The Human Seriousness of Play*. New York City: Performing Arts Journal Publications.
Waddington, Keir. 2000. *Charity and the London Hospitals, 1850–1898*. Woodbridge: Boydell & Brewer.
Wall, Barbara. 1991. *The Narrator's Voice: The Dilemma of Children's Fiction*. New York: St Martin's Press.
Weber, Max. 1991. *From Max Weber: Essays in Sociology*. London: Routledge.
Wheeler, Elizabeth A. 2013. 'No Monsters in This Fairy Tale: *Wonder* and the New Children's Literature'. *Children's Literature Association Quarterly* 38 (3): 335–50.
Williams, Raymond. 1973. *The Country and the City*. London: Chatto & Windus.
Wilson, Kim. 2011. *Re-Visioning Historical Fiction for Young Readers: The Past through Modern Eyes*. New York: Routledge.

Wolfe, Cary. 2003. *American Culture, the Discourse of Species, and Posthumanist Theory*. Chicago: University of Chicago Press.
Wood, Christopher. 2006. 'Piero della Francesca, Liminologist'. In Steffen Bogen, Wolfgang Brassat and David Ganz (eds), *Bilder, Räume, Betrachter: Festschrift für Wolfgang Kemp*. Berlin: Reimer, pp. 252–6.
Young, Helen. 2010. 'Approaches to Medievalism: A Consideration of Taxonomy and Methodology through Fantasy Texts'. *Parergon* 27 (1): 163–79.
Zagal, José P., and Michael Mateas. 2010. 'Time in Video Games: a Survey and Analysis'. *Simulation Gaming* 41 (6): 844–68.
Zornado, Joseph. 1997. 'A Poetics of History: Karen Cushman's Medieval World'. *The Lion and the Unicorn* 21 (2): 251–66.

Index

Note: 'n' after a page reference denotes a note number on that page.

Alexander, Michael, 183n1
Allan, Cherie, 184n8
Altschul, Nadia, 1, 3, 184n1
anachronism, 7, 26–7, 29, 39, 58, 176
　see present past
animals in medievalist texts, 9,
　132–54
　anthropomorphic, 150–3
　and actor-network theory, 133–44
　and monstrosity, 125–8
　as narrators, 141–4
　magical and metaphorical, 144–50
Appadurai, Arjun, 14, 160
Armstrong, Philip, 136
Arthurian narratives, 5, 8, 33–5, 79,
　138–41, 154
　in post-disaster fiction, 42, 58–61
authenticity, 2, 6, 25, 26, 27–31, 54,
　76, 176, 179
Avi
　Crispin: At the Edge of the World,
　104–5

Bailey, Mark, 187n5
Baker, Steve, 191n8
Bakhtin, Mikhail, 173–5
Barnhouse, Rebecca, 6–7, 29–31
Barr, Helen, 191n5
Bayless, Martha, 72
Baynton, Martin
　Jane and the Dragon, 22–4, 183n4
Beck, Ulrich, 13
Bedard, Michael, 185n10
Bennett, Jane, 13, 17–20, 134, 136,
　144, 150
Berger, Peter L., 166
Bergson, Henri, 9, 40, 44, 155–8, 165
Bérubé, Michael, 89
Biddick, Kathleen, 184n1
Bloom, Clive, 77–9
bodies in medievalist texts, 9, 165–6

animal, 132–54
　disabled, 85–106
　monstrous, 46, 107–31
　racialised, 80–2, 99–103, 108, 117
Bogost, Ian, 56, 57
Boston, Lucy M., 186n2
　The Stones of Green Knowe, 64–71
Botting, Fred, 2, 71, 73–4, 75,
Bourdieu, Pierre, 18
Bown, Nicola, 109, 111, 188n1
Branford, Henrietta
　Fire, Bed & Bone, 141–4, 154
Breslin, Theresa, 185n10
　Dream Master Nightmare, 52–5
Brooks, Peter, 124
Buckingham, David, 168, 170
Bui, Diem-My T., 107
Burke, Peter, 168
Bursztynski, Sue
　Wolfborn, 125–8, 190n22
Butler, Catherine, 35, 55, 184n6
Bradford, Clare, 8, 58, 183n3, 186n4,
　186n18, 187n12, 189n3
Byrd, Robert, 93

Cadden, Mike, 120
camp (performances) in medievalist
　texts, 21–2
Carey, Janet Lee
　Dragon's Keep, 120, 123–5
Carter, Charlie, 184n3
　Battle Boy: Black Prince, 52, 55
Cast, Kristin, and Cast, P. C., 187n10
　Marked, 81–2, 84, 108
Cecire, Maria Sachiko, 152
Chakrabarty, Dipesh, 12–13, 42
Chappell, Shelley, 125
Chaucer, Geoffrey, 5, 32, 64
childhood, 7
　and enchantment, 13
　and innocence, 73, 181

children's literature, 2, 5
  and socialising agendas, 4, 11–12, 42, 108, 181, 182
children's literature studies, 2–10
  and anxieties over accuracy, 6, 9, 25–6
  and historicism, 5–6, 26, 29
chivalry, 56, 138–41, 152, 158, 177
Clark, John, 185n6
Cohen, Jeffrey Jerome, 63, 79, 107, 108, 110, 125, 126, 184n2
Cole, Babette
  Princess Smartypants, 156–8, 161
Colebrook, Claire, 161
Collins, Fiona M., 26
comic medievalism, 15, 20, 21, 50, 79, 155, 158, 160, 161, 162, 163, 166, 167, 171, 172, 173
  carnivalesque, 173–5
  defined, 156
  see also humour
Cooper, Helen, 110, 188–9n2
Cooper, Susan, 186n2
  The Boggart, 55, 64, 82–4, 187n13
  The Boggart and the Monster, 64
Cosslett, Tess, 141, 142
Crane, Susan, 133, 138, 191n1
Craven, Allison, 94
Critchley, Simon, 9, 155–6, 171, 173, 177, 192n1
Crossley-Holland, Kevin, 6, 141, 154, 191n2
  At the Crossing-Places, 138
  Gatty's Tale, 18–20
  King of the Middle March, 140–1
  The Seeing Stone, 138–40
Cushman, Karen
  Catherine, Called Birdy, 27–33
  The Midwife's Apprentice, 134–8, 154

D'Arcens, Louise, 4–5, 53–4, 166, 169, 170, 182, 183n3, 185n11, 192n4
Davis, Kathleen, 1, 3, 184n1
Deary, Terry, 165, 169
  Horrible Histories books, 2, 164–9, 192n4
  The Measly Middle Ages, 165, 166–7
  The Smashing Saxons, 165–6
  Vicious Vikings, 168–9

Derrida, Jacques, 9, 108–9, 113–14, 118, 123, 137–8, 139
Dinshaw, Carolyn, 9, 41–2, 50, 51, 62, 184n1
disabilities in medievalist texts, 9, 85–106
  and aesthetic nervousness, 87, 88, 93, 98, 108
  and narrative prosthesis, 86–7, 98, 101, 103, 104
  and normates, 87, 95, 103–4
  and race, 99–103
disenchantment, 12, 13

Eco, Umberto, 181, 182
education, 164, 166–7, 170, 185n12
edutainment, 169–70
Elliott, Janice
  The Empty Throne, 58–61
enchantment and medievalism, 12–20, 39, 40, 116, 139, 148, 150, 182
  and border-crossing, 19–20, 134, 144–6
  history of, 13–15
  see also disenchantment
exceptional figures in medievalist texts, 23, 28, 32–3, 92–3, 139, 161
Eyler, Joshua, 86, 187n2

fantasy, 6, 8, 9, 12, 13, 144, 152, 171
  and ironic imagination, 14, 31
  and deconstruction, 25, 31, 171–9
  as social practice, 14, 15–18
  paranormal, 80–2, 109–114, 119–25
Federico, Sylvia, 184n1
Felski, Rita, 134
feminism, 28, 32, 130
  second-wave, 23–4, 32, 156–8
  and post-feminism, 114
Ferry, Luc, 133
Fletcher, Charlie, 43, 46, 48
  Ironhand, 46, 48, 49, 185n5
  Silvertongue, 47–8, 49, 185n5
  Stoneheart, 46–7, 48,
Foucault, Michel, 9, 62, 114, 116, 122
Fradenburg, L. O. Aranye, 3, 7, 8, 133, 183n2
de France, Marie, 126, 127, 190n20

Index

Frow, John, 183n3
Fudge, Erica, 133, 137

Gaiman, Neil
  The Graveyard Book, 43–6, 61
Galloway, Alexander R., 56
Garland-Thomson, Rosemarie, 9, 87, 91, 95, 97, 103, 104, 105, 107, 188n3
genre, 9, 12, 24, 32, 36, 61, 63, 109, 170, 183n3
Ginger Snaps (film), 126, 128–31, 190n21
Good, Jonathan, 193n15
gothic, 2, 43, 61, 63, 71–9, 80, 81, 82–84, 94, 108, 115, 128
  architecture, 17, 18, 43, 64, 71–9, 183n1
  narratives, 2, 9, 61, 63, 75, 77
  and postcolonialism, 128–31
Graham, Judith, 26
Grosz, Elizabeth, 9, 40–1, 42, 43, 44, 45, 47, 66, 71
Gurevich, Aron, 173

Haraway, Donna, 132
Hartman, Rachel
  Seraphina, 120–4, 125, 190n17
Harvey, David, 9, 74, 84, 187n8
Hazen, Barbara Shook, and Ross, Tony
  The Knight Who Was Afraid of the Dark, 158–60
historical fiction, 6, 8, 9, 12, 18, 24, 25, 26–7, 29, 30–1, 63, 85, 99, 104, 132–3, 138, 141, 155
  deconstructive, 25, 31–2, 33–5, 36, 175
  historiographic metafiction, 175–9
historiography, history, 24–5
  and children's literature, 25, 31–5, 175–9
  theories of, 9, 11–12, 24–35, 39
  in schools, 167–8
  see also historical fiction
Hollindale, Peter, 120
Holsinger, Bruce, 1, 133, 184n1, 190n13, 191n1
Horrible Histories (television series), 169–71

How to Train Your Dragon (film), 87–91, 160–3, 175–6, 188n4, 192n2, 192n3
humour, 6, 50, 163–4, 172
  and gender, 20–4, 156–8, 160–1
  and heroic figures, 56, 158–60
  and the Horrible Histories, 164–71
  in *How to Train Your Dragon*, 160–3
  theories of, 9, 155–6, 177, 192n1
  see also comic medievalism
The Hunchback of Notre Dame (film), 71–9, 93–5, 98, 187n7
Hutcheon, Linda, 126–7, 171, 176, 178, 179

irony, 14, 31, 87, 147, 155, 161, 163, 176, 179
Islam (in medievalist texts), 8, 24, 99–103, 117

Jacques, Brian, 151, 182, 191n9
  Redwall, 151–4
Jameson, Fredric, 119, 121
Jinks, Catherine, 155, 193n14
  Pagan's Crusade, 175–9
  Saving Thanehaven, 55, 56–8, 61
Jones, Diana Wynne, 172
Jones, Gwyn, 192n5
Jordan, Sherryl
  Wednesday Wizard, 50–2

Karlyn, Kathleen Rowe, 124
Keightley, Thomas, 111, 187n13
Kelly, S. E., 185
Kline, Daniel T., 5, 185n15
Knight, Stephen, 5, 184n7
Kutzer, M. Daphne, 64

Laird, Elizabeth
  Crusade, 99–103
Lang, Andrew, 111
Langton, Jane, 28–9, 32
Latour, Bruno, 9, 133–44, 147
Le Goff, Jacques, 86
Le Guin, Ursula, 119–20
Lerer, Seth, 7
Levina, Marina, 107
Lewis, C. S., 6, 152

Lindqvist, John Ajvide
  Let the Right One In, 114–19, 131
Linton, Simi, 101
Lowenthal, David, 11, 27
Loyn, H. R., 192n5
Lukács, Georg, 26–7
Lupack, Barbara Tepa, 5
Lynch, Andrew, 5, 60, 61, 119–20, 182, 183n3

Macleod, Anne Scott, 29–30
Mallan, Kerry, 21, 186n4
Marr, Melissa, 109
  Wicked Lovely, 110–14
masculinity, 20–1, 54, 56, 72, 77, 95, 99, 139, 158, 179, 191n3
Mateas, Michael, 56
Mathijs, Ernest, 128–9
Matthews, David, 183n1
McCallum, Robyn, 186n4
McGillis, Roderick, 4
McHugh, Susan, 144
McNaughton, Colin, 158
Mead, Richelle, 189n9
  Vampire Academy, 8, 80–2
medievalist tourism, 49–55
medievalism, 2–3, 7–8, 11, 12, 48, 63, 79, 154, 181–2
  and gothic, 2, 43, 63, 71–9, 80, 81, 82–84, 94, 108, 115, 128
  defined, 2
  recursiveness of, 2, 9, 39, 42, 71, 79, 181–2
medievalist aesthetic, 16–18, 48, 72, 85
medievalist texts for children
  and distancing strategies, 8, 20–24
  and gender, 8, 20–3, 35, 77, 85, 122, 156–8
  and barbarism, 7, 42, 51, 71, 165–6, 169
  and romanticised representations, 7, 42, 51, 65–6, 70, 133
  and transnationalism, 79–84
  as introduction to the medieval, 5, 182, 190n14
medievalism studies
  and animal studies, 133, 191n1
  and medieval studies, 3–5
  defined, 3

memory, 11, 25, 40, 46, 60, 66, 84, 103, 143
  and memorialisation, 67
metafiction, 9, 15, 25, 31, 33, 35–7, 43, 175
Metzenthen, David, 185n10
Metzler, Irina, 86, 187n2
Mickenberg, Julia L., 85
Middle Ages, 1, 3, 7–8, 27, 29, 30, 39, 41, 49, 56, 61, 133, 155, 181
  architecture of, 46, 62, 63, 64–79
  and alterity, 4, 135, 41, 164
  and disabled bodies, 85–6, 106
  and modernity, 1, 7, 41, 49–55, 156
  eighteenth-century view of, 2, 71, 73, 75, 79
  Enlightenment view of, 1, 7, 71, 111
Miller, Mirian Youngerman, 6
Milne, Lesley, 164
Mitchell, David T., 9, 86–7, 88, 91, 95–6, 98, 100, 101, 102, 104, 107
monstrous identities in medievalist texts, 9, 44, 45, 46, 59, 107–31, 172–3
  and the *arrivant*, 9, 108–9, 113–14, 118, 123, 128, 131
  and disabilities, 91, 107
  and spatiality, 73–4, 75–9
  cultural meanings of, 107–9, 110, 113–14, 115–17, 122–3, 125, 128–31
Montesino, Norma, 190n12
Montgomery, L. M.
  Anne of Green Gables, 79–80
Mopurgo, Michael, 185n10
Mulkay, Michael, 160
Munsch, Robert, and Martchenko, Michael
  The Paper Bag Princess, 20–24, 158, 161
Munslow, Alun, 25

nationalism and nationhood, 8, 24, 59–61, 62, 67, 70, 79, 117–18, 121–3, 125, 143, 152–3, 164
Nel, Philip, 85
Nesbit, E., 64–6, 70, 186n2
Norden, Martin F., 93–4

nostalgia, 42, 49, 50–51, 54, 61
  and fantasy, 119
  and imperialism, 51

O'Donovan, Hallie, 35, 55, 184n6
Orme, Nicholas, 30
Owen, Alex, 12

parody, 36, 48, 56, 75, 88, 109, 156–7, 163, 170, 172, 174, 176–9
past future, 26, 32, 33
past present, 26, 32
Pierce, Tamora, 191n6, 191n7
  Terrier, 144–7, 153–4
postcolonialism, 51, 63, 128, 130
Pratchett, Terry, 109, 155, 172–5, 193n9, 193n10, 193n11, 193n12, 193n13
Prendergast, Thomas, 3, 4
present past, 11, 33, 35, 39, 41, 85, 87, 92, 93, 95, 99, 103, 133, 139, 141, 156, 175
  defined, 26
  compare past future, past present
Preston, Richard, 193n7
Price, Susan
  Foiling the Dragon, 52, 54–5
Pugh, Tison, 5, 6, 30, 57–8, 185n15
Punter, David, 94

Quayson, Ato, 87, 88–9, 93, 98, 100, 108
Quindlen, Anna
  Happily Ever After, 52, 54, 55

Reeve, Philip, 155
  Here Lies Arthur, 33–5
  No Such Thing as Dragons, 180–1, 182
Rice, Anne, 2
Ricoeur, Paul, 40
Robinson, Alan, 11, 26–7, 31–3, 35, 39, 41, 49, 85, 87, 92, 93, 95, 99, 103, 133, 139, 141, 156, 175
romance, 21, 32, 69, 79, 81, 95, 119
  paranormal, 2, 9, 63, 77, 109–15, 121–5, 189n3
  tropes, 48, 56–7, 79–80, 147, 150
Rooney, Monique, 122

Rosaldo, Renato, 51
Rosoff, Meg
  How I Live Now, 68–70
Royle, Nicholas, 108, 113

Saler, Michael, 12, 13–14, 183n2
satire, 50, 54, 164, 170
Scala, Elizabeth, 184n1
Scanlon, Margaret, 168, 170
Schlitz, Laura Amy
  Good Masters! Sweet Ladies!, 91–3, 95, 97, 98
Scott, Robert A., 72
Sellar, Walter Carruthers, and Yeatman, R. J.
  1066 and All That, 164
Sharpe, Jim, 168
Simmons, Clare, 183n1
Snyder, Sharon L., 9, 86–7, 88, 91, 95–6, 98, 100, 101, 102, 104, 107
spatiality, 9, 19, 43–44, 46, 62–84
  and built environment, 46–9, 63, 64–79, 80–2
  and journeys, 52, 74, 80, 83, 178–9
  and natural world, 58, 60–1, 69–70, 133, 148
  and the spatial turn, 9, 62–3
Stagg, Kevin, 107
Stephens, John, 4, 30, 31, 184n9, 186n4, 191n3
Stiefvater, Maggie, 109
  Lament, 110–14, 131, 189n8
Stott, Andrew, 169, 173, 175
Strohm, Paul, 173, 184n1
Sugars, Cynthia, 128
Sutcliff, Rosemary, 6, 187n1, 188n6
  The Witch's Brat, 95–9
Sutcliff, Rosemary, and Clark, Emma Chichester
  The Minstrel and the Dragon Pup, 147–50, 154

Tally, Robert T., 62
temporality, 7, 40–61
  and asynchrony, 40–2
  and multi-temporal fantasy, 42–9
  and time-travel narratives, 49–55
  and medievalist video games, 55–8
  in post-disaster fiction, 58–61

Tolkien, J. R. R., 6, 14, 119–20, 152, 171, 183n2, 190n15
Trigg, Stephanie, 3, 4, 5
Turner, Victor, 65

Waddington, Keir, 188n7
Wall, Barbara, 66
Weber, Max, 12
Weisl, Angela Jane, 5, 6, 30, 57–8, 185n15
Westall, Robert
 Ghost Abbey, 74–7
 The Stones of Muncaster Cathedral, 77–9
Whatley, Bruce
 Hunting for Dragons, 15–18, 20

Wheeler, Elizabeth A., 85
Wiesner, David
 The Three Pigs, 36–9, 43, 183–4n4
Wilde, Jane, 111
Williams, Raymond, 83
Wilson, Kim, 29, 49
Winthrop, Elizabeth
 The Castle in the Attic, 82
Wolfe, Cary, 150–1, 154
Wood, Christopher, 150

Young, Helen, 6, 12

Zagal, José P., 56
Zornado, Joseph, 31

Printed and bound by CPI Group (UK) Ltd, Croydon, CR0 4YY